MODERN FRENCH
MARXISM

For Jo and Thomas

MICHAEL KELLY

Modern French Marxism

The Johns Hopkins University Press
Baltimore, Maryland

First published in Great Britain in 1982 by
Basil Blackwell, Publisher
108 Cowley Road, Oxford OX4 1JF

First published in the United States of America in 1982 by
The Johns Hopkins University Press
Baltimore, Maryland 21218

Library of Congress Catalog Card Number 82-47973
ISBN 0-8018-2906-2

Printed in Great Britain

Contents

Introduction

Nationally and internationally, French Marxists have played a crucial role in the social and political changes of the past century. For almost half of that time, their practical importance has been complemented by a theoretical contribution of equally remarkable proportions. Despite this, and sometimes even because of it, French Marxism has been ill served in the English-speaking world. Little known and less understood, its contours have generally been perceived through the distorting mirrors of impatience and antipathy. Though its political importance is often acknowledged, its intellectual wealth remains almost unexplored. There are, it is true, exceptions to this picture. Some few individual theorists have been singled out for particular attention. Most notably, the innovative approach of Louis Althusser and his circle attracted considerable interest among young Marxists during the early and mid-1970s. And the earlier attempts of Jean-Paul Sartre to marry Marxism with his existentialist principles also aroused some belated support on the 'New Left' at the same period. Outside these intellectual enclaves, French Marxism has obtained some limited and piecemeal recognition in the study of politics, economics, history and sociology, but virtually none in the field of philosophy. Moreover, the ideas have almost invariably been seen in isolation from the historical and cultural context in which they were elaborated. The object of this book is to give a sympathetic but critical survey of the development of Marxist thought in France, and to analyse the contributions which French Marxists have made on certain central questions of philosophy and social thought. In this way it may also help to redress the patchy and distorted view of French Marxism which is still widely held, and convey something of the richness and diversity of its philosophical traditions.

The notion of Marxist philosophy immediately poses conceptual problems for readers accustomed to the division of knowledge and enquiry prevalent in English-speaking countries. Many British philosophers are reluctant to concede that Marxism has any significant philosophical dimension, since it has little to say on most of the problems which commonly preoccupy them, and can only with difficulty be translated into the terminology of their intellectual framework. The reluctance is not confined to Marxism, but extends to much of contemporary European thought, since most cultures allow a broader understanding of the term 'philosophy' than does the 'Anglo-Saxon' tradition. In consequence, recent years have seen the spread of the hybrid category of 'social thought' to describe the enquiry into general principles of thought, related to politics, society and the human and social sciences. Typically it includes theoretical discussions which fall neither into the narrow view of philosophy nor into a recognized scientific discipline. Such discussions are pre-eminently the domain of Marxism, and what the French and others call Marxist philosophy corresponds broadly to what in English might be termed Marxist social thought.

The philosophy or social thought of Marxism comprises not only a conception of history and society, usually designated historical materialism, but also a conception of the more general principles of development and relation in the world, often termed dialectical materialism. It is this latter that forms the major focus of this study, embracing a network of problems which include the nature and status of thought, especially philosophy and social thought; its relation to the natural world, to human society, and to the sciences which study them; and the types of rationality appropriate to investigate such questions.

French Marxist reflection on these issues begins with the key concepts of dialectics and materialism, used by Marx and Engels to characterize their approach. Dialectics is taken to offer a rational framework within which the movement and interrelation of natural, social and conceptual processes can be comprehended. Materialism is taken to affirm the priority of the material world over the thought which reflects on it. A recurrent point of reference is the relationship between the materialist dialectic of Marx and the idealist dialectic of Hegel from which it emerged historically. Debate on these questions has ramified into a complex and diverse philosophical culture, and the following pages will hope to show something of its richness and depth, as well as its historical roots and practical importance.

Any intellectual movement has both a cognitive and a social dimension. That is, it has a conceptual structure, however rudimentary, which seeks to provide knowledge of the world; and it articulates and organizes, however indirectly, the experience and activity of people in society. In the case of Marxism, both dimensions are recognized and asserted in its ambition to be both scientific and revolutionary. How far French Marxism has progressed in the scientific understanding of the world or the revolutionary changing of it is a matter on which assessments will vary. But this book seeks to provide elements towards a firmer basis for judgement. On a cognitive level, the various philosophical issues in question are critically analysed to draw out their theoretical and practical implications, strengths and weaknesses. On a social level, they are placed in their historical context, and related to the changing configuration of French politics and society, and to international relations. The shifting interrelations of social and cognitive content are traced often in fine detail, especially where that interrelation is itself a point of contention in debate.

The organization of the material follows as far as possible the logic of its internal development, though inevitably the need for selection and division imposes something of its own pattern. As will be observed, Marxism led a mediocre life in France until the 1930s. The short first chapter therefore aims to situate the problems, both historically and conceptually, as they stood before that time. A brief account of the major relevant statements by Marx and Engels is followed by short surveys of the development of Hegelian and Marxist ideas in France up to 1929. Thereafter the chapters proceed chronologically, examining the significant contributions to debate on materialism and the dialectic, in their intellectual and historical context.

As far as possible, the most interesting, influential, or representative work has been given special attention at the expense of other less noteworthy contributions. For this purpose, focus has been centred on varieties of Marxism broadly associated with the communist movement, at the expense of the 'New Left' or Trotskyist tendencies, which are extensively discussed in other studies. Similar but even more compelling reasons underlie the absence of many of the Christian, existentialist, structuralist or post-structuralist writers who have seen themselves in some sense as Marxist. Most of those omitted on this basis have made little or no notable contribution to debate on materialist dialectics, so that their absence is not a major loss to the subject under consideration. Any subsequent work which attempts to discuss in any detail the multitude of currents claiming a close or distant affinity to Marx or Marxism will practically involve a complete intellectual history of modern France. The writings studied from the most recent period also reflect an inevitable degree of personal choice, since the passage of time has not yet revealed how important or influential they have been. But the writers chosen are all in some sense representative and, I hope, stimulating.

In the gestation and preparation of this book, I have received more material and intellectual assistance than I can adequately acknowledge. In particular, I should like to thank University College Dublin for generously allowing me the leave of absence necessary to complete the work. I am also grateful to the library staff of the College, who have been particularly helpful to me at all times, and to the Institut des Recherches Marxistes in Paris for access to valuable source material. I am deeply indebted to many colleagues and friends with whom I have discussed the various problems of the subject-matter, and to many others of my friends and family for their assistance and encouragement. I hope they will forgive me for not singling them out individually. I should, however, like to express my special gratitude to Jo Doyle, my wife, for her indispensable, unfailing and many-sided help and support.

1

Beginnings

1845 – 1929

Marx, Engels and the Hegelian dialectic

My dialectical method is not only different from the Hegelian, but
is its direct opposite. To Hegel, the life-process of the human brain,
i.e., the process of thinking, which, under the name of 'the Idea',
he even transforms into an independent subject, is the demiurgos
of the real world, and the real world is only the external,
phenomenal form of 'the Idea'. With me on the contrary, the ideal
is nothing else than the material world reflected by the human
mind, and translated into forms of thought.

The mystifying side of the Hegelian dialectic, I criticised nearly
thirty years ago, at a time when it was still the fashion. But just as I
was working at the first volume of 'Das Kapital', it was the good
pleasure of the peevish, arrogant, mediocre Ἐπίγονοι who now
talk large in cultured Germany, to treat Hegel in the same way as
the brave Moses Mendelssohn in Lessing's time treated Spinoza,
i.e., as a 'dead dog'. I therefore openly avowed myself the pupil of
that mighty thinker, and even here and there, in the chapter on
the theory of value, coquetted with the modes of expression
peculiar to him. The mystification which dialectic suffers in
Hegel's hands, by no means prevents him from being the first to
present its general form of working in a comprehensive and
conscious manner. With him it is standing on its head. It must be
turned right side up again, if you would discover the rational
kernel within the mystical shell.

Karl Marx, Afterword to the second German edition of Capital,
24 January 1873, English edition (London, 1970), 19–20

Karl Marx never gave a systematic account of his philosophy,
understood in the narrower sense. Successive generations of Marxists
have regretted the fact and argued over what such an account might
have contained. They have also debated at length what its absence
implies. But the inescapable fact remains that no such text exists.

Claims have been made on behalf of two introductions which he wrote
to his *Critique of Political Economy* (1859), but neither of them meets the
necessary conditions. The first, written in 1857, contains lengthy
discussion of methodology, but is incomplete, unrevised and was
unknown for almost a century, until 1953.[1] It also poses serious
problems of interpretation, some of which will be examined in later
chapters. The second, which replaced the first and was published as a
preface to the work in 1859, is a famous text in which Marx gives a brief
account of his personal development and the most celebrated short
statement of his historical materialism.[2] But philosophical questions, in
the restricted sense, are not even broached. Neither text is the missing
exposition of Marxist philosophy.

It is true that during his early twenties, Marx wrote voluminously
about philosophy. It was his passion. And some commentators have
sought to interpret the writings of these years, the early 1840s, as the
substantive philosophy of Marxism as a whole. A full discussion of this
viewpoint cannot be undertaken without entering into the debates on
humanism and alienation which have nourished many volumes of
discussion. These are deliberately left aside in the present study in
favour of the philosophical questions posed by Marxism after it reached
the main conclusions which characterize its distinctive conception of
history and society. At this stage, soon after Marx's association with
Friedrich Engels had begun in 1844, they decided, as Marx said, to
'settle accounts with our erstwhile philosophical conscience', by jointly
writing the manuscript now known as *The German Ideology* (1845 – 46).
In it the young men worked out 'the opposition of our view to the
ideological view of German philosophy'.[3] The implications of this
process remains contentious and, as later discussion will show, some
commentators have taken it to mean the rejection of philosophy as
such. After 1846, by a mutual division of labour sustained over a
lifetime, Marx devoted his attentions to the urgent problems of political
economy, culminating in *Capital*, while Engels specialized in matters of
the natural and human sciences and philosophy. For this reason,
though the two men were in constant consultation over each other's
work, there is no further writing on philosophy in Marx's hand.

The usual sources for an account of Marxist philosophy are therefore
the works of Engels, in particular his lengthy polemic against the
German theorist Eugen Dühring, usually known as *Anti-Dühring* (1880),
and his pamphlet *Ludwig Feuerbach and the End of Classical German
Philosophy* (1888). More recently the fragments collected as *Dialectics of
Nature*, written from 1873 to 1886 and first published in 1925, became a
further source. Engels' works are not treatises addressed to professional

philosophers, but they set out the philosophical framework of Marxism with clarity and precision.

Some commentators have disparaged Engels' formulations, arguing that they are not by Marx's hand, do not correspond to Marx's conceptions, and cannot validly be counted as Marxist. His philosophical conclusions are especially singled out for criticism on this basis. However, such a view is without historical or textual foundation. The closeness of Marx's and Engels' collaboration and the frankness of their relationship leave little room to suppose a major undiscovered divergence on such important questions of overall perspective. More pertinently, the scattered comments which Marx occasionally made on topics relating to philosophy serve only to corroborate the more developed expositions of Engels.

There is, at least, no dispute that the methodological and philosophical positions of Marxism developed out of Hegelian philosophy and the criticism of it by Marx and Engels in the mid 1840s. So much is certain, though views on how Marxism emerged and how it relates to Hegel diverge considerably. Much of the controversy which the present study is concerned with refers back more or less explicitly to this issue. There were, of course, other important theoretical and practical sources for Marxism as a whole. But no discussion of its conceptual procedures and general philosophy can evade the question of their relation to Hegel.

Like many thinkers quite remote from either Marxism or Hegelianism, Marx and Engels regarded Hegel as the last great systematic philosopher of Western Europe. With him, they thought, philosophy had reached its highest point of development. In common with many of their German contemporaries, they belonged initially to the Young Hegelian movement which sought to develop the revolutionary implications of his thought. Engels later offered the following assessment:

> The Hegelian system was the last and most consummate form of philosophy, in so far as the latter is represented as a special science superior to every other. All philosophy collapsed with this system. But there has remained the dialectical method of thinking and the conception that the natural, historical and intellectual world moves and transforms itself endlessly in a constant process of becoming and passing away. Not only philosophy but all sciences were now required to discover the laws of motion of this constant process of transformation, each in its particular domain. And this was the legacy which Hegelian philosophy bequeathed to its successors. [4]

What was revolutionary about Hegel was therefore his conception of change and development as the fundamental reality. Earlier philosophers had articulated the same view, but Hegel's originality lay in formulating a way of thinking which could grasp the 'constant process of becoming and passing away'. However, this way of thinking – dialectics – was embedded in a deeply conservative system of idealist philosophy, which Hegel had constructed. While they recognized the great power and value of the Hegelian dialectic, Marx and Engels rejected the idealist philosophy that enveloped it.

The materialist dialectic which they espoused holds a relation of both continuity and discontinuity with its idealist predecessor. But whereas Hegel devoted lengthy volumes to his conception of dialectics, the founders of Marxism were content with a few brief indications of their conception of it. Hence, the difficulties of defining a precise relationship between Marxism and Hegelianism have constituted many of the contentious points attending the elaboration of materialist dialectics in subsequent Marxist philosophy.

The classical statement of the relationship, the one to which all debate eventually returns, is Marx's own assessment at the end of his afterword to the second German edition of *Capital*, part of which is quoted at the head of this section. But, as with most crucial texts, it has become the starting point, rather than the final word, in the recurring discussion. Despite its concision and clarity, it has fuelled more than a century of controversy. Almost every phrase has given rise to intense disputes over its precise interpretation and implications. Many of them will be examined in the present work, but an initial census can usefully indicate some of the questions raised. Is Marx's dialectic simply a method or is it a philosophy, or both? Likewise Hegel's? Does Marx use an opposite method or an opposite philosophy? How far does the rejection of idealism affect the nature of the dialectic? Is Marx's criticism of Hegel a limited modification or a complete rejection? What is the 'mystifying side' and how far does Hegel mystify the dialectic? Does Marx's 'coquetry' affect the substance or simply the presentation of his analyses? In what sense is Marx a 'pupil' of Hegel, and is it limited to *Capital*? What takes place in the process of turning Hegel right side up? And what is the 'rational kernel', what the 'mystical shell'?

Essentially, the problems can be expressed in terms of Marx's 'inversion' of Hegel. In what does the process consist and does it contain or lead to any structural changes in the Hegelian dialectic? References to Hegel are scattered throughout *Capital* and through most of Marx's other writings, but the brief statement quoted here is the most explicit judgement on his general attitude to his predecessor. More extended examination of the Hegel question was left to Engels, who spent some time discussing it, particularly towards the end of his life.

Engels frequently quoted Marx's statements as a condensed expression of their common position. Sharing Marx's respect for the 'mighty thinker', he recognized the great wealth of Hegel's thought, where 'one finds innumerable treasures which today still possess undiminished value'.[5] He also acknowledged that in his writings 'there is much that is botched, artificial, laboured, in a word, wrong in point of detail'. The defects largely stemmed, in Engels' view, from the idealist viewpoint which was a crucial limitation. Hegel, he explained, held that instead of thoughts in the brain being more or less abstract pictures of actual things and processes, things and their evolution are 'the realized pictures of the "Idea", existing somewhere from eternity before the world was'. 'This way of thinking', he concluded, 'turned everything upside down, and completely reversed the actual connection of things in the world.'[6]

On the other hand, Engels emphasized the revolutionary character of dialectical philosophy, which holds that 'nothing is final, absolute, sacred', which 'reveals the transitory character of everything and in everything', and for which nothing endures except 'the uninterrupted process of becoming and passing away'.[7] Hegel's great achievement he suggested, was to enunciate this philosophy and attempt to 'trace out the internal connection that makes a continuous whole of all this movement and development'.[8] In contrast, he said, the overall system, which Hegel felt compelled to construct, was conservative, dogmatically declaring itself to be absolute, in contradiction with the revolutionary implications of his method. Consequently, depending on whether a person leant towards the system or the method, quite opposing conclusions could be reached concerning particularly religion and politics.

The contradiction between the system and the dialectical method, he felt, was an incurable one, but it showed the way out of the labyrinth and made Hegel's the last great philosophical system in the classical sense. The search for an impossible absolute truth was now replaced by the pursuit of 'attainable relative truths along the path of the positive sciences, and the summation of their results by means of dialectical thinking'.[9]

Engels' analysis clarifies some of the lapidary formulations of Marx's statement, and proposes answers to some of the outstanding questions. His distinction of Hegel's system as against his dialectical method makes it clear that Marxism adopts the dialectical method without its systematic expression, but whether the dialectic is a philosophy remains unsolved. Engels, like Marx, uses the term 'philosophy' in several senses, depending on the context. The Hegelian system is for him the end of German philosophy and even of all philosophy in the classical sense. But dialectical philosophy remains revolutionary and valuable.

At least one distinction may be proposed, between philosophy as the construction of definitive intellectual systems, and philosophy as a way of thinking and reasoning. The first, static, sense excludes Marxism, the second, dynamic, sense includes it. In the latter sense, Marxism incorporates the dialectical method. But there is also the suggestion that it incorporates the results of dialectical thinking, including the criticism of philosophical systems and the 'summation' of scientific discoveries. Whether it may legitimately be inferred that Marxism is therefore a philosophy in some sense is a question that has provoked much controversy. It relates to what Marx means by 'settling accounts with our erstwhile philosophical conscience'. Is Marxism a new philosophy or the end of philosophy? The interpretation of Marx's relation to Hegel has a vital role to play in the answer.

It was already clear, from Marx, that he considered Hegel's dialectic to be mystified by his idealism. The suggestion that with Hegel the dialectic was 'standing on its head' is already a paraphrase of Hegel's own characterization of his idealist viewpoint. In his *Phenomenology of Mind* (1807), Hegel spoke of the need to understand reality as an 'inverted world' (*verkehrte Welt*) in which the negation of things by the idea of their opposites represented the truth of those things.[10] In the sense that, for him, the truth of the world lay in ideas and mind, Hegel deliberately sought to stand the conventional view of reality on its head. In repeating this assessment, then, Marx and Engels are not indulging in the type of unkind caricature which is sometimes supposed. Their materialist viewpoint asserts that ideas are reflections of the world rather than the reverse, hence turning the 'inverted world' 'right side up'. In this sense materialism, whether or not it is viewed as philosophy, is plainly the opposite of idealism, which is a philosophy. Correspondingly, Marx's dialectic is the opposite of Hegel's in that it follows an opposite direction, proceeding from the world to ideas. The dialectic is therefore the 'rational kernel', idealism its 'mystical shell'.

Despite the satisfying metaphorical solution, Hegel is not such a simple nut to crack. Marx acknowledges that the dialectic suffered mystification in Hegel's hands; Engels speaks of aspects that are botched or plain wrong. Evidently, the Hegelian dialectic cannot be simply adopted unchanged by Marxism, albeit in inverted form. Even the fact of inversion would suggest the need for some modification: ceilings can hardly be expected to serve as floors without some reconstruction. The interrelation of Hegel's idealist philosophy and his dialectic raises the question of how far they are separable and in what form Marx appropriated the dialectic. Part of the answer lies in the notion of a contradiction between the dialectic and the total system in Hegel. The dialectic, if it intrinsically undermined the system, must have been in a healthy state from a materialist viewpoint. But even the concept of contradiction, a Hegelian concept, implies an interpenetration of the opposed aspects, and in turn poses the question of how much of each aspect survives in the eventual resolution of their conflict.

The possible complexities of the answer have left later generations of Marxists ample scope for debate. The closely connected issues of the relations between Marx, Engels and Hegel, the status and content of philosophy, and the nature of materialist dialectics, have continuously stood at the centre of controversy. The texts which have been quoted, far from closing discussion, have been variously adduced and traduced in support of quite divergent positions. To propose a single exclusive interpretation of Marx's and Engels' statements would preempt an important ‘part of the debates to be studied in the forthcoming pages. More important, it might foster the erroneous impression that philosophical questions can be resolved by exegesis of authoritative texts. Further discussion of Marx and Engels would go beyond the present purpose of setting the initial terms of discussion. The issues raised will be taken up in the context of French Marxism and its development.

Marxism in France before 1917

La France aura fait attendre Karl Marx. C'est un paradoxe que nous l'ayons connu si tard, alors que nous subissons depuis longtemps son influence, indirecte et gênée il est vrai: le marxisme menait dans notre pays une vie médiocre.

Pierre Gérôme, ‘Le marxisme pénètre en France’, Europe,
15 août 1935, 611

The implantation of Marxism in France was a long, painful and uneven process. Organically bound to the working class, its progress followed the rise and fall of the socialist movement and mirrored the

development of the conflicts within it. From the beginnings of the
Guesdist movement in the late 1870s, the economic and political
analyses of Marx and Engels spread widely through the French labour
movement, albeit in an elementary and at times distorted version. By
the turn of the century the general principles of historical materialism
were generally known and accepted by socialists, even though they were
often deformed by a variety of foreign accretions. It was a much longer
task to introduce the philosophical principles of Marxism into a
working class suspicious of abstractions and an intelligentsia profoundly
steeped in bourgeois ideology.

Marx's own connections with France are well known. From the time
of his early months of political exile in Paris during 1844 and 1845, and
his exhilarating experience of the French socialist movement, he
maintained throughout his life a close interest in France. Some of his
most memorable and influential essays were devoted to developments
there: *Class Struggles in France 1848–1850*, *The 18th Brumaire of Louis
Bonaparte*, and *The Civil War in France*. But it was not until the last
years of his life that Marx's conception of socialism began to take root in
French political culture. There was only one professed Marxist among
the leaders of the Commune: Léo Frankel, a Hungarian by birth, whose
solitary efforts to give the Commune a Marxist direction were assisted
from London by Marx. Frankel's work was cut short by the slaughter of
the *communards*, and the International Workingmen's Association to
which he belonged was ruthlessly harried by a government anxious to
stamp out all forms of socialism. Marx's reputation among the surviving
socialists working in clandestinity was gravely compromised by the
nomination of three disastrous representatives for the International in
France. The Bordeaux agent vanished without a trace; the Paris agent
abjectly repudiated socialism at his trial in early 1873; and the Toulouse
agent turned out to be a police spy who secured the conviction of nearly
forty Internationalists in the area. The French socialist movement, such
as it was, continued to find its theoretical nourishment in the moralistic
syndicalism bequeathed by Pierre-Joseph Proudhon, or in the
revolutionary putschism of Auguste Blanqui.

The first significant promotion of Marxist ideas in France was the
work of Jules Guesde and the small group of socialists around him.
During his exile after the fall of the Commune, Guesde developed from
a confused form of anarchism to a collectivist socialism close to that of
Marx, whose work he encountered in the late 1870s after his return to
France. Guesde embarked on an energetic campaign to popularize the
new ideas through lectures, pamphlets and the review *Egalité*, which he
founded in 1877. The efforts of Guesde and his colleagues led to the

foundation in 1880 of the Parti ouvrier français, whose programme was consciously Marxist. Marx himself had, at Guesde's instigation, drafted the preamble to the programme, and broadly approved the specific demands it made.

Throughout the 1880s and into the early 1890s, Marxist ideas were vigorously disseminated, not only by the Guesdists but also by Marx's daughter and son-in-law, Laura and Paul Lafargue, and by fellow socialists Benoît Malon and Gabriel Deville. Their work could be found in many popularizations and in a variety of journals, among them Guesde's *L'Egalité* (1877–82), *Le Socialiste* (from 1885), the weekly organ of the Parti ouvrier, and Malon's socialist forum *La Revue socialiste* (from 1885). The vigour with which the ideas were propounded was, however, not matched by their clarity or profundity. The level of theoretical development can be gauged from incidents like the public debate between Marx's other son-in-law Charles Longuet and Jules Guesde in 1881, or later the exchange of articles in 1894 between the socialist leader Jean Jaurès and Paul Lafargue. In both cases, a confused and woolly idealism was opposed by a crudely mechanical material determinism. The subtlety and penetration of Marx's thought was not reflected in the interpretations of his French followers. The extent of the adulteration can be judged by Engels' response to Gabriel Deville's widely read popular digest of Marx's *Capital*. While he resigned himself to seeing it appear in French, he categorically forbade any translation into English or German lest Marx's thought be deformed and discredited in countries with a stronger grasp of theory. Nonetheless, the dynamism of the Guesdists and the debates they aroused did at least implant the beginnings of a Marxist culture and pave the way for later advances.

One striking exception to the prevailing conceptual poverty was the emergence in the mid-1890s of Georges Sorel as a perceptive and original theorist. A retired engineer, Sorel threw himself into analysing and discussing the major problems of Marxist theory. He drew on material from current international debates and established particularly close links with Italian Marxists grouped around Antonio Labriola. His prolific work for the socialist journals *L'Ere nouvelle* and its successor *Le Devenir social* was a major effort to reformulate Marxism in terms which escaped the sterile opposition of idealism and mechanical materialism, and to propose a cogent critique of contemporary bourgeois sociology. Sorel's work was somewhat eclipsed in the controversies over revisionism as the century turned, and he moved to a brand of syndicalism which led him to flirt with extreme right-wing groups, though later again he declared himself a Leninist in the wake of the

October Revolution. He is still best known for his essay *Réflexions sur la violence* of 1906, which has earned him a reputation for violent and irrational anarchism, but his earlier importance in the history of Marxism is beginning to be recognized.

Sorel was isolated from the main movement of socialism in France and his work left little lasting trace, but he did render the service of promoting the circulation of Marxist writings from other countries, particularly Italy and Germany. He was not alone in this, of course, and the 1890s saw a considerable number of translations of important works. The works of Marx and Engels had already begun to be published during the 1880s, under the impulse of the Guesdists, the Lafargues and their associates. *Capital*, first translated almost unnoticed in 1872, was reprinted half a dozen times in the 1880s and 1890s, although it was best known through Deville's unsatisfactory digest. The *Communist Manifesto* first appeared in French, in New York, in the same year of 1872, but was not published in France until 1885. Some two dozen French editions appeared before the First World War. As the century turned, Marx's writings on French historical developments, the Commune, 1848, and the Second Empire, were readily available, as was his *Critique of Political Economy* (1859) and *Wages, Prices and Profits* (1865). Of his work in which philosophical questions were raised, his early *Critique of Hegel's Philosophy of Right* (1843) was translated in 1895, and *Misère de la philosophie* (1847) was reprinted the following year, though the latter was more concerned to demonstrate the poverty of Proudhon's *ersatz* Hegelianism than to define Marx's own conception of the dialectic. On the other hand Engels' *Socialism: Utopian and Scientific* was in circulation from 1880 and his *Anti-Dühring*, from which it was extracted, was published in full in 1911. His *Origin of the Family, the State and Private Property* appeared in 1893 and an important anthology of his writings, *Religion, philosophie, socialisme* (1901) was published soon afterwards by Paul and Laura Lafargue.

The international debates within Marxism were echoed to some extent in the socialist press of the period. They generally focused on the political controversies and polemics which raged within the socialist movement during these turbulent years, but there was also room for philosophical discussions presented by the Italian Labriola, the Russian George Plekhanov,[11] Dutch socialist Christian Cornélissen[12] and others. To the work of foreign theorists can be added the scholarly researches of French writers outside the socialist tradition into philosophical issues related to the place of Hegel in Marxist theory.

Before the First World War, there was therefore some basis on which French socialists could judge the nature of the materialist dialectic and

the relationship between Marx and Hegel, drawing on their own
political and philosophical traditions, and on work produced by the
international socialist movement.

In comparison with the level of theoretical activity among German,
Italian and Russian socialists, the French appear distinctly
underdeveloped, especially in their contribution to Marxist philosophy.
It may be true that the reunified Parti socialiste unifié (SFIO) implicitly
agreed after 1905 that 'la théorie divise, la pratique unit', and covered its
divergences with a theoretical silence.[13] At all events, in the decade
which preceded the war and that which followed it, little progress was
made in developing Marxist theory in France beyond the stage it had
reached in 1900. When the beginnings of a new advance emerged in the
1920s it came in a changed world, where the political and social forces
had been dramatically restructured both by the Great War and by the
revolutionary upheavals which accompanied it.

Hegel in France

Tout ce qui est réel est rationnel, tout ce qui est rationnel est réel,
avait-il dit. On peut s'armer de ce principe pour maintenir ce qui
est, et pour consacrer tous les progrès, pour demeurer stationnaire
et pour provoquer des révolutions, pour légitimer le quiétisme
politique, comme aussi l'impatiente ardeur des changemens [sic].

A. Lèbre, in La Revue des deux mondes, 1 janvier 1843, 18

The attempts of French Marxists to unravel the complexities of the
dialectic did not take place in an intellectual vacuum, as is sometimes
supposed. On the contrary, their reflections drew on a well-established
current of French socialism, which was familiar with Hegelian ideas and
held the German philosopher in respect and esteem as an early
exponent of revolutionary theory. They could also draw on a weaker,
but still important, academic tradition of Hegel studies, concerned with
mostly religious aspects, but not excluding valuable work on the
rational structures of dialectic.

The commonly received academic view has it that after more than a
century of ignorance and neglect, Hegel's thought suddenly erupted in
the centre of French intellectual life to occupy a place of unexpected
prominence, which it still holds. Whatever its attractions and
convenience, that view does not correspond to historical reality. Hegel
was not introduced into France by the existentialists in the 1940s or
even the 1930s, however much they contributed to his subsequent

popularity. In fact, he had long been known and studied by the French socialist and progressive movement, whose interest was primarily responsible for the attention which philosophers of other persuasions focused on him.

A. Lèbre's judicious observation of 1843, that Hegel's principles could legitimize either political quietism or the impatient ardour for change, was accurate in pointing to two diametrically opposed tendencies inherent in Hegel's thought – the conservative and the revolutionary.[14] They were represented by a corresponding opposition among those who discussed his ideas in France. The resulting polarization in French attitudes to Hegel has structured discussion of his ideas since his own lifetime. Succeeding generations of socialists maintained a sympathetic interest in the philosopher, from Leroux and the Saint-Simonians through Proudhon to Herr and Jaurès. Since the First World War the French communists have continued the tradition by promoting his cause as an ancestor of Marxism and the progressive movement. On the other hand, the largely conservative philosophers of the French university responded by a conspiracy of silence, at times breaking into public expressions of hostility, and occasionally, but rarely, exploring the possibilities of adapting Hegelian ideas to their own forms of conservative idealism. Only in the decade preceding the Second World War did the latter tendency begin to flourish, more than thirty years after Right-Hegelian movements had held sway in Britain, the United States, Germany and Italy. The basic conflict between Left and Right in the Hegelian succession is the major cause of the illusion that, in the words of one recent commentator, following the 'utter absence of interest in Hegel', there was an 'abrupt turn to Hegel in the 1940s', which signified 'a break with traditions of thought'.[15] A brief survey of Hegel's implantation in France confirms the extent of the conflict and reveals the pre-eminence of socialist thinkers in introducing Hegel into French intellectual life.[16]

During his lifetime, Hegel had been an early admirer of the French Revolution, and later of Napoleon. He had close contacts with French intellectual life, including occasional visits to Paris, where he exercised a strong influence on the young Victor Cousin, before the latter rallied to the conservative July Monarchy and abandoned Hegel with other progressive ideas and aspirations of his youth. After Hegel's death, in 1831, a number of presentations and expositions of his thought appeared in histories of philosophy, but, apart from one or two enthusiastic germanists, academic commentators were inclined to treat it with caution, pointing to the radical consequences drawn by militant Young Hegelians in Germany. Generally, it was Saint-Simonians like

Prosper Enfantin, socialists like Pierre Leroux and progressive thinkers like Jules Michelet and Edgar Quinet who introduced, and made active use of, Hegelian conceptions. Much of their interest centred on his pantheism, whether, like Enfantin, to develop a religious metaphysic for their socialism, or, like Leroux, to tease out the progressive spirit from its metaphysical encumbrances. From the late 1830s onwards, the major French socialist writer, Pierre-Joseph Proudhon, was deeply impressed by Hegel's dialectic, even though it was imperfectly transmitted and understood, as Marx vigorously demonstrated in his *Misère de la philosophie* (Paris, 1847).[17] In Proudhon's defence, it might be pointed out that, until the mid-1850s, the only French translation available was of Hegel's *Aesthetics*.

The presence in Paris in the 1840s of a large population of political exiles emphasized the radical possibilities of Hegel's dialectic, for among them were many Germans of the Young Hegelian movement, including Marx and Engels, as well as revolutionaries who, like Mikhail Bakunin, came from other countries or traditions but held Hegel in high esteem. In the aftermath of the Europe-wide upheavals of 1848, Hegel's name was commonly linked with revolution. Characteristic of this association is the Comtesse de Gasparin's popular story *L'Hégélien* of 1858.[18] Set in 1849, it relates a brief encounter between a very respectable French lady traveller and the dangerous but dashing captain of a revolutionary militia unit. The Hegelian captain is last seen disappearing over the German border with his men, and it is with a mixture of (social and political) relief and (sentimental) regret, that the lady later learns of his brutal execution by Prussian government troops.

Parallel to the revival of the socialist movement in France and internationally in the 1860s came a brief upsurge of academic interest in Hegel. The major factor was probably the French translation of Hegel's *Encyclopedia of Philosophical Sciences* which appeared in instalments over twenty years from 1859. Even then, it was the work of a dedicated Italian Right-Hegelian, Augusto Véra, distinguished more by his enthusiasm than his competence. At the same period, positivists like Renan and Taine were exploring the possibilities of using Hegelian idealism to construct non-Christian religious philosophies. But generally the spiritualist reaction shied away from Hegelianism, considering that, in the words of Emile Beaussire, 'c'est le matérialisme sous le nom d'idéalisme objectif'.[19] Reticence turned to bitter hostility from this quarter in the wake of the Franco-Prussian War and the Commune, with Hegel reaping opprobrium on the one hand for the works of German nationalism and on the other for those of revolutionary socialism.

With the exceptions of Quinet and Michelet, French socialism during three-quarters of the nineteenth century was excluded from the university, and regarded with suspicion and hostility. Those socialists who, like Proudhon, wrote theoretical works, were less concerned to write about earlier thinkers than to use their ideas, where appropriate, in their own analyses. With the involvement of increasing numbers of intellectuals in the socialist movement, the 1880s began to see a new concern to turn the apparatus of academic enquiry on to the socialist tradition and its important ancestors, combined with the beginnings of an acceptance by the university that such subjects could properly be studied in academic terms. Hegel benefited from the academic labours of leading socialist intellectuals like Lucien Herr, Victor Basch, Charles Andler and Jean Jaurès. The latter two both devoted large sections of their doctoral theses to examining Hegel's relation to German socialism, and Herr's article on Hegel in the *Grande Encyclopédie* played an important role in the development of interest in Hegel from the early 1890s to the approach of the Great War.[20]

The growing distribution of works by Marx and Engels gave added impetus to the study of Hegel, who was increasingly discussed in terms of his influence on Marx. A Sorbonne thesis of 1907 was devoted to that sole question,[21] and the topic was further evoked at a session of the Société française de la philosophie, which was devoted entirely to Hegel.[22] But by this time the Hegelian revivals in the rest of Europe and in America were also attracting attention, and important studies appeared in France which, while acknowledging the Marxian connection, were concerned mainly with Hegel's philosophy as a rational ordering of human knowledge, quite apart from any practical or political implications. Georges Noël's classic work on the *Logic* was the best of these.[23] War, again, and the revolutionary upsurge which followed in its wake, introduced a hiatus in the developing interest. But Hegel had become too deep-rooted during the thirty years preceding the Great War for the interruption to be more than temporary.

The 1920s were marked by a further noticeable growth in Hegel's importance in France. Socialists like Andler, Herr, Basch and Edmond Vermeil occupied important posts in the Sorbonne, the Ecole normale supérieure and the Collège de France. Their teaching was influential in spreading knowledge of Hegel's ideas. Two significant developments of the 1920s were the resurgence of interest in the religious dimension of his thought and a new interest in the value of his dialectical reason. Philosophers like Emile Bréhier and Paul Archambault pointed to the religious origins of his ideas, and directed students like D. D. Rosca and Jean Wahl towards Hegel's early works in which the religious preoccupations were more prominent.[24] On the other hand, one of the most sympathetic commentators in the rationalist tradition was the philosopher of science, Emile Meyerson, who saw Hegel's assertion of the unity of reason as a possible foundation for a new form of scientific rationality, and as a weapon against positivism.[25]

Since the early nineteenth century, the scandal of Hegel's socialist associations had been aggravated by his unorthodox religious position: he was a protestant, widely regarded as a pantheist, and even, some thought, an atheist. That still made him a risky reference point for French academic philosophers even when they were otherwise attracted to his ideas. However, these inconveniences might have been overcome, as they were in Germany, Italy, Britain and the United States, had it not been for the close identification felt between Hegelian philosophy and the Prussian state. It is undoubtedly true that the Franco-Prussian War of 1870–71 prevented France from experiencing the kind of Hegelian revival that occurred among its neighbours. As a result, Hegel's thought was effectively barred from the French universities for most of the century following his death. The Hegel revival of the 1930s and 1940s, the supposed 'break with traditions of thought', was nothing other than his readmission into the accepted canon of official academic philosophy.

Hegel's readmission into respectable society was made possible by the long-standing interest of French socialists in his historical contribution to socialist theory. The periodic spates of national anti-germanism were less influential among socialists, particularly since these spates either contained, or were accompanied by, campaigns of repression against the labour movement, and especially against its socialist leadership. The ideological extermination of Hegelian philosophy after 1871, in particular, was accompanied by the physical extermination of tens of thousands of *communards*, and followed by a physical and ideological witch-hunt against socialists of all descriptions. But in the last two decades of the nineteenth century it was the socialists who reintroduced Hegel into French intellectual life. Building on that work after the Great War, it was they too who made the major contribution to 'naturalizing' Hegel to the point where his ideas became an integral part of contemporary debate.

The 1920s

Les renaissances de l'esprit correspondent à la découverte d'une matière nouvelle. Cette découverte succède à une période sans matière, période de convulsions inconscientes, en dépit d'une conscience tout apparente: débauche d'artifices et de complications irréelles; période de nuances, de raffinements, en un mot: scolastique.

Georges Politzer, 'Introduction', L'Esprit, 1, mai 1926; reprinted in his Ecrits, I (Paris, 1973), 23

The holocaust of the Great War and the enormous upheavals which followed it worked a dramatic transformation in French socialism. The general acquiescence in a patriotic 'union sacrée' was slowly replaced by a militant pacifism and the surging desire to bring in a new social order. Henri Barbusse's powerful anti-war novel *Le Feu*, which appeared in the summer of 1916, was a rallying point for this new movement. It sold a quarter of a million copies by the end of the war. Grouped around Barbusse were many young socialist intellectuals searching for an alternative to the discredited and defunct Second International, among them writers like Raymond Lefebvre, Jean-Richard Bloch and Paul Vaillant-Couturier. From the end of 1917, they and older writers like Anatole France and Romain Rolland looked to the October Revolution in Russia to show the way in which a new socialist society might be built. Even many who hesitated to endorse the Bolsheviks under Lenin were drawn towards support for them by revulsion at the Allied intervention and savage blockade against the young Soviet republic, the more so since it continued long after the end of the war in Europe and claimed the lives of several French sympathizers, including Raymond Lefebvre.

The political and ideological ferment of the post-war months produced an irresistible leftward swing in the SFIO, culminating in the decision of its Tours congress in late 1920 to adhere to the Third, Communist, International. The consequent division into two parties, a majority communist and a minority socialist, was one aspect of the fragmentation and decline of French socialism which characterized the 1920s. Over the years, large numbers of writers and intellectuals passed through the newly formed communist party (SFIC), which was itself wracked by successive crises as opposing tendencies struggled for leadership against a background of falling support and growing repression. The most publicized intellectual flirtation of these years was the decision of the surrealist group to join the party in 1927. That writers like Breton, Eluard and Aragon should have been drawn to an organization which was at the time both highly sectarian and pervaded by anti-intellectualism is perhaps surprising, and apart from Aragon, most surrealists left again shortly afterwards. But it also indicates something of the intellectual attraction which the communist ideal exerted.

In the domain of ideas, the spread of Marxism was by no means immediate. Marxist culture in France was generally as mediocre after the war as it had been before it. For the most part it was nourished by the debates surrounding Lenin and the development of the Soviet Union. The communist party made an early effort to circulate Lenin's major works, in conformity with the Comintern policy of promoting Marxism-Leninism. But the effort flagged amid internal squabbles, and until the late 1920s the only works of Marx and Engels to be republished at the party's instigation were the *Communist Manifesto* and *Socialism: Utopian and Scientific*. The gap was largely filled by the enormous undertaking of Jacques Molitor's translation of the complete works of Marx and Engels, published by Alfred Costes. Nearly half of the sixty or more volumes appeared between 1924 and 1928, almost all devoted to political and economic works. But three volumes, published in 1927, were given over to Marx's early philosophical writings, including *The Holy Family* (1844), his doctorate (1841), and the *Contribution to Hegel's Philosophy of Right* (1843). These constituted an important addition to the known materials which could assist the development of Marxist philosophy in France, even if the editing and the translation left much to be desired. In the same year, 1927, there also appeared a translation of the influential work of George Plekhanov, *Fundamental Problems of Marxism* (1908). This classic short study emphasized the importance of Hegel's philosophy as the 'algebra of revolution'.[26] Plekhanov emphasized that it was not applied to the burning problems of practical life by Hegel himself, and that it was left to Marx and Engels to realize its revolutionary potential by setting it 'right side up' on a materialist basis. He recognized the contribution of German idealism to the formulation of the dialectic, and closely related Hegel's analysis to that of Engels. Plekhanov pointed out, however, that Hegel's dialectic was itself largely derived from practical experience, and therefore readily lent itself to a materialist interpretation.

From the point of view of French Marxist philosophy, the most important event of the 1920s was the appearance in French in 1928 of Lenin's major philosophical work *Materialism and Empirio-criticism* (1908), the first volume of his *Collected Works* to be translated. In many respects, it marks the beginning of the new stage of development of Marxist philosophy in France, occurring, as always, some years after the resurgence of Marxist political and economic theory. Lenin's book offered a wide-ranging exposition of Marxist philosophy and rapidly became the standard treatise on the subject. It was, however, a polemical work primarily aimed to defend the materialism of Marxism. Consequently, it contained little extended discussion of the dialectic as such, and confined its discussion of Hegel largely to questions relating to his idealism. Valuable though the work was, it tended to divert attention from the rational contribution of Hegel to Marxism, even though, as other works later showed, Lenin himself held Hegel's dialectic in high esteem.

As the 1920s closed it was still true that the main works of Marxist philosophy published in France were the work of foreign theorists. What was conspicuously absent was any significant effort on the part of French Marxists, or non-Marxists for that matter, to explore the philosophical implications of the classical works of Marxism, to articulate them in the context of the France of their time, and to develop them beyond the level of the popularizing outlines in which they still largely remained. But the foreign monopoly was only temporary. A patient but intensive work of assimilation was proceeding, the necessary preliminary to any worthwhile contribution.

Study groups were formed by young intellectuals at the Ecole normale supérieure and in other institutions. The 'Philosophies' group of the middle and late 1920s drew together young philosophers of the calibre of Georges Politzer, Paul Nizan, Henri Lefebvre, Georges Friedmann and Pierre Morhange. Small and usually shortlived reviews appeared, like *Philosophies* itself (from 1924), *L'Esprit* (from 1926, and not to be confused with the Catholic *Esprit* founded in 1932), and *La Revue marxiste* (1928). They articulated something of the new direction, which was also intermittently reflected in Romain Rolland's *Europe* (founded in 1923) and Henri Barbusse's *Monde* (founded in 1928, and not to be confused with the post-1945 newspaper *Le Monde*). These scattered and largely unco-ordinated groups slowly developed a more confident grasp of Marxist theory, as distinct from the often woolly conceptions of socialism that they had inherited from their elders. Groping and uncertain though their beginnings were, their efforts laid the foundations for the blossoming of French Marxist philosophy which occurred in the 1930s.

References

1   K. Marx, *Grundrisse* (London, 1973), 83–111. The appearance of the Berlin edition of 1953 is the time at which the German text became known and generally available, though a limited edition was published in Moscow in 1939.
2   K. Marx and F. Engels, *Selected Works* (London, 1968), 180–184.
3   *Ibid.*, 182–183.

4   F. Engels, *Anti-Dühring* (London, 1947), 34.
5   F. Engels, 'Feuerbach and the End of Classical German Philosophy', in Marx and Engels, *Selected Works*, 584–622, p. 590.
6   Engels, *Anti-Dühring*, 34–35.
7   Engels, 'Feuerbach', 588.
8   Engels, *Anti-Dühring*, 34.
9   Engels, 'Feuerbach', 590.
10 G. W. F. Hegel, *The Phenomenology of Mind* (London, 1966), 202–209.
11 Georges Plekhanov, 'La philosophie de Hegel', *Ere nouvelle*, octobre 1894, 138–146; novembre 1894, 258–280.
12 Christian Cornélissen, 'La dialectique hégélienne dans l'oeuvre de Marx', *La Revue socialiste*, février 1901, 185–200.
13 See Daniel Lindenberg, *Le Marxisme introuvable* (Paris, 1975), 104.
14 A. Lèbre, 'Crise actuelle de la philosophie allemande: Ecole de Hegel, nouveau système de Schelling', *Revue des deux mondes*, 1 janvier 1843, 5–42. See quotation at the head of this section.
15 Mark Poster, *Existential Marxism in Postwar France* (Princeton, 1975), 3–5.
16 For a more detailed discussion of the points in this section, see Michael Kelly, 'Hegel in France to 1940', *Journal of European Studies*, xi (1981), 29–52.
17 In K. Marx and F. Engels, *Collected Works*, VI (London, 1976), 105–212.
18 Comtesse A. E. (Valérie) de Gasparin, 'L'Hégélien' in her collection of stories *Les Horizons prochains* (Paris, 1858), 112–136.
19 Emile Beaussire, 'Le centenaire de Hegel en 1870', *Revue des deux mondes*, 1 janvier 1871, 145–161.
20 Charles Andler, *Les Origines du socialisme d'Etat en Allemagne* (Paris, 1897); Jean Jaurès, *Les Origines du socialisme allemand* (Paris, 1892); Lucien Herr, 'Hegel', in *Grande Encyclopédie*, XIX (Paris, n.d.), 997–1003, which appeared in 1893–94; Victor Basch, *Les Doctrines politiques des philosophes classiques de l'Allemagne* (Paris, 1927).
21 Léopold Leseine, *L'Influence de Hegel sur Marx* (Paris, 1907).
22 René Berthelot, 'Sur la nécessité, la finalité et la liberté chez Hegel', *Bulletin de la société française de la philosophie*, avril 1907, 115–140. Berthelot's paper was followed by a discussion, also reproduced in the *Bulletin*, in which pp. 183–184 are particularly relevant to the Marx/Hegel debate.
23 Georges Noël, *La Logique de Hegel* (Paris, 1897).
24 Cf. Emile Bréhier, *Histoire de la philosophie allemande* (Paris, 1921); Paul Archambault, *Hegel, choix de textes et étude du système philosophique* (Paris, 1927); D. D. Rosca, *L'Influence de Hegel sur Taine* (Paris, 1928); Jean Wahl, *Le Malheur de la conscience dans la philosophie de Hegel* (Paris, 1929).
25 Emile Meyerson, *De L'explication dans les sciences* (Paris, 1921).
26 G. V. Plekhanov, *Fundamental Problems of Marxism* (Moscow, 1977), 40.

2

The Irruption

1929–1939

Marxism and the crisis of the 1930s

Or, voici que tout change; depuis quelques années, depuis la
grande crise économique, on voit se multiplier les éditions des
principaux ouvrages de Marx et d'Engels . . . . les études marxistes
foisonnent.

Pierre Gérôme, 'Le marxisme pénètre en France', Europe,
15 août 1935, 612

Du moins n'a-t-il échappé à personne que l'irruption, vers 1930, du
matérialisme dialectique dans les débats publics et jusque dans
l'Université était un fait nouveau et de première grandeur.

Lucien Sève, 'Transformation de la philosophie française', La Pensée,
janvier – février 1960, 88

The Wall Street Crash of October 1929 provoked a moral and
ideological reaction in France long before its economic and political
efforts became noticeable there. The collapse of Western structures of
trade and finance took almost two years to strike the relatively
cushioned French economy, plunging it into a deepening crisis which
continued thoughout the 1930s. Even before the shock wave struck, the
anticipation of it had spread dismay and confusion through the
country, throwing into question the values and ideas which dominated
French culture. As the material effects grew more severe, so the cultural
effects intensified. The five years from 1929 to 1934 witnessed an
effervescence among the young generation of intellectuals as they tried
to renew and recast the tottering ideologies inherited from their elders.
In particular the traditions associated with the right-wing and centrist
groupings of the Third Republic fell rapidly into disrepute as they
appeared not only unable to understand the very palpable crisis, but
also incapable of any meaningful action in response to it.
The crisis in the economy thus precipitated a cultural crisis of far-

reaching importance. The discredit which fell upon the various forms of conservatism, nationalism, pragmatism, liberalism and their ilk provided a crucial opportunity for Marxism to make important advances as a coherent and effective alternative ideology, offering persuasive analyses and a programme of action in response to the crisis. The residual Marxist inspiration among the social democrats undoubtedly played some role in popularizing Marxism, but the primary vehicle for Marxism in France was unquestionably the Communist Party. It was to the PCF that many young intellectuals turned in search of a world view which would arm them to understand and change the decaying world they saw around them. The PCF was active in various movements grouping intellectuals in the defence of culture, against fascism, for peace and in other progressive causes. Its militancy and commitment in practice attracted many to its side and led them to give serious attention to the theoretical principles it stood for. At the same time the party was reorganizing itself under Maurice Thorez, who became its secretary in 1930, and who laid great importance on the development of Marxist theory. As a result of his initiatives a huge effort of publication was undertaken, and study groups, reviews, lectures, schools, discussions and other forms of intellectual activity were promoted.

In France, as in other countries, many of the most educated and talented members of the intelligentsia were drawn to Marxism. Well-publicized examples came from the ranks of writers, artists, film-makers, natural and social scientists, among others. There were also a number of young philosophers who turned their minds to researching and developing the principles of Marxist theory in their own specialist area. To the young groups and small reviews of the middle and late 1920s were added new ones like *Avant-poste* (1933) and *Bifur* (1930), as well as the substantial monthly *Commune* which played a major intellectual role from the time of its foundation in 1933 by Aragon and Vaillant-Couturier. *Europe* moved closer to Marxism during the same period and both it and Barbusse's *Monde* began to reflect and encourage the growing interest in questions of Marxist philosophy. Even Emmanuel Mounier's progressive Catholic review *Esprit* evinced a growing curiosity in the development of Marxist ideas. The study groups of the Cercle de la Russie neuve and its successor the Association pour l'étude de la culture soviétique played a major part in fostering discussion and original thought on philosophical questions, manifested in a number of important published works. This new generation of Marxist philosophers contained some brilliant names. Some of them – Paul Nizan, Georges Politzer, Jacques Decour, Jacques Solomon and Henri

Mougin – died prematurely during the Second World War, or as a
result of it. Others, like Henri Lefebvre, Auguste Cornu, René
Maublanc, Roger Garaudy and Georges Cogniot survived to make
important contributions to post-war Marxist debate.

After the riots and demonstrations of February 1934, the
politicization of the French intellectuals grew rapidly. The rising tide of
the Popular Front movement drew communists, socialists and liberal
democrats together in concerted action, promoting the exchange of
ideas and values. A growing awareness of common problems provided
the atmosphere in which the cogency of Marxist analyses was
increasingly recognized. The disoriented quest for intellectual
innovation of the early 1930s gave way to the polarization of two hostile
blocks based on traditional class alliances. But the balance of power was
shifting, and in the camp of the growing labour and progressive
movement, the position of the communists (and hence of Marxism) was
consolidated and strengthened. The same picture was discernible on an
international level, with the forces of fascism meeting a hardening
resistance, organized in groups such as the anti-fascist Amsterdam-
Pleyel movement of Barbusse and Romain Rolland, and symbolized in
the fight to defend the Spanish republic. Foremost among the anti-
fascists were the Marxists, but as their prestige and influence grew so did
the hostility of their opponents.

Concurrent with the rising activity of French Marxists, increasing
numbers of Marxist writings from other sources became available, in the
shape of a continuing proliferation of works by its founders and a
growing number of works by Lenin and other Soviet writers. The
Costes edition of the complete works of Marx and Engels was
substantially finished by 1938, though by present-day standards it was
very far from being complete, and several of the works in it suffered
from poor editorial standards. Most noteworthy of the series, from a
philosophical viewpoint, was the appearance in 1937 and 1938 of
volumes containing Marx's 1844 economic and philosophical
manuscripts, the subject of much ensuing controversy, and the joint
work *The German Ideology* (1845–46), in which he and Engels
undertook to settle accounts with their former philosophical
conscience.

The PCF publishing houses ensured that practically all the major
known works of Marx and Engels were published or republished, and
available in cheap editions. They initiated the practice of thematic
anthologies from their works, devoted to current social and political
questions, but also to cultural topics such as literature, art, philosophy
and religion.[1] With the aid of the Soviet foreign languages publishing

house, they also made available the works of Lenin in similar fashion, beginning the publication of his collected works, a project which the war interrupted after eight volumes had appeared.

Commercial publishers saw the existence of a growing market, and Gallimard in particular published several important works by Marxist intellectuals, including editions by Lefebvre and Guterman of anthologies of Marx and Engels, and of Hegel. Of particular significance was the edition, by the same writers, of part of Lenin's philosophical notebooks. Published as *Cahiers sur la dialectique de Hegel* (1938), it included the central text of the notebooks, a conspectus of Hegel's *Science of Logic*, which Lenin had read and commented in 1914. The conspectus clearly reveals Lenin's respect for the Hegelian dialectic and the time and energy he devoted to its study. More perhaps than any other text, it stimulated French Marxists to reappraise the importance of Hegel in the materialist dialectic.

The first concern of the young French Marxist philosophers of the 1930s was to put to practical use the principles they had conscientiously studied, rather than to develop a reformulation of them. Paul Nizan expressed it forthrightly when he explained the need for a new philosophy in France, adding: 'il n'est pas question d'une invention, d'une création miraculeuses, mais d'un ralliement à la philosophie de Marx et de Lénine'.[2] He took it for granted that an adequate Marxist philosophy existed which was there to be appropriated and used. His own attack on bourgeois philosophy in *Les Chiens de garde* (1932), or his friend Georges Politzer's attack on Bergson in his pamphlet *La Fin d'une parade philosophique: Le bergsonisme* (Paris, 1929) are characteristic of the prevailing attitude.

Nizan saw philosophers as divided between those who supported the comfortable exploiting bourgeoisie and those who were on the side of the workers, the exploited and suffering majority of humanity. Philosophy was therefore similarly divided, and while not denying the efficacity of ideas, Nizan insisted that their effects were essentially social. Marxism was seen primarily as a political weapon of the working class in its struggle for revolutionary social change, and secondarily as an intellectual weapon enabling its holder to subject opposing views to devastating criticism. There is a rare vigour in *Les Chiens de garde* which can be found in many of the writings of these years. The crusading force of the new generation of Marxist intellectuals was fuelled by a heartfelt rejection of the complacency and conservatism of the Sorbonne, and by high progressive aspirations touched with revolutionary romanticism. To these factors may be ascribed the unilateral and oversimplified positions which they espoused on certain issues. The cognitive dimension of philosophy was a major victim, overshadowed by an acute awareness of the social, and notably political, dimension. The stark polarization of society in the interwar years, reflected in the 'class against class' policy of the Communist International during the late 1920s and early 1930s, served to confirm the simple dichotomy which Nizan and his comrades perceived in philosophy.

These circumstances did not foster a prolonged attention to the specifically philosophical questions within Marxism, much less an extensive examination of its unquestionably bourgeois intellectual roots. The first efforts in this direction were embodied in the pioneering thesis on the young Marx which Auguste Cornu defended at the Sorbonne in 1934.[3] Cornu proposed an intellectual biography which traced the formation of Marx's thought from his early Hegelianism to the formulation of historical materialism in 1845. The importance of his study lay less in the reappraisal of Marxist principles than in the demonstration of their intellectual origins in Hegelian philosophy, and in the presentation of a range of historical material which was otherwise little known or studied. Following the conventions of doctoral theses of the time, it was largely expository and avoided making overt judgements, which might have been considered provocative. The most he ventured was in his conclusion, where he suggested that if the dialectic is a law of real development as Marx thought, rather than a form of thought, then Marxism is basically true.[4]

Cornu's view of the dialectic did not propose any fundamental distinction between Hegel's and Marx's other than its transposition from a form of pure thought to a theory of social and economic development. More generally he saw Marx as essentially a successor to Hegel, and wrote elsewhere that 'cette doctrine de l'action qui sert de fondement à tout le système marxiste, se rattache étroitement à la philosophie de Hegel et constitue l'aboutissement, le terme dernier de la pensée romantique allemande'.[5] His emphasis on the German basis of Marx's thought can be related partly to the academic context in which the thesis was written. A student of the germanist and socialist Charles Andler, to whom he dedicated the work despite Andler's hostility to its general orientation, Cornu was concerned primarily with intellectual developments in Germany of the 1840s, and devoted his supplementary thesis to Moses Hess and the Left-Hegelian movement. The consequent narrowing of focus led him to dismiss or neglect the French and English sources of Marx's thought, and the effects of the historical circumstance on his evolution.

Whatever the shortcomings of the work, Cornu's thesis played an important role in introducing Marxism into the French university.

More significantly, it drew attention to the Hegelian roots of Marx's thought and made available a wealth of little-known material, including the *1844 Manuscripts*, which had appeared in German only two years before Cornu's book was published. It therefore occupied a central place in the reappraisal of Marxist philosophy which was beginning to emerge in the middle 1930s.

Whereas Cornu's work was primarily an individual effort, the same period saw the beginnings of a concerted attempt to organize the collective work of Marxist intellectuals. The small groups and reviews of the late 1920s were an early expression of the need to work together, but tended to assemble côteries of like-minded individuals with a limited impact beyond their immediate circle. Henri Barbusse's weekly *Monde* was an exception in basing its appeal very broadly, but if its appeal was to intellectuals, its content was more concerned with political militancy than with theoretical questions. And the diversity of its interests and perspectives was so great that it survived scarcely a month after Barbusse's death in September 1935. The monthly *Commune* was founded in July 1933 by Paul Vaillant-Couturier and Louis Aragon as the organ of the Association des Écrivains et des Artistes Révolutionnaires, and tried in the area of culture to emulate *Monde*'s breadth of appeal. But in the area of science and philosophy it proved more difficult to bring Marxist intellectuals together.

The establishment in 1929 of the Cercle de la Russie neuve brought together Marxist scientists of stature: the great physicist Paul Langevin, the great psychologist Henri Wallon, and several colleagues of scarcely lesser talent. They were joined by other social scientists and by philosophers to the point at which, from 1933 onwards, the *commission scientifique* of the Cercle was able to produce a series of papers of original research on Marxism in relation to philosophy and the sciences. The first collection of these essays was published in 1935, edited by Wallon under the title *A la lumière du marxisme*, and was followed by a second volume under the same title two years later.[6] Containing more than a dozen essays, the first volume dealt with a range of subjects in the natural and human sciences as well as questions of the dialectical method and materialism. Dominating the latter section was an important study by the philosopher René Maublanc on the relation of Marx and Hegel.[7] Maublanc was, with Georges Politzer, one of the first French Marxists to attempt a comprehensive exposition of Marxist philosophy, and he sought to clarify, in his study of Marx and Hegel, the nature and status of the materialist dialectic.[8]

Developing Engels' distinction between idealism and materialism, Maublanc sees Marx's originality in the rejection of Hegel's system as idealist, while retaining the logical method used to construct it: the dialectic. He acknowledges the richness and invention of Hegel's philosophy, but argues that its collapse was related to the subordination of nature and history to the idea. When the world changed, the profound conservatism of the Hegelian system left it unable to match the change. Marx alone provided a comprehensive critique of Hegel, integrating his dialectic with materialism, where other Left-Hegelians also abandoned the system, but took the unsatisfactory options of a dialectical idealism (Bruno Bauer, Max Stirner) or a non-dialectical materialism (Ludwig Feuerbach). Maublanc sees the 'inversion' process as a common-sense rejection of idealism, leaving the rational dialectic as a method which reflects the movement of the world, and is guaranteed by its success in practice.

For Maublanc, as for most of his contemporaries, the Hegelian dialectic was transferred, in an inverted form, into Marxism. The method was seen as radically separable from the idealist system and not noticeably affected by its natal environment. Maublanc devoted some time to analysing Hegel's logic, and considered the dialectic to be his major achievement, constituting 'la logique de toute philosophie contemporaine'.[9] On the one hand, he may be criticized for not examining any transformation of the dialectic subsequent to its inversion. But, on the other hand, the relative neglect into which philosophy had fallen among French Marxists made Maublanc's essay something of a rehabilitation. In another pamphlet of the same year, Maublanc pointed out the influence of the German Social Democrats, especially Kautsky and Bernstein, in excluding Hegel and the dialectic from the accounts of Marxism current in the French socialist tradition.[10] In this light, Maublanc's work takes an important step in emphasizing, against the scholasticism of the Second International theorists, and against the disdain of much French academic philosophy, the importance of the Hegelian dialectic in the formation of dialectical materialism.

On the level of Marxist philosophy, Maublanc undoubtedly initiated a crucial rediscovery. His role was all the more important because of his age and background. A generation older than Nizan or Politzer, Maublanc was a pupil of Anatole France, grew up in the rationalist tradition, and, now in his forties, held a philosophy post at the prestigious Paris lycée Henri IV. Though not a member of the PCF until the occupation, he was a committed Marxist and an influential fellow-traveller. His discussion of the dialectic in 1935 not only broke new ground for the period, it also stood (among philosophers and party militants alike) as an authoritative statement of the Marxist view.

A new elaboration

La méthode, pour perdre la forme limitée de l'hégélianisme et
devenir une raison moderne, doit subir une nouvelle élaboration.
Elle n'est pas comme une boîte que l'on vide de son mauvais
contenu pour y mettre un contenu meilleur. Elle ne se prend pas à
Hegel comme une pièce de machine. L'unité du matérialisme et de
la dialectique transforme ces deux termes.

Henri Lefebvre and Norbert Guterman, Introduction to Lénine,
Cahiers sur la dialectique de Hegel *(Paris, 1938), 1967 edition, 16*

Among the prolific young Marxist intellectuals of the generation after
Maublanc, most were more concerned to apply their principles rather
than examine the finer points of their history and structure. But there
were two notable exceptions: Henri Lefebvre and Norbert Guterman,
who devoted enormous energy to exploring these domains. Fascinated
from the early 1930s by the possibilities latent in Marx's early writings,
the two philosophers produced a series of joint works exploring the new
themes offered. Many of the early writings dealt with Hegel, among
them a section of the *1844 Manuscripts* dealing with Marx's critique of
the Hegelian dialectic. Lefebvre and Guterman made and published the
first French translation of it in 1933.[11] Their 1934 edition of selected
works by Marx and Engels drew heavily from the early writings, and
their essay *La Conscience mystifiée* (Paris, 1936) set similar material to
work in a critique of ideology, culture and thought in bourgeois society.

Soon after the appearance of the Russian original, the polyglot
Guterman and Lefebvre began work on a translation of Lenin's
Philosophical Notebooks, of which the central text, on Hegel's *Logic*, was
published in 1938. The extent of their accumulating interest in Hegel
can be judged by their publication of a selection of his works the
following year. Their analysis of his relevance to Marxism is set out at
length in the 130-page introduction to their translation of Lenin's
notebooks, which introduced a radical reinterpretation of the question.
Its influence in the 1930s was curtailed by the outbreak of war and the
ensuing censorship, but it has been amply repaid by a wide circulation
since its reissuing in 1967 in a popular paperback format.

In their introduction, dated September 1935, Lefebvre and Guterman
declare that Lenin's notebooks reveal a new depth and complexity in
the process of inverting the Hegelian dialectic. They distinguish a form
and a content of Hegelianism, neither of which is readily separable from
the other. Part of Hegel's content therefore passes into dialectical
materialism. Of Hegel's theory, they argue, some can simply be

translated into modern terms and retained, some must be rejected outright or entirely upturned, while other aspects lie between the two extremes. The dialectical method must therefore receive a new elaboration which will take account of the effect materialism and the dialectic have upon each other when united in the Marxist synthesis. The inversion of Hegel thus appears as one moment in a wider process of reformulation of the revolutionary philosophy of Marxism.

The effort of reflection represented by this analysis marks it out qualitatively as a major step in the development of French Marxist philosophy and an attempt to come to grips with the complexities of the Hegelian system. Its novelty does not, however, go without dangers. The traditional distinction between the dialectical method and the idealist system is subverted, first by its restatement as a distinction between form and content, second by the assertion that, since the two are inseparable, part of the content passes into Marxism, where it is reworked. The advantage of this subversion is to show the intimate bond between method and system and to counter the tendency to a simple mechanical view of the process of separating them. On the other hand, Lefebvre and Guterman open the way to a substantial importation of new Hegelian elements into Marxism, since the method, or form, is declared adopted after mere 'translation' into modern terms, and the system, or content, is selectively incorporated, subject to reworking.

A second, allied, subversion occurs with the concept of inversion. It is used as a synonym for the transposition of Hegelian concepts, and also to indicate the correction of an undesirable misapprehension over ontological priority. The mechanical view of the operation is again replaced by a more complex conception. But the notion of inversion is reduced to that of an adjustment, removing an important error of procedure but not fundamentally undermining the results of a great intellectual tradition. Here as elsewhere, the two writers introduce a new subtlety of analysis at the expense of Hegelianizing Marxism.

Guterman and Lefebvre go on to examine the contribution of Hegelian ideas to a series of questions in Marxist philosophy: the theories of contradiction, truth, consciousness, and degrees of reality; the concepts of essence and appearance, overcoming (*Aufhebung*), practice and alienation. Of these, the first one concerns the central structure of the dialectic – contradiction – and occupies a crucial position in the Marxist conceptual framework. The two writers rapidly trace the development of the consciousness of contradiction to the point where Hegel united it with a consciousness of historical movement to found dialectics as a science. Hegel then abandoned the concrete history of dialectical awareness, his *Phenomenology*, for an abstract history of the idea, his *Logic*. But since he was able to derive an objective dialectic from dialectical consciousness, thereby founding an ontology, it is difficult to avoid Hegel's procedure without confining the dialectic to an internal movement of mind, which the classics of Marxism follow Hegel in refusing to do.

Lefebvre and Guterman propose to resolve the problem by distinguishing contradiction in being from the consciousness of contradiction which reflects reality. This, they argue, results in a more consistent dialectic than even Hegel achieved, because the attempt to reduce real contradictions to expressions of dialectical logic encloses reality in a closed and eternal ideality, deprives it of life and opens the way to an outdated and impoverished pluralist view. Contradiction in reality, they affirm, is the dynamic force of progress, valued not for its own sake, but because it is the motor of movement. Consequently, the dialectical method is not only a method of analysis, the procedure of seeking contradictions in things, but also the reflection in thought of the tumult of seething matter, the ascension of life, the epic of evolution, rising above successive catastrophes: in short, the entire cosmic drama.

This picture, arising from Lenin's reading of Hegel, binds the subjective and objective dialectics together in a global vision. It invests the dialectical method with the riches, not of an ideal system, but of the material universe. Thought is no longer a neutral instrument of analysis but an exciting dimension of reality in which the laws of movement of the material world are reflected. The vivacity of Lefebvre's and Guterman's account is undeniable. But their Marxism, consistent with their view of inversion, remains a philosophical system, albeit a more exhilarating one than the idealism they criticize. The process of reflection is conceived as taking place entirely within thought, and the existence of practical sanctions and determinants is but barely hinted at. The grandeur and dignity of human thought is justly asserted, but in emphasizing its internal dynamism they tend to cloak its dependence on social existence. The ontological priority of being over thought, which they recognize, has not merely a cognitive importance, in determining what is known, but also an epistemological importance, in determining how knowledge is produced. It is on this last point that Lefebvre and Guterman reveal, by omission, the limitations of their espousal of materialism, and the excessive autonomy they attribute to the dialectic. The limitations of their materialism were not irremediable in principle, provided the neglected dimensions were suitably nurtured. But as their thought developed, it became increasingly apparent that the Hegelianizing dynamic of their interpretation could only exacerbate the incipient dematerializing of the dialectic.

The self-inverting dialectic

Peut-être est-il possible de dépasser l'hégélianisme en son propre nom, et du dedans, en partant de ses propres contradictions, en gardant l'essentiel de son mouvement. Peut-être faut-il accepter dans son immensité – nature, spontanéité, action, cultures si diverses, problèmes nouveaux – le 'riche contenu' de la vie. S'il déborde notre pensée, s'il nous faut l'explorer et l'approfondir sans pouvoir l'épuiser, il faudra aussi lui ouvrir la pensée.

Henri Lefebvre, Le Matérialisme dialectique *(Paris, 1939),*
1974 edition, 50

Having taken up permanent residence in the United States, Norbert Guterman ceased to have any major part in the progress of French Marxism after the mid-1930s. New York's gain was Paris's loss, but his colleague Henri Lefebvre pursued their common researches with determination and vigour. Quite the most successful product of his pen was the short but dense study which Lefebvre published on the eve of the war, *Le Matérialisme dialectique* (Paris, 1939). Written as an attempt to state in concise form the major principles of Marxist philosophy, the essay was immediately acclaimed. Though banned and burnt during the occupation, it was influential in attracting many intellectuals to Marxism, and in stirring an awareness of the complexity and subtlety of its philosophy. Even to the present day it continues to exercise a widespread influence.

Lefebvre begins by outlining the superiority of the Hegelian dialectic over formal logic, based on the dialectic's attempt to achieve a synthesis of the concept and its content, and therefore a synthesis of thought and being. He describes how Hegel resolves the contradiction between being and non-being in the third term of becoming, which is continual development, ultimately grounded in the Idea or Mind. But he points out that Hegel's system falls into formalism, since he seeks to derive content from its concept, and does not resolve or suppress contradictions in reality, only in ideas. Nonetheless he feels that Hegel's ambition to unite thought and being, the ambition of all philosophy, is valid, and that, following the internal movement of Hegel's dialectic, it is possible to achieve an acceptance of the content which will henceforth direct the development of the concept. He claims that this is the course broadly followed by Marx and Engels from 1843 to 1859, at the end of which they arrived at their final position.

Lefebvre traces their successive criticisms of Hegel's theory of the state, of religion and of alienation, particularly in the *1844 Manuscripts*. He accepts only a limited influence for Feuerbach's materialist critique of Hegel, and is at pains to emphasize how intellectually poor Feuerbach was in comparison to Hegel, and how critical Marx and Engels were of his limitations, even while they were praising his humanism. He sees the historical materialism of *The German Ideology* (1845 – 46) as a unity of idealism and materialism, which is turned against Hegel, Feuerbach and philosophy generally. Not until 1858, he argues, did the dialectic make a return to Marxist thought, with Marx's rediscovery of Hegel's *Logic* and Engels' subsequent elaboration of the dialectic as an indispensable element of dialectical materialism, in which 'idéalisme et matérialisme sont non seulement réunis mais transformés et dépassés'.[12] Marx's dialectic, though the opposite of Hegel's in status, retains for Lefebvre the same categories as Hegel's, and as a method of exposition is simply the reconstruction in thought of the internal movement of the concrete content. Consequently, he suggests, Marxism gives a dynamism to the static Hegelian dialectic. Where Hegel sought the ultimate resolution of contradictions in Mind, Marx finds it in practical activity, Praxis.

It would require a lengthy exposition and commentary to do justice to Lefebvre's closely argued text, but even a brief survey reveals the seriousness of his project to assert the Hegelian element in Marxism. It also reveals the far-reaching implications inherent in his stance. On a purely historical level, there are clear limitations to Lefebvre's account. Hegel is treated as almost the sole theoretical source of Marxism. The reduction of Feuerbach's role is controversial enough, but the omission of any serious consideration of French socialists and English economists is clearly a misrepresentation. His dating of Marxism is equally contentious: 1843 for the emergence of historical materialism and 1859 for dialectical materialism. In fact, the dates are entirely fixed by Marx's attitude to Hegel, beginning with his first critiques and ending with his rediscovery of the *Logic*, and presumed reintegration of the Hegelian dialectic. No significance whatsoever is accorded to Marx's and Engels' own account of their development, and no intervening date is considered as marking any important changes. In themselves the historical problems are of secondary import, but they reflect a Hegelianization which leads to an extensive reinterpretation of the development of Marxism. The rewriting of history, while serious enough, is of a piece with Lefebvre's redrafting of Marxist theory.

The view that Marxism is an outgrowth of Hegelian philosophy is central to Lefebvre's argument. He proposes to 'dépasser l'hégélianisme en son propre nom, et du dedans', suggesting that Marx essentially developed the dialectic along the lines of its own innate orientation. To some extent this suggestion echoes Marx's and Engels' acknowledgement of the inherently revolutionary potential of the dialectic, which was tending to burst the Hegelian system apart. But the perception of an internal contradiction between dialectic and system is not equivalent to accepting it as the motor of Marxism's development.

However much the Hegelian dialectic may undermine the primacy of the concept over the content, it did not 'invert' itself, as Lefebvre suggests. Nor would a 'self-inverted' dialectic be materialist, but rather an even more subtle form of idealism. The reason for this can be explained in terms of the relation between concept and content. In the Hegelian system the concept is the truth of its content and therefore accepted as the reality. If the content were seen to 'spill over' its concept it would be possible to argue that the concept needed closer definition or even reformulation, without thereby conceding the reality or primacy of the content in principle. Even if the reality of the content were conceded, its primacy would not necessarily follow. A content is intelligible only in terms of something in which to contain it. But if reality is, by definition, 'contained', then its container, in this case concepts or thought, must be at least coextensive with it and inseparable from it. The content cannot then have primacy or priority over its concept; at best they may be co-equal. But since materialism requires the primacy and priority of being over thought, Lefebvre's subtly inverted dialectic falls short of being materialist.

To foist a non-materialist dialectic on Marx is both an aim and a result of Lefebvre's Hegelianism. In the process, he expressly excludes the intervention of substantially non-Hegelian elements in Marx's development. Were he to admit them, it would lend force to the view that the inversion of the dialectic had to be undertaken from a standpoint outside the Hegelian system, and indeed outside of philosophy itself. His treatment of Feuerbach is consistent with the rest. He asserts that 'l'étude du développement de la pensée marxiste ne montre pas une "période feuerbachienne" mais une intégration et en même temps une critique continue de la pensée de Feuerbach'.[13] The denial that Marx or Engels went through a Feuerbachian period is not only against the evidence available to Lefebvre in 1939, but is proven to be flatly wrong by a letter, published in 1958, which Marx wrote to Feuerbach in August 1844. Enclosing an essay of his own for the philosopher's scrutiny, Marx declared:

I am glad to have an opportunity of assuring you of the great respect and – if I may use the word – love, which I feel for you. Your *Philosophie der Zukunft* and your *Wesen des Glaubens*, in spite of their small size, are certainly of greater weight than the whole of contemporary German literature put together.

In these writings you have provided – I don't know whether intentionally – a philosophical basis for socialism, and the Communists have immediately understood them this way.[14]

Whatever its limitations, Feuerbach's materialism was taken, as late as mid-1844 when Marx was completing his Paris *Manuscripts*, to provide the 'philosophical basis for socialism'. Lefebvre's view therefore appears plainly in the unflattering light of an attempt to excise philosophical materialism from Marxism, even where it unquestionably existed. Moreover, he characterizes Feuerbach himself as being essentially a Hegelian, albeit of an inferior variety, minimizing the importance and consistency of his materialism and his critique of Hegel. In thus emphasizing the undoubted deficiencies of Feuerbach, he operates a wide reductionism which ignores not only Marx's views of 1843–44, but also Engels' well-known acknowledgement of the philosopher's importance, written from the vantage point of mature reflection in 1886. Consequently Marx's own materialism is virtually assimilated to an aspect of internal conflict within Hegelian philosophy.

Lefebvre's silence concerning the role of socialism and political economy in the development of Marxism is likewise a means of encompassing it within Hegel. Non-Hegelian intellectual influences are passed over, and so are important practical experiences, of political activity and of the growing capitalist economies. Without these important elements, there is no way of explaining Marx's development except as internal to Hegelian philosophy. Without an external materialist standpoint, how can Hegel be stood upright on his feet? Even if his feet can be distinguished from his head, how is it established which is up and which is down? In the space of pure thought, ideas are weightless. The Hegelian system might rotate endlessly in such conditions, defining up and down solely in relation to itself. In Feuerbach's materialism and in their own practical activity, Marx and Engels found the basis for a standpoint in relation to which they could orient the Hegelian dialectic and set it on a materialist footing.

The non-materialist ramifications of his Hegelian dialectic are further manifested in Lefebvre's curious characterization of historical materialism as 'l'unité de l'idéalisme et du matérialisme'.[15] The apparent paradox of how materialism can be both materialist and idealist is illuminated by the self-inverting dialectic. Lefebvre depicts Hegelian idealism inverting itself to assimilate Feuerbach's materialism. But he conceives the resulting 'historical materialism' as a philosophical product which at the same time exposes the inadequacy of philosophy, with its ideological illusions. The tension, or struggle, between the two antithetical philosophical positions therefore produces a dialectical passage to a higher level, that of 'praxis'. In this way he argues 'le matérialisme historique accomplit la philosophie en la dépassant'.[16]

With philosophy left behind, having served its purpose, what is left is the materialist conception of history. Later, in 1858, the Hegelian dialectic is added to it as a method of working, and the two elements combine to form dialectical materialism. But Lefebvre is careful not to admit any philosophical content to finished Marxism. At most, he refers to 'la pensée marxiste'. Philosophical materialism therefore disappears, having been 'transcended', from the synthesis of historical and dialectical materialism, which for Lefebvre constitutes Marxist thought.

The transcending of philosophy is a theme drawn from *The German Ideology* (1845–46), in which Marx and Engels 'settled accounts' with their 'erstwhile philosophical conscience'. Lefebvre quotes this text to present Marxism as the end of philosophy as such. Consequently, he rejects the possibility of constructing a systematic Marxist philosophy, on the grounds that Marx never repudiated his position expressed in *The German Ideology*.[17] Certainly Engels considered that philosophy 'has been expelled from nature and history' in so far as it has been replaced by science, although he conceded a role for it in 'the theory of the laws of the thought process'.[18] But both Engels and Lefebvre speak of a characteristic Marxist theory, conception, thought, and world view. To some extent Lefebvre is playing with words. When Marx and Engels initially rejected philosophy, the term meant for them the speculative idealism of classical German philosophy. They did not, then or later, fall into the positivist mistake of denying the value of general conceptualizations based on the laws of thought and the natural and social sciences. In particular they did not shrink from making 'philosophical' statements about the determination of thought by being, rather than the contrary. The real end of philosophy was not the abandonment of general principles, of intellectual syntheses or of conceptions of the world. It was the demonstration that thought does not create the world or even itself, that consciousness must seek elsewhere than in itself the foundation of its own existence and development, and the principles of movement of nature and history. It was the overweening ambition of speculative philosophy, not all

philosophy as such, that Marx and Engels rejected. Lefebvre's purpose
in rejecting philosophy, in the broad sense, is at least partly to overcome
the problem of philosophical materialism. His own Marxism
(philosophy or world view) studiously restricts materialism to the
function of a title, and evacuates the materialist content both from
Marx's development and from his mature theory. In place of
materialism he offers an updated, self-propelling Hegelianism whose
idealism is nominally disowned but substantially retained.

Stalin and dogmatism

Dialectical materialism is the world outlook of the Marxist-
Leninist party. It is called dialectical materialism because its
approach to the phenomena of nature, its method of studying and
apprehending them, is *dialectical*, while its interpretation of the
phenomena of nature, its conception of these phenomena, its
theory, is *materialistic*. . . . When describing their dialectical
method, Marx and Engels usually refer to Hegel as the philosopher
who formulated the main features of dialectics. This, however,
does not mean that the dialectics of Marx and Engels is identical
with the dialectics of Hegel. As a matter of fact, Marx and Engels
took from the Hegelian dialectics only its 'rational kernel', casting
aside its idealistic shell, and developed it further so as to lend it a
modern scientific form.

> J. V. Stalin, Dialectical and Historical Materialism *(1938)*;
> New York edition, 1940, 5

Dogmatism as a way of thinking, whether in ordinary knowledge
or in the study of philosophy, is nothing else but the view that
truth consists in a proposition, which is a fixed and final result, or
again which is directly known.

> G. W. F. Hegel, *Preface to* Phenomenology of Mind
> (London, 1966), 99

Of all the discussions of Marxist philosophy to appear during the 1930s,
unquestionably the most influential was the famous short essay by
Joseph Stalin extracted from the *Short Course of History of the CPSU*.
Published under the title *Dialectical and Historical Materialism* (1938), it
has aptly been described by Isaac Deutscher as 'a crude digest of the
Marxist theory of dialectics'.[19] Its crudeness lies in the simplified and
schematic summary it gives of Marx's and Engels' thought. But its

simple schematism is also its pedagogic strength, which was reinforced, until after his death by the prestige and authority of the Soviet leader.

Cutting through complex interrelations, Stalin distinguishes the dialectical method from the materialist theory. He acknowledges that Hegel 'formulated the main features of dialectics' and identifies Hegelian dialectics as the 'rational kernel' which Marx and Engels took and developed further after casting aside the 'idealistic shell'.[20] The dialectical method is then explained in terms of four principles which distinguish it from metaphysics: that nature is 'a connected and integral whole'; that it is 'a state of continuous movement and change'; that development occurs as 'a transition from quantitative changes to qualitative changes'; and that the process of development is 'a disclosure of the contradictions inherent in things and phenomena . . . a "struggle" of opposite tendencies'.[21] Philosophical materialism, for Stalin, is characterized by three principal features which oppose it to idealism: it holds the world to be material, composed of matter in motion, developing in accordance with its own laws; it asserts that matter or being is an objective reality, existing independent of, and prior to, mind, which reflects it; and it believes that the world and its laws are fully knowable, knowledge of those laws being established as objectively true by means of practice and experiment.

As a plain man's introduction to Marxism, Stalin's exposition is clear and readily understood. However, its sweeping generalizations and neat distinctions are deceptively simple. The dialectical method, developed to grasp a shifting and complex reality, comes to resemble a blunt instrument in Stalin's hands. That which in Marx and Engels was a supple and responsive guide to enquiry, becomes a rigid and imperious set of rules. Materialism, in turn, appears impoverished. The robust child and guardian of Marx's and Engels' quest for scientific knowledge becomes an arbitrary and disembodied credo in Stalin's formulation. Materialism and the dialectical way of thinking were intimately bound together in Marx's synthesis; in Stalin's system they are distinct and separate components. These criticisms, though valid, would be of relatively minor importance if the work in question were a brief introduction aimed at an unsophisticated audience. They assume major importance, however, when they concern a work which for most of fifteen years was widely regarded as the definitive statement of Marxism. Because of the yawning discrepancy between its historical importance and its cognitive value, the many other more detailed objections which could be levelled at the essay will be left for examination in later chapters concerned with the efforts to exorcise Stalin's ghost from Marxist philosophy after his death.

Stalin's work was circulated in large numbers throughout France in the few months preceding the outbreak of war as an effective means of promoting a knowledge of Marxist philosophy: 300,000 copies of the *Short History*, which contained it, were sold in nine months. Its influence is therefore more visible in the post-war period than in the 1930s, where it was a latecomer to the theoretical scene. But influential as it was, both at the time of its appearance and later, Stalin's essay was not blindly adopted as the final word on all philosophical matters, even by those communist writers who professed the greatest allegiance to his ideas. True, during the worst Cold War years, from 1949 to 1952, it was often taken as a point of retrenchment on which communists could close ranks. But it was exceptional, rather than the rule, for philosophers to resort to exegesis of Stalin's analysis as such. More commonly, their tendency was to take for granted his distinction of a dialectical method and a materialist philosophy, treating them as separate components. A parallel division was therefore introduced into their view of Hegel whose idealist philosophy was counterposed to his dialectics. The dialectical method was implicitly accepted, though it tended to be assumed that Engels' reformulation was sufficient and dispensed Marxists from re-examining Hegel himself. The 'inversion' process, referred to in the afterword to *Capital*, was not mentioned by Stalin, but rejection of the idealist shell was held to cover what Marx meant.

Lefebvre later described his *Matérialisme dialectique* as an episode in the struggle against dogmatism, and singled out Stalin's essay as a primary culprit in the tendency to dismiss Hegel's and Marx's own early works.[22] Whatever reproaches Stalin's essay deserves, it does fully acknowledge Hegel's elaboration of the dialectic. However, its incipient tendency to counterpose dialectic and materialism did lead in practice to an over-concentration on materialism at the expense of the dialectic. Hegel, as the arch-idealist, was undoubtedly a victim of this process. On the other hand, Lefebvre's charge of philosophical dogmatism is entirely unhelpful. It is true that, by the early 1960s, dogmatism became a codeword for any intellectual tendencies associated with Stalin, but it has limited value as a concept with which to analyse the struggle of ideas which was taking place.

It may be useful to recall Hegel's definition of dogmatism, as 'the view that truth consists in a proposition, which is a fixed and final result, or again which is directly known'.[23] Hegel, in contrast, sought to emphasize the importance of reasons and the process of enquiry behind propositions as an integral part of truth. Marx developed the same idea, attacking dogmatism as the tendency to argue from abstract and unsupported premises. Even Stalin denounced dogmatism, pointing out

that Marxism is not a collection of dogmas, and that 'some of its
formulas and conclusions cannot but change in the course of time'.[24] In
none of these senses can the prevailing view of Hegel be dismissed
simply as dogmatic. It is true that Stalin, in his philosophical essay, and
others who emulated him, presented Marxism in a dogmatic manner,
but the substance of their argument is not rebutted by pointing out this
fact.

In a more constructive spirit it could be argued that Stalin's schematic
manner of presentation was largely responsible for the separation of the
dialectic from materialism, and thus in turn for a suspicion of Hegel, so
that ultimately dogmatism is to blame. Such an interaction of form and
content was certainly present in Stalin, but his contribution was only
part of the Marxist position and he was even a latecomer in the debate,
which was already well established. Where the label dogmatism is
fundamentally inadequate is in referring ideological divergences to
differences of form, particularly to a manner of presentation. It suggests
that the truth of a position is established by its mode of expression.
Although a position may be vitiated by dogmatic presentation, it is not,
conversely, the case that the truth of any position is enhanced by a non-
dogmatic expression. Equally, conclusions enunciated dogmatically may
be capable of substantial restatement in non-dogmatic form.

Hence, although dogmatism played a part in the Marxist resistance to
Hegel, it is entirely possible that equal resistance might be reached from
a non-dogmatic analysis. For example, the attack on his idealist system
could be muted on the grounds of the system's considerable materialist
content, but on the other hand, his dialectic might be discovered to be
more deeply infected with idealism than had earlier been allowed.
However that may be, the charge of philosophical dogmatism also
obscures the crucial fact that the struggle of ideas was not conducted
purely within a closed intellectual system, but in a context of intense
political and ideological struggle.

In this perspective it is helpful to invoke the more ancient sense of
dogma as a principle imposed by authority, and accepted by virtue of
the person or body enunciating it rather than by virtue of its inherent
rationality, persuasiveness or truth. It is undoubtedly the case that
Stalin's authority and prestige tended to impose his formulations,
discouraging critical discussion. Dogmatic acceptance of ideas because
they were Stalin's does not have any necessary bearing on the truth
value of the ideas, and it would be entirely perverse to reject them
simply because they carried a charge of authority. But dogmatism has a
very important bearing on the social and political existence of the ideas.
In particular, it raises questions of the forms of organization within the

Marxist movement, the state of class conflicts, and the development of the struggle for socialism both in France and internationally. The ascendancy of Stalin within the Soviet Union and within the Third International were substantially established by the early 1930s. Among French Marxists his approach and achievements were looked to as a model, even if they were neither fully known nor fully emulated. But it would be a misleading oversimplification to ascribe the success in France of Stalin's view of Marxism purely to the imposition of a foreign model of political action and organization. To a considerable degree, Stalin's schematic and dogmatic conception of philosophy which prevailed immediately before the Second World War and intermittently until the late 1950s, responded to the political and ideological conditions facing Marxism in France at the time. A beleaguered movement was often glad to turn to a simple manifesto which could furnish clear slogans.

In defence of materialism

Pendant que la bourgeoisie devenue conservatrice s'est détournée du matérialisme, celui-ci demeura intact dans les larges masses du peuple français. L'avant-garde du prolétariat révolutionnaire adopta le matérialisme moderne: le matérialisme dialectique et le matérialisme historique qui constituent, comme l'écrit l'*Histoire du Parti bolchévik*, 'le fondement théorique du communisme, les principes théoriques du Parti marxiste'.

Georges Politzer, 'La philosophie des lumières et la pensée moderne',
Cahiers du bolchévisme, *juillet 1939, in his* Écrits, *1*
(Paris, 1973), 126

French Marxists were generally reluctant to go as far as Lefebvre or Guterman in embracing Hegelian ideas, and felt a consequent hesitation in developing their understanding of the dialectic beyond Stalin's cryptic outline. Their attitude was conditioned by the general state of ideological struggle in France and internationally, which in turn was conditioned by social and political developments. The growing polarizations of the late 1930s intensified the battle of ideas, and placed Marxists in something approaching a state of siege. Though they had made important advances in establishing the credibility and influence of dialectical materialism, they found their beliefs even more strongly attacked than before. The extension of Marxism socially also brought an increased danger of dilution and compromise in matters of principle.

As always, the most direct assault continued to be directed against the adherence to materialism.

On a philosophical level, the overwhelming predominance of idealism in French and European academic circles confronted Marxists with the urgent task of asserting the value of materialism, and its importance in Western thought. In France, the materialist tradition had been virtually written out of the history of philosophy. A pall of disrepute, perpetuated by ignorance, had fallen over even its most illustrious representatives, whether the great names of classical antiquity: from Democritus to Epicurus and Lucretius; or those of France's own brilliant intellectual past: from Gassendi to Diderot and the Encyclopédistes. In such circumstances, a necessary emphasis on the defence of materialism frequently led to the dialectic's being relegated to an undeservedly minor role.

Hegel inevitably fell into some neglect as materialism held the centre of Marxist attention. He was, after all, an idealist, and in his lectures on the history of philosophy he had made harsh judgements on some of the early materialists. Paul Nizan's essay Les Matérialistes de l'antiquité (Paris, 1938) noted with disapproval the many calumnies Hegel had heaped on Epicurus.[25] The main reference text for the Marxist philosophers of this period, Lenin's Materialism and Empirio-criticism (1908), was concerned primarily with defending materialism against a variety of more or less subtle forms of idealism. But even in this work Hegel is not simply identified as an idealist. His refutation of Hume's and Kant's attack on cognition is commended; the superiority of Hegel's objective idealism over subjective realism is noted; his analysis of freedom and necessity is approved; and his role in formulating the dialectic is recognized, though not elaborated on. Though neglected, Hegel was not forgotton by Lenin, and the young Marxists defending materialism in the 1930s followed his example.

Georges Politzer, probably the most brilliant of the Marxists of his generation, was characteristic. He identified materialism as the cutting edge of progressive thought, adopted by the bourgeoisie in their revolutionary struggle against feudalism, but abandoned in haste once their power was secured. In modern times, he said, the working class had taken up materialism as a weapon in its own struggle against capitalism.[26] But second to materialism, and ultimately inseparable from it, rationality was also a powerful means of pushing forward human progress. In this respect Hegel deserved recognition as a great defender of reason against reactionary obscurantism. Like the philosophes of the Enlightenment, Hegel had also been excluded or misrepresented by the French education system. For the most part it had wanted nothing to do with his rational dialectic, preferring to consider him, if at all, as an eccentric metaphysician. Politzer endeavoured, in 1939 in the newly founded Marxist journal *La Pensée*, to defend Hegel against the neo-positivism of Albert Bayet, the Kantian idealism of Léon Brunschvicg, and the irrationalist vitalism of Henri Bergson.[27] He asserted the revolutionary value of his dialectical reason as an important contribution to the modern rationalism constituted by Marxism.

Hegel's rational dialectic was also amply recognized in the philosophy lectures which Politzer gave at the Université Ouvrière from 1932 to 1936. Though dominated by the affirmation of materialist principles, they included considerable elucidation of the dialectic. Published as a primer of Marxist philosophy after the war under the title *Principes élémentaires de la philosophie* (Paris, 1945), Politzer's conceptions have continued to be influential, as may be judged from the 200,000 copies of the *Principes* sold over thirty years. Unfortunately this very accessible introduction to Marxism gives at best an indirect view of Politzer's analysis since it is a reconstitution based on a student's notes from 1935–36, and has been revised and reorganized by various hands. But it can readily be observed that Politzer presents a fuller and more complex account than Stalin's essay, and that Hegel and the dialectic are at least adequately served.

It would therefore be wrong to depict French Marxists of the 1930s as anti-Hegelian, though in comparison to Lefebvre and Guterman they certainly appear lacking in enthusiasm. In some ways, they repeated Marx's own development. In the dozen or so years after his emergence from German idealism Marx showed scant respect for Hegel, only to return to his former mentor's defence when it seemed that the dialectical method itself was threatened with extinction. The parallels can even be extended to the social situations. Marx championed the materialist cause against the resurgent idealism of a bourgeoisie consolidating its position after the revolutionary upheavals of 1848. The French Marxists faced an even more ferocious retrenchment of the bourgeoisie after 1917 and the upheavals following the end of the Great War. It would be inaccurate to attribute the aggressive materialism of either Marx or the French Marxists of the 1930s to a planned policy: it was determined primarily by the conditions then prevailing. But it is possible to conclude that, at least in ideological terms (that is in terms of the social dimension of thought), materialism was perceived by friend and foe to be the most fundamental principle of Marxist philosophy. Engels and Lenin after him were wont to point out that the basic question in philosophy is the relation of being to thought.[28] Depending on which is given priority, either materialism or idealism result. If this is the primary theoretical question, it is strikingly appropriate that in the most difficult struggles of Marxism in two centuries it should also be the primary ideological question.

The primary question, however, is not the sole question, and if Lefebvre's protest against anti-Hegelianism is to be appreciated for its full value, it should be seen as a timely reminder that the materialism defended by Marxists must be dialectical. Although he may have neglected to emphasize the dialectic, Marx never abandoned it in his work. Lefebvre's fear was that French Marxism, and for that matter international Marxism, was not inherently immune from such an abandonment. It is unfortunate, however, that his intervention showed such clear signs of abandoning materialism in favour of an idealist dialectic. His rectification thus lost most of its force among his Marxist comrades, beleaguered by idealism of another stamp, and paradoxically reinforced their reservations about Hegel. The result was an overall loss to Marxist philosophy.

The irruption of dialectical materialism in France was a tangible fact of the 1930s. But the path was rough and thorny. If Marxists stumbled and erred it was the price they paid for their advance. But casting a retrospective glance over the decade, it is striking how rapidly that advance came. From the faltering steps of the small groups of isolated young intellectuals to the confident stride of a self-conscious movement, Marxist culture had taken a firm hold in French life. The 1930s posed many grave historical challenges, and it was their determined attempts to confront them that won Marxists their place. The antifascist movement, the Popular Front, the battle for Spain and the struggles of the working class and democratic forces were the fire in which French Marxism was tempered. It was by virtue of these social and political conflicts that a demand and an audience for Marxist philosophy were created, even among the intellectuals who constituted its first and major constituency. More than any other school of thought, Marxism reflects the conflicts of its time. The divergences and deficiencies of the different accounts of dialectical materialism are a clear witness to that.

If materialists were insufficiently dialectical and dialecticians insufficiently materialist, it was in part at least because of their circumstances. They were, after all, attempting to construct a new Marxist culture, strong enough and complex enough to meet the needs of a turbulent era, and drawing on both the wealth of international Marxism, and the rich intellectual traditions of France. But their problems were also inherent in the nature of Marxism. The materialist dialectic at the heart of its philosophy embodies tensions and complexities which offer endless scope for variation. A consistent materialism cannot finally be exhausted by conceptualizations. A dialectical approach to change and interrelation cannot be stated in definitive form. In their attempts to assimilate dialectical materialism, reformulate it to meet the needs of the day, and contribute to its creative development, French Marxists fell into many pitfalls and made many mistakes. They fell short of achieving their ambitions because those ambitions were so high. At the end of the decade, however, they had established a thriving culture of Marxist philosophy which, for all its faults, was dynamic and productive. It was the solid basis on which its later achievements were constructed.

References

1 *Sur la littérature et l'art*, edited by Jean Fréville (Paris, 1936); *Études philosophiques* (Paris, 1935); *Sur la religion*, edited by Lucien Henry (Paris, 1936).
2 Paul Nizan, *Les Chiens de garde* (Paris, 1960), 114, first published in 1932.
3 Presented at the Sorbonne as 'La jeunesse de Karl Marx' in 1934, it was published as *Karl Marx, l'homme et l'oeuvre* (Paris, 1934).
4 See quotation at the head of this section.
5 Auguste Cornu, 'Karl Marx et la pensée romantique allemande', *Europe*, 15 octobre 1935, 199–216, pp. 199–200.
6 *A la lumière du marxisme, essais* (Paris, 1935); and same title, volume II (Paris, 1937).
7 René Maublanc, 'Hegel et Marx', in the collective work *A la lumière du marxisme, essais* (Paris, 1935), 189–232.
8 Cf. René Maublanc, *La Philosophie du marxisme et l'enseignement officiel* (Paris, 1935); Georges Politzer, *Principes élémentaires de la philosophie* (Paris, 1945), based on a lecture course of 1935–36.
9 Maublanc, 'Hegel et Marx', 198.
10 Maublanc, *La Philosophie du marxisme*.
11 'Critique de la dialectique hégélienne', *Avant-poste*, juin 1933, 32–39; août 1933, 110–116.
12 H. Lefebvre, *Le Matérialisme dialectique*, 7th edition (Paris, 1974), 78.
13 *Ibid.*, 59.
14 K. Marx, Letter to L. Feuerbach, 11 August 1844, in K. Marx and F. Engels, *Collected Works*, III (London, 1975), 354.
15 Lefebvre, *Le Matérialisme dialectique*, 66.
16 *Ibid.*
17 See also the 'Avant-propos' to the 1961 edition, *ibid.*, 11.
18 F. Engels, 'Feuerbach and the End of Classical German Philosophy', in K. Marx and F. Engels, *Selected Works* (London, 1968), 621.
19 Isaac Deutscher, *Stalin* (London, 1966), 379.
20 See quotation at the head of this section.

21   J. V. Stalin, *Dialectical and Historical Materialism* (New York, 1940), 7–11.
22   See 'Avant-propos' to the 1961 edition, Lefebvre, *Le Matérialisme dialectique*, 5.
23   See quotation at the head of this section.
24   J. V. Stalin, *Marxism and Problems of Linguistics* (Peking, 1972), 53, first published in 1950.
25   P. Nizan, *Les Matérialistes de l'antiquité* (Paris, 1971), 44.
26   See quotation at the head of this section.
27   G. Politzer, 'La philosophie et les mythes', *La Pensée*, avril–juin 1939, 15–38, reprinted in his *Ecrits*, I (Paris, 1973), 128–179.
28   Cf. Engels, 'Feuerbach', 593.

3

War and Post-war

1939–1948

Marxism and the Second World War

Vous vous rappelez aussi l'aveu concluant de Drieu-la-Rochelle:
'Presque toute l'intelligence française est contre nous.' Et le journal
de Doriot confirmait: 'Les 9/10ᵉ au moins.'

*Georges Cogniot, Les Intellectuels et la Renaissance Française
(Paris, 1945), 16*

From September 1939 onwards the French Communist Party and its
activities were declared illegal, and the organization was obliged to
resort to clandestinity. Marxism as such was not banned by the French
government during the 'phoney war', though its conditions of existence
were made considerably more difficult. In the odd interlude period
between the declaration of war and the fall of France, Marxists
continued to write and publish, even though they had to proceed with
great circumspection. Lefebvre's *Le Matérialisme dialectique* made its first
appearance with Alcan at this time. The prohibition of his party was a
major reason why Lefebvre systematically omitted any specific reference
to communism, and why no concrete political issues were broached in
the book. Ironically, these omissions increased the book's appeal to
non-committed readers, and later commentators have even seen them
as its major strength.

One of the culminating intellectual achievements of the 1930s was the
foundation in the spring of 1939 of the Marxist review *La Pensée*.
Subtitled 'revue du rationalisme moderne', it was sponsored by Paul
Langevin, Henri Wallon and Georges Cogniot, and saw its role as
broadly encouraging a progressive culture rather than narrowly
proselytizing on behalf of the Communist Party. The review drew on
the scientists of the Cercle de la Russie neuve: Marcel Prenant, Georges
Teissier, Jacques Hadamard, Jacques Solomon, as well as young
intellectuals like Georges Politzer, Henri Mougin and Jacques Decour,
and historians like Pierre Vilar and Albert Soboul. Sympathetic non-

Marxists, such as Jacques Monod and Mikel Dufrenne, also contributed in their specialist areas.

The third issue of *La Pensée* appeared in the autumn of 1939, reduced to 64 pages, little more than a third of its previous size. Because it was not a specifically communist publication it was not forbidden, but with many of its contributors in uniform or in prison, it was unable to produce a further edition until after the Liberation. The creation of the review, however, marked a qualitative advance in the activity of French Marxists in the area of theory, providing an important base on which subsequent progress was built.

The events of the occupation from the spring of 1940 to the summer of 1944 have frequently been narrated. The pre-eminent role of communists in the Resistance won many French intellectuals for the party and many more for Marxism. Politzer, Decour and Solomon played a heroic part in founding the 'Université libre' movement. The clandestine paper of the same name appeared regularly from October 1940 and produced some hundred issues by the time of the Liberation. The same men were also instrumental in producing the clandestine journal *La Pensée libre* as a continuation of *La Pensée*. Only one issue of the journal appeared, in February 1941 within nine months of the German invasion. It included an attack on the racist theories of the Nazi ideologist Rosenberg, and a critique of Bergson's obscurantism on the occasion of his death, noting the embarrassment of the new authorities over the non-aryan status of Bergson, a Jew, whose ideas they generally found appealing. Politzer in particular contributed lengthily, and his attack on Rosenberg was reprinted, in an enlarged and improved version, as a clandestine pamphlet, *Révolution et contre-révolution au XXe siècle* (February 1941).[1]

Further publications in the series were prevented by the arrest of Politzer, Solomon and Decour, and by their subsequent execution as hostages in May 1942. As the repression intensified, the possession and distribution of Marxist literature became more difficult. The German occupying authorities, ably assisted by the Vichy regime, banned books by the dozen, organizing large-scale book-burning and massive destructions of any printed matter that could be regarded as even remotely subversive. Marxist writings were to the forefront among those destroyed and proscribed. But as Politzer pointed out, the assault included most of the French and international socialist writers and the thinkers of the enlightenment as well as large sections of French and world literature.[2]

The repressive and authoritarian regime rapidly alienated from itself the majority of writers and intellectuals, repelled by the naked assault on the values of culture and intelligence. All but a small minority refused to reject the bulk of their national heritage and traditions in favour of the reactionary medieval and fascist values being urged on them. The schools and universities went into covert or declared dissidence, rallying where possible to the defence of their members who came under attack. One of the first and most successul examples was the campaign launched on behalf of the great Marxist physicist Paul Langevin, arrested in October 1940, imprisoned and then released. But others followed. Very often Marxists were the main targets of repression and also the leaders of opposition to it. In this way a degree of unity was established which had not previously existed, with Marxists cast in a leading role in defence of the values of French thought and culture.

The inaccessibility of even basic works was a considerable setback for the development of the growing interest in Marxism. The battle of ideas did not stop, however, and the relative freedom of liberals or progressive Catholics to spread their views, albeit in diluted form, was an added handicap to Marxists. Non-Marxist thinkers who were associated with the Resistance were able to express their philosophical opinions more or less openly. Camus's Le Mythe de Sisyphe appeared in 1942, and Sartre's weighty L'Etre et le néant the following year; the Catholic reviews Esprit and Temps nouveaux were published during 1940 and 1941. Marxists were, however, deprived of the same freedom, and because of the limited and dangerous circumstances in which they wrote, were able to do little more than attempt to counter the worst of the right-wing and fascist propaganda which circulated freely with official subvention and approval.

The courage and heroism of many French people in opposing the occupation and its consequences is a matter of public record and legitimate pride. The growing organization of the Resistance movements enabled some continuity of publications to be achieved, though often at terrible cost in lives and suffering. The clandestine publications of the Communist Party included a widely circulated series of printings of central Marxist texts: the Communist Manifesto; Wages, Prices and Profits; Wage Labour and Capital; Socialism: Utopian and Scientific; State and Revolution and others. But the predominant orientation of Marxists was towards the active struggle for liberation of their country, rather than towards the development of theoretical questions. Most probably the distinguished Resistance record of prominent Marxists did more to confer prestige and authority on their beliefs than did more purely intellectual considerations. Certainly the occupation and liberation period witnessed a large-scale movement among intellectuals to join the Communist Party and to embrace the ideas of Marxism, preparing for the philosophical renewals that took place in the post-war period.

Crucial though the practical experience of resistance was in developing the influence of Marxism, it could not completely replace the cultural and intellectual activities which the occupation rendered almost impossible. In philosophy especially, it was hard to replace a militant intellectual journal of the calibre of *La Pensée libre*; it was harder still to replace the brave and talented intellectuals who died for their principles. Moreover, the clandestine press from the *Cahiers du bolchévisme* to *Les Lettres françaises* were increasingly concerned with the needs of the moment and the political questions of the nation's future. Philosophy was well down the list of priorities for which producers, distributors and readers of clandestine publications could be asked to risk their lives.

Hence at the Liberation, Marxist philosophy was in the paradoxical situation of enjoying unprecedented prestige while lacking the most elementary resources for communicating its principles to the avid public. The stock of Marxist books, pamphlets and journals was practically eliminated, and the difficult conditions of the economic reconstruction placed severe constraints on the amount that could be printed. These problems were overcome in the course of time, but the physical elimination of many of the best Marxist writers and thinkers was a catastrophe of quite a different order.

French Marxists realized with particular acuteness the truth of Stalin's often repeated dictum that 'man is the most precious capital'. The death of so many militant Marxist intellectuals was deeply felt. Among the philosophers alone, the toll was cruel. Georges Politzer in particular could not easily be replaced, for he was the most brilliant and energetic Marxist philosopher of his generation, but Jacques Decour and Jacques Solomon were also badly missed. Nizan, killed in the fighting of May 1940, had been estranged from the party over the German–Soviet pact of non-aggression, but his talent as a Marxist writer and philosopher could have been most valuable inside or outside the PCF. Henry Mougin, ten years younger than these, survived a few months after his return from a German concentration camp, long enough to show how heavy a loss his death was. More names could be added to the martyrology of Marxist philosophers to set alongside the grim list of historians, scientists and other intellectuals who died for their Resistance activities. But those named suffice to indicate the magnitude of the task faced by their survivors and successors in restoring Marxist philosophy to its pre-war level of quality and scope, let alone improving and extending it to deal with the new and complex problems of the post-war era.

Liberation and reconstruction

Héritiers du réalisateur Voltaire, de l'Encyclopédie à la fervente
pensée technique et du cartésianisme animé de nobles soucis
pratiques, les intellectuels s'uniront pour coopérer à la
reconstruction du pays, au relèvement de ses ruines.

Georges Cogniot, in Les Intellectuels et la Renaissance Française
(Paris, 1945), 23

The Liberation propelled Marxism into the forefront of French
intellectual life. In a way that would have been inconceivable in the
1930s, it became a central reference point, not only for its adherents and
sympathizers, but also for the other currents of thought which had
previously kept it at a very firm distance. The most vehement of its
opponents were discredited and silenced during the first months of the
post-war period, having mostly been compromised by their activities
during the occupation. Neo-Hegelians, existentialists, progressive
christians, christian-democrats, socialists and liberals professed a
respectful recognition of Marxism, even when they did not go further
and adopt Marxist analyses to their own intellectual frameworks.

But Marxists were, initially at least, ill equipped to take full advantage
of their sudden popularity. The severe depletion of their human and
material resources by the long years of repression, the hybrid ideologies
of many of their newer supporters, and the urgent social and political
tasks of national reconstruction, all militated against the rapid
development of Marxist ideas. Naturally Marxists, particularly the
Communist Party, made every effort to supply the needs expressed. But
demand greatly exceeded the possibilities of supply, and by the time the
gap was closed the ideological shutters of the Cold War were beginning
to descend. Even as late as the autumn of 1947, the PCF was deploring
the low level of theoretical training among many of its members, even
some in senior positions.[3] Roger Garaudy's complaint of 1945 that
intellectuals were far too often supporters without being activists,
continued to be an accurate reflection of the ideological leeway
Marxism had to make up.

During the years 1944–47, Marxist philosophy in general, and the
materialist dialectic in particular, suffered from the lack of creative
development. The national role in government played politically by the
PCF, the problems of political unity and relations between the
competing ideologies in France were key determinants in shaping the
philosophical priorities of Marxists.

As a result of the presence in government of communist ministers up to the spring of 1947, considerable emphasis was placed on the roots of Marxism in French thought. Roger Garaudy was particularly identified with the promotion of the French sources of Marxism-Leninism. He declared that 'Le communisme est sorti du mouvement de l'esprit français ... né du trésor de pensée rationaliste et d'action révolutionnaire de la France du XVIIIᵉ siècle, de la France de 89, de 48, de 71'.[4] Materialists and revolutionaries of the eighteenth and nineteenth centuries were invoked as ancestors. Though there was good cause to present these French connections, Garaudy failed to stress that Marxism had as often been developed in the criticism of their errors as in the adoption of their principles, and his presentation gave a one-sided picture of the formation of Marxism, as he was later obliged to acknowledge. But, more crucial for the philosophy of Marxism, the French precursors were not exponents of the dialectic. With the partial exception of Diderot, their materialism was largely of the mechanical variety, and they did not in any case provide the philosophical context from which Marxism emerged historically. The mid-1940s therefore saw a very welcome and long-overdue renaissance of French Enlightenment studies, in which Mougin, Garaudy, Lefebvre and many other Marxist scholars participated, but they did little to raise the level of Marxist philosophy itself.

One by-product of the attention focused on the eighteenth century was the formation of a project to produce a dialectical encyclopedia. Henri Wallon, Paul Langevin and Frédéric Joliot-Curie were anxious to sponsor its preparation, and Henri Mougin, until his untimely death, worked extensively on it.[5] The directorship was assumed by the prominent biologist Marcel Prenant. Like Diderot's *Encyclopédie*, it was to be a rational dictionary of the arts, sciences and technology, constructed according to an overall conception and offering an integrated account of human knowledge and achievement. Its proposers pointed out that no contemporary bourgeois publication could envisage such a plan because bourgeois ideology could no longer propose a unified conception on such a scale. Hegel's had probably been the last attempt to produce this type of encyclopedia. Marxism, on the other hand, they argued, offered the only all-embracing world view which might make the project possible, and it would serve the rising working class in the same way as the *Encyclopédie* had served the rising bourgeoisie under the Ancien Régime. Attractive though it was in 1945, the encyclopedic project proved unrealizable in practice. The progress of two centuries would have required massive resources of material and manpower to encompass it. Commercial encyclopedias were plentiful, and however defective their conception might be, they could command far greater resources in production and distribution. Nonetheless, the project went ahead until the deteriorating political situation made it economically unviable, politically difficult, and ideologically secondary to many more urgent tasks.

Considerations of political unity contributed to mute discussion of the more divisive aspects of dialectical materialism. It was increasingly recognized by social democrats and Catholics that the materialist conception of history was a powerful and productive account of society and its development. They were willing to espouse large parts of this account provided it could be divorced from a more general commitment to philosophical materialism. In the case of Christians it was evident that their religious faith could not be reconciled with it. In the case of social-democrats, like Léon Blum or Maximillien Rubel, their socialist convictions were based on an essentially ethical view, which rejected the possibility of any objective or scientific foundation. Since the christian-democrats, social democrats and communists composed the principal political forces of liberated France there was definite advantage for Marxists in not pointing too sharply to the philosophical differences between a fully consistent dialectical materialism and the various attenuated forms of Marxism which were widespread. These differences were not, of course, denied or ignored. They were frequently asserted in the various expositions of Marxism which appeared.[6] But there was little attempt to engage in lengthy theorizations in the area of disagreement, and the parties concerned were generally content to agree to differ.

If there was a mutual non-aggression pact between the political ideologies in coalition, there was no such agreement on the broader ideological level, especially so far as the new and fashionable existentialist movement was concerned. The extraordinary popularity of existentialism in the first five years after the war presented a major challenge to Marxism in the social strata to which it was newly spreading: students, the urban petty bourgeoisie and the intelligentsia. Even among committed Marxists, the strong injection of Hegelianism, which Lefebvre and others had introduced, provided a favourable tilth in which the seeds of existentialism might germinate. Much time and thought was directed by Marxist intellectuals to the examination and criticism of existentialism, particularly in the implications for morality of its theory of freedom, for psychology of its theory of subjectivity, and for politics of its theory of commitment. Several books were devoted to the subject: Mougin, Lefebvre and Jean Kanapa each contributed one, as did the prominent Hungarian Marxist George Lukács; and innumerable shorter studies appeared in reviews.[7]

A great deal has been written on these debates, most comprehensively by Mark Poster in his valuable *Existential Marxism* (Princeton, 1975), though his presentation is caught in the unenviable contradiction of an undisguised contempt for the Marxist critics combined with a general appropriation of their criticisms. It is not the present intention to review the various arguments and polemics which were deployed, but to point out that they related little and indirectly to the nature of the materialist dialectic. Certainly they were much concerned to assert the value of materialism against the idealist bases of existentialism, and to reject the latter's philosophical categories in favour of Marxist ones. Certainly, too, they were concerned to assert the rationality of the Marxist dialectic against the irrational foundations of the existentialist account of human existence. But in each case the result was much more a use of Marxist dialectics than an examination of it, though at times the polemical orientation undoubtedly led to an excessively unilateral presentation which did scant justice to the dialectic.

Overall, the result of the first three post-war years was a significant spread of Marxism in social extension, but little advance in deepening understanding of the materialist dialectic, as the central core of Marxist philosophy. But work was progressing and at least two of the scholars who had made signal contributions to it in the 1930s continued to do so in the 1940s. Henri Lefebvre and Auguste Cornu both produced important studies. But they were no longer alone in exploring their respective interests and their work came under increasingly informed scrutiny and consequently increased challenge.

Towards an objective idealism

Lorsqu'il s'agit de *cette question précise*: 'Quelle est la portée exacte de nos moyens de connaître? Quel est le rapport entre nos idées sur le monde et ce monde lui-même? Notre pensée peut-elle connaître le monde? Pouvons-nous, dans nos idées et nos conceptions du monde, nous faire une image de la réalité?', l'opposition entre le matérialisme et l'idéalisme cesse d'être absolue . . . . Sur ce point déterminé il y a accord entre les *idéalistes objectifs* et les *matérialistes*.

Henri Lefebvre, Logique formelle, logique dialectique
(Paris, 1947), 27

The synthesizing intelligence of Henri Lefebvre placed him to the fore among post-war Marxist philosophers. His position was further consolidated by a remarkably prolific pen. In the year 1947 alone, apart from a new edition of *Le Matérialisme dialectique*, he published in book form a study of Descartes, two short studies of Marx, a *Critique de la vie quotidienne* and an important treatise on formal and dialectical logic, in addition to articles and papers. Nor was the year uncharacteristic, for those which preceded and followed it saw scarcely fewer important works in diverse fields. During this period, Lefebvre was accorded more recognition and support from his communist comrades than at any other time of his career. *La Pensée* published an article of fulsome praise by the young Jean Kanapa at the end of the year, commending him as a model of 'la philosophie vivante'.[8] But the simmering idealism of Lefebvre's dialectic was scarcely diminished, bringing him into more explicit conflict with his fellow Marxists as time passed.

The relative evacuation of materialism which has already been discerned was at the centre of the problem. In his short exposition *Le Marxisme* (Paris, 1948) for the popular 'Que sais-je?' paperback series, Lefebvre dealt with materialism only indirectly, preferring to emphasize the dialectical nature of Marxism. His chapter on Marxist philosophy held two sections only: one on the dialectical method, and the other on the theory of alienation. He did acknowledge the importance of an objective, real foundation for human thought, but it was to stress the difficulties it posed for traditional methods of thought, which needed to be given the greater depth of dialectical reason. His view was that the search for truth through the contradictions of thought, and the objective basis of contradictions in reality, should both be admitted simultaneously. While, from the point of view of thought, his view is consistent with materialism, from the point of view of reality, it falls short of accepting the priority of being over thought, and therefore short of materialism.

As a popular introduction to Marxism, his short book has much to recommend it, and it may be unjust to tax Lefebvre with the precise formulation. On the other hand, the interpretation proposed has undoubtedly exercised a widespread influence, to judge by the popularity of the work, which sold well over a quarter of a million copies in the thirty years after its publication. At all events, his precise attitude to materialism is set out in detail in the 1947 treatise on logic.

Originally planned as the first of eight volumes to be written by Lefebvre in a series entitled *A la lumière du matérialisme dialectique*, the work *Logique formelle, logique dialectique* (Paris, 1947) was intended to determine the exact relations between formal and dialectical logic, and to rehabilitate the means of knowledge: reasoning, the concept or notion, and the idea.[9] Conscious that some readers would react against the seeming overemphasis on Hegel, Lefebvre recalled Lenin's high estimate of Hegel's *Logic* and warned against oversimplified versions of materialism. On the other hand he dissociated himself from the kind of neo-Hegelianism currently being elaborated by writers like Alexandre Kojève. Lefebvre postponed full discussion of the materialist elaboration of the Hegelian dialectic to a later volume, which was never produced. But in the introductory chapter, on the theory of knowledge, he broached the question of materialism in some detail.

Philosophically, he agreed, idealism and materialism were absolutely opposed and incompatible: the sciences and knowledge in general presuppose an external world, an object which is known, and which is the primordial element. Rejecting idealism, which in its various forms admits the primacy of thought over the world, Lefebvre pointed out that there is agreement between materialism and objective idealism in affirming the possibility of human knowledge of the world. Moreover, he suggested that the contribution of objective idealists has historically been greater than that of materialists in the development of a conceptual apparatus, and in particular of logic. He stressed that the naïve, practical conviction of the existence of things independently of human consciousness is at the basis of materialism: it cannot be theoretically demonstrated since it starts from a 'postulate' and is proved only by its internal coherence, its content, its practical consequences and its agreement with practice and the results of the sciences. Lefebvre rejected the crude accounts of mind and matter proposed by mechanical materialism, and emphasized that modern (that is, dialectical) materialism recognizes the real and active existence of thought, distinct from, but bound to, nature. He accepted that the world is not identical with our sensations of it, but asserted that, with the application of knowledge and practice to sense perceptions, the real depths of nature can be penetrated.

Lefebvre's account was undoubtedly important in asserting the active nature of human knowledge. There was a tendency among some materialists and even some Marxists, to hold that consciousness contained little more than a passive reflection of objective reality, underestimating the work of elaboration and organization undertaken by thought in the production of an adequate representation of that reality. On the other hand, he appears in the process to have reversed the error, leaving little or no active or dynamic role in knowledge for extra-mental factors. The historical emergence of consciousness in natural, biological and social reality is briefly acknowledged, and the hypothetical independence of nature and society from thought are accepted, but these acknowledgements scarcely go beyond a token gesture. The theoretical materialism is therefore not amplified into a practical materialism where the world interacts with thought instead of being acted on by it.

This problem is related to Lefebvre's contentious assertion of an alliance between objective idealism and materialism. The assertion is directly aimed at refuting Stalin's statement that idealism 'denies the possibility of knowing the world and its laws, . . . does not believe in the authenticity of our knowledge, does not recognize objective truth'.[10] Stalin amalgamates several types of idealism in his statement, and it is clear that his view is quite inadequate to summarize them all, however pertinent it may be in some cases. In particular, the Hegelian theory of knowledge has a complexity which cannot be exhausted in such a blunt fashion. To that extent Lefebvre is right to challenge, however implicitly, Stalin's analysis. On the other hand, he does not escape from a similar charge himself, since it is by no means clear that objective idealism can be so readily reconciled with materialism. Stalin's strictures were aimed at the subjective idealists, but also specifically against the Kantian tradition, which surely belongs to objective idealism. If Lefebvre were to include Kant among the objective idealists, it is hard to see how he could sustain his defence of their alliance with materialism on the theory of knowledge. But this criticism does not go to the heart of the matter, since by 'objective idealism' Lefebvre is primarily indicating Hegel.

The 'precise question', quoted above, on which Lefebvre sees an agreement between objective idealism and materialism, is in fact four questions, whose content is not identical. Taking them in reverse order, it can be seen that the agreement between even Hegel's objective idealism and materialism is less than perfect. First: can we in our ideas of the world make a picture of reality? For Hegel ideas are reality and the world is unreal, becoming real only by virtue if its incorporation in ideas. Hence the knowledge process, far from making a picture of reality from ideas of the world, makes the world real by picturing it in ideas. Second: can our thought know the world? Hegel's system has thought unfolding itself out of itself and embracing the world in the process. Ultimately thought is itself the world, but in so far as thought can be said to know itself, that is, to be knowledge, then it might be agreed that our thought can, for Hegel, know the world. Third: what is the relation between our ideas on the world and the world itself? In Hegel's view, the natural and social world is a product, and alienation, of the idea. The relation of our ideas to it is therefore one of retrieval, seeking to subsume the world (back) into our ideas, rendering it rational and therefore real. Finally: what is the exact scope of our means of knowledge? The question has strictly no meaning for Hegel since the achievement of the Absolute Idea is both a means and an end, and indeed the content of the entire knowledge process. Our ideas are not therefore just a means of knowing the world but that which knows, that which is known, and that which is to be known.

From this brief examination it is evident that the Hegelian theory of knowledge does not concord with a materialist view. Nor can its idealist context be placed in parentheses to obtain the same structure of knowledge as that pertaining to materialism. If it is agreed that the priority of mind or matter is the first, or fundamental, philosophical question, as Lefebvre accepts, then it is difficult to envisage the resolution of the question being a matter of indifference in determining the precise relation between thought and the world, as Lefebvre appears to suggest. It is entirely reasonable to argue that the idealists made great strides in refining the conceptual apparatus of knowledge, but the relation of that apparatus to the world cannot remain unaffected by the prior option of idealism. The historical examples instanced by Lefebvre, namely Hegel and Descartes, illustrate the point clearly. In neither case is their theory of knowledge reducible to a materialist theory without extensive alteration. Hegel has already been examined; Descartes' dualism and his notion of innate ideas are scarcely compatible with a thorough going materialism. Hence Lefebvre's suggestion of an agreement between objective idealism and materialism in their theory of knowledge is visibly without historical foundation.

One further possibility remains. It is perhaps possible to construct an objective idealism in which there is no subordination of thought to being and in which their relationship might be such as to permit the same structure of knowledge as exists in a materialist account. The similarity would necessarily be limited, but in the absence of a specific theory, the nature and extent of the limits can only be a matter of speculation. In the event, Lefebvre's own interpretation of Marxism comes close to fulfilling the necessary conditions. The priority of matter is purely residual, since it is a postulate of which no more can be said philosophically than that it exists 'hors de notre conscience, sans nous, avant nous'.[11] The transition from priority to simultaneity is perceptible in his later *Le Marxisme*, as has been noted, and involves no significant restructuring of Lefebvre's theory of knowledge. His extensive reworking of the Hegelian dialectic clearly led him increasingly away from the dialectical materialism to which he aspired, and towards a renovated form of objective idealism.

Back to Hegel

La discussion qui a eu lieu ici au sujet de Hegel est assez étrange. Ceux qui y ont participé ont enfoncé des portes ouvertes. Il y a longtemps que la question de Hegel est résolue. Il n'y a aucune raison de la poser à nouveau.

A. A. Jdanov, 'Sur l'histoire de la philosophie', Europe, novembre 1947, 44–66, p. 59

As the post-war philosophical recovery gathered momentum, Marxists increasingly turned to the intellectual roots of dialectical materialism as the starting point for their further enquiries. In particular, attention focused more insistently on Hegel, who was no longer the preserve of a few specialists like Lefebvre and Guterman. The phenomenon was not confined to France, but was widespread throughout Marxism internationally. In some quarters the movement came as a surprise. The Soviet Communist Party's Secretary in charge of ideology, Andrei Zhdanov, gave a particularly noted expression of this surprise. His view, quoted above, was that the question of Hegel had long been settled and there was no need to go back over it. In one sense he was right: the inversion and materialist appropriation of Hegel's dialectic was and remains an acknowledged part of Marxist philosophy, and an assault on them is bound to undermine Marxism itself. But in many more senses he was badly wrong.

The summary statement of Hegel's role given in Stalin's essay could hardly be expected to satisfy Marxist philosophers, even if they accepted its general orientation. Any more elaborated statement would therefore necessarily have to re-examine the question. Moreover, an authentic Marxist analysis of the question could not be satisfied with a reiteration of Marx's and Engels' views on Hegel, however crucial they might be, but would have also to examine Hegel himself. Even in the development of Marxism proper, the vast Hegelian apparatus deployed by its founders would need to be made explicit. Apart from the exegesis of their writings to expose the method contained in them, a close scrutiny of the original Hegelian dialectic would obviously be valuable since Hegel enunciated his methodological principles at great length while Marx and Engels did not. And finally, the irreducible historicity of Marxism precludes it from becoming a set of disembodied philosophical propositions. Consequently, any exposition of its philosophy must necessarily include the origins in Hegel and any attempted development must include a reappraisal of those origins. Its historicity also entails that Marxism can never be definitively stated in a fixed and final form.

The inevitability of change and development ensures that reappraisal of its origins will continue to be an integral part of Marxist philosophy. The question of Hegel is not therefore settled, nor will it ever be settled: on the contrary, the raising of the question will remain one of the strongest indications that Marxism retains its vitality and its capacity to develop.

The patient labours of Auguste Cornu continued to nourish discussion in France on the relation between Marx and Hegel. His doctoral thesis of 1934 established him as an authority on the crucial formative years of Marx, and in 1948 he published a further study on the period under the title *Karl Marx et la pensée moderne*. Like his earlier work, it stopped at 1846 with *The German Ideology*, but it was concerned primarily to trace philosophical filiations. Cornu examined in turn the German rationalist and romantic thinkers, culminating in Hegel and leading to the Young Hegelian movement from which Marxism emerged. He saw the *1844 Manuscripts* as a decisive turning point in Marx's development but pointed to the relegation of their ideological preoccupations to a subordinate place in his mature doctrine. Cornu outlined the main ideas which Marx retained from the Hegelian philosophy of his youth: the unity of thought and being, the dialectical development of reality, and the rationalization of reality. Together these ideas formed a complex which went considerably beyond the view that Hegel contributed to Marxism only a dialectical method.

The unity of thought and being exists in Hegel by virtue of the primary and all-embracing status of thought in his system. Cornu's argument is that the materialist inversion of Hegel retains the same relationship with the terms inverted: thought is a product, and part, of being. The 'union nécessaire' of the two is therefore based on the recognition of this fundamental principle. One consequence of the principle is to undermine the separation of method and system, both in Marx and in Hegel. The necessary union of thought and being precludes the isolation of the dialectical method as simply a set of rules for enquiry, as it also precludes the isolation of the materialist or idealist conception of the world as simply a set of ontological presuppositions. While no direct application is suggested, Cornu's enunciation of the principle of unity could be directed at a number of his contemporaries, who run the risk of abstract, utopian or dogmatic tendencies. But perhaps most pertinently, Stalin's crude pedagogical separation of materialism from the dialectic is implicitly criticized.

The conception of the dialectical development of history, engendered by the oppositions and contradictions inherent in all living reality, is in many respects linked to the principle of unity. In parentheses, Cornu's use of the term 'réalité vivante' permits an ambiguity as to whether all reality is described as 'living', or whether the dialectic is restricted in its operation to organic matter and its organization. The second interpretation would reflect the position of neither Hegel nor Marx, even though some commentators have held it to be defensible. If Cornu intended such a position, his essay would have been more controversial than he apparently thought it, and the possibility may, for practical purposes, be disregarded. His view, then, is that for Marx as for Hegel the basic forms of relation and change must exist at all levels of reality. The dialectical movement of thought and being in general is necessarily linked to the dialectic of history, which like all reality has the motive power of opposition and contradiction as its dynamic. Again, the dialectic is seen not only as a method of historical analysis but also as the structure of historical reality: one further reason for asserting the necessary unity of thought and its object.

Cornu's third principle, that the efficient cause and final aim of dialectical development is the increasing rationalization of reality, is apparently a paradox. On the one hand, it appears to make thought the motive principle of reality, while on the other hand it makes rationality an end-product of the development of reality. As a statement of the grandiose Hegelian conception of the idea unfolding itself through history, it is succinct and accurate. But as a statement of the materialist dialectic? There can be no doubt that, in the Marxist view, reason is a historical product, reflecting in consciousness the structures of nature and human practice. Moreover, it is also held that human consciousness strives increasingly to gain rational mastery over nature and society, introducing 'rationalization' as a motive force in historical development. The paradox of being both a product and a cause is therefore resolved. But it remains questionable whether the principle corresponds to a Marxist view. Certainly the role of human rational activity becomes greater as history advances: the scientific and technological revolution, and the growth of social and economic planning, among other things, are constant reminders of the fact. But Cornu appears to suggest that reason is both the motor and the goal of history, whereas the classical Marxist formulations invariably place class struggle as the motor of history, as the fundamental form of contradiction in historical societies.

In order to reconcile the two views it would be necessary either in some way to reduce class struggle to the expression of a rational urge, or else to posit rationality as a form of being independent of, and prior to, human consciousness. In the first case, the result is a clearly idealist position in which ideas ultimately govern the world. In the second case, the result is cosmic vision which may be acceptable at the highest level of abstraction, but holds many dangers in its concrete expression, because it abstracts the distinctions between the different forms of dialectical movement in nature, society and thought; because it regards the dialectic as a known and invariable structure which operates in a regular and foreseeable pattern; because it supposes a final outcome of dialectical movement; because it supposes a teleological process in which the end plays a determining role in initiating its own production; and because it is in constant danger of falling into the idealism of Hegel's cosmology which begins and ends with the idea and its self-movement. It is true that Marx's early writings were still strongly Hegelian in inspiration and the cosmic idealist conception still informed his thinking before *The German Ideology*. The celebrated description of the proletarian revolution as the realization of philosophy was first published in the *Deutsch-Französische Jahrbücher* of 1844, and undoubtedly echoed the notion described by Cornu. His view was that 'philosophy cannot be made a reality without the abolition of the proletariat, the proletariat cannot be abolished without philosophy being made a reality'.[12] The realization of philosophy is closely bound to the notion of 'rationalizing' reality, and the originality of Marx's view in 1844 was to associate the process intimately with the emancipation of the proletariat where previously it had been regarded as essentially the work of philosophers. On further investigation, Marx discovered that social and political developments, far from being subordinate, or even equal, to philosophical processes, were in fact their condition and explanation. This materialist conception of history was set out extensively in *The German Ideology*. Cornu's view therefore runs the risk of freezing Marx's development at an early formative stage, where it could still in many respects be assimilated to a Hegelian position.

The latent dangers of Cornu's analysis were aggravated by the general conception of his book. Although it carried the subtitle *Contribution à l'étude de la formation du marxisme*, the book was accompanied by an editorial note explaining that it lacked any extended discussion of the role of French socialism, eighteenth-century materialism or classical economics, since it had originally been conceived as a study of the relation between Marx and Hegel. If the book is taken in the spirit of its original intentions, then at worst it might be argued that Cornu overstates the Hegelian content of the Marxist dialectic. If taken in the spirit of the title and subtitle, there is no doubt that the book would constitute a major distortion of Marxist theory. In either case it was a clear indication that Hegel was a major growth point for Marxist philosophers.

The implications of Cornu's analysis were not confined to the growing pains of Marxism, however. The intellectual context of post-war France gave the problem of Hegel an extension and complexity which had been foreshadowed in the 1930s. To speak of Hegel was to take position on a range of ideological issues, the terms of which were being modified by the spreading revival of Hegel spearheaded by the non-Marxist neo-Hegelian movement.

The emergence of a mystified and neo-religious dialectic in the 1930s can be traced to the work of Jean Wahl, whose inspiration animated the secularized interpretations of Alexandre Kojève and Jean Hyppolite. As the Second World War ended, their work acquired an authority and status which placed them among the intellectual masters of French academic philosophy, and made them almost cult figures with a generation of young intellectuals. The roots of this popularity have been variously stated. Certainly the collapse of traditional bourgeois values could be widely seen to accompany the fall of the Third Republic, confirmed in the experience of occupation and resistance. The dramatic advances for socialism on a world scale underlined the historical fragility of the capitalist social order, shaking the security of old certainties in all fields of human experience. Such certainties were further shattered by the massive destructions of the war, the horrific butchery, cruelty and inhumanity which the fascist regimes were shown to have practised, and by the nascent realization that Hiroshima and Nagasaki signalled the birth of weapons which might ultimately destroy the entire human race.

A philosophy of anguish, conflict, and the isolation, freedom and responsibility of the individual had strong appeal for the youth of this generation. Sartrean existentialism was the principal supplier of such a philosophy, but in many respects the rediscovered Hegelian dialectic offered a more ecumenical theoretical expression of the existentialist position. Not only did it relate personal experience more comprehensively to social structures, suggesting affinities with Marxism, but it also eschewed the blunt atheism of Sartre and gave the transcendent dimension of experience a potential opening on to theology.

Alexandre Kojève's *Introduction à la lecture de Hegel* (Paris, 1947) and Jean Hyppolite's *Genèse et structure de la Phénoménologie de l'esprit de Hegel* (Paris, 1946) were the fundamental texts of the neo-Hegelian revival. Hyppolite in particular took a leading role in propagating Hegel, writing many articles, some of which were published as *Etudes sur Marx et Hegel* (Paris, 1955), and two other important books: *Introduction à la philosophie de l'histoire de Hegel* (Paris, 1948) and *Logique et existence, essai sur la logique de Hegel* (Paris, 1953). Apart from the work of Marxist writers, already examined, there were several Catholic studies, notably Henri Niel's substantial *De la médiation dans la philosophie de Hegel* (Paris, 1945), Paul Asveld's *La Pensée religieuse du jeune Hegel* (Paris, 1953), and a book, *Aux Sources de la pensée de Marx: Hegel, Feuerbach* (Paris, 1947), and a series of essays collected subsequently as *Etudes hégéliennes* (Louvain, 1958), by the Louvain philosopher, Franz Grégoire.

The religious commentators, understandably, had only a marginal effect on the development of the materialistic dialectic, but Kojève and Hyppolite occupied a position much closer to Marxism, and in many respects formed a bridge between it and the views of Sartre, Wahl and the Catholics. Their analyses were sympathetically read in Marxist circles, particularly between 1945 and 1949, and a degree of convergence is apparent between their thought and that of younger Marxists like Jean Kanapa and Jean-T. Desanti, as well as Lefebvre and Garaudy.

From the point of view of Hyppolite and Kojève, Marxism appeared as a development, among others, within the Hegelian tradition. Kojève, for example, declared in 1946 that 'toute interprétation de Hegel, si elle est plus qu'un bavardage, n'est qu'un programme de lutte et de travail (l'un de ces "programmes" s'appelant *marxisme*)'.[13] Insisting on the political significance of Hegel, he tended to see the German philosopher as the *éminence grise* of several contemporary movements, a view not without plausibility in the context of the late 1940s. However, the Hegel of Kojève, Hyppolite and their school was the Hegel of *The Phenomenology of Mind* rather than of the *Logic*. Kojève's celebrated *Introduction à la lecture de Hegel* (1947) was a commented reading of the *Phenomenology*, and Hyppolite's major work, his two-volume *Genèse et Structure de la Phénoménologie de l'Esprit de Hegel* (1946), was a careful and detailed exegesis of it. The importance of this orientation is that it produced an almost existentialist Hegel, concerned primarily with the analysis of human experience. How well the *Phenomenology* responded to existentialist preoccupations can be gathered from Sir James Baillie's assessment of it as an unparalleled rational ordering of the life of the human spirit.[14] The exploration of experience and the attempt to establish basic principles for understanding it, these were the very stuff of the existentialist project. In the *Phenomenology* they found a rich source on which to draw, and many of Hegel's categories and analyses passed into the common currency of post-war thought. Self-estrangement, the self and desire, the conflict and duplication of self-consciousness, the unhappy consciousness and the relation of lord and bondsman (rendered in French as *Maître* and *Esclave*), these became key themes in existentialist and neo-Hegelian discussion.

For the Marxists, on the other hand, Hegel's main achievement was centred on his *Science of Logic*. This weighty volume contains a lengthy elaboration of the categories of his dialectic, and at the same time a developed statement of his system as a whole. If it is accepted that Hegel's major contribution to Marxism was his rational dialectic, then the *Logic* undoubtedly appears as the central text to consult. Lenin recognized this, and devoted much study to the work. His notebooks reveal the extent of his interest and contain the famous aphorism that 'It is impossible completely to understand Marx's *Capital*, and especially its first chapter without having thoroughly studied and understood the *whole* of Hegel's *Logic*. Consequently half a century later none of the Marxists understood Marx.'[15] The importance of Lenin's advocacy in stimulating Marxists to study Hegel is difficult to overstate. Already before the war the notebooks had received wide attention as a result of the labours of Lefebvre and Guterman, and they were widely quoted throughout Marxist studies, including Stalin's notorious essay. However, until the appearance of a full French edition in 1955 they were largely transmitted in various selected, second-hand forms. The influence of Engels gave further impetus to the developing interest with the publication in French in 1952 of his *Dialectics of Nature*, containing discussions of the various categories of dialectics in terms which took up many of Hegel's analyses in his *Logic*.

As had been the case with socialist and spiritualist interpretations since the nineteenth century, so now Marxist and neo-Hegelian views of Hegel occupied different intellectual territories. Where one delved into the hidden structures of individual experience, the other hammered out general laws of matter in motion. Where one developed a subjective dialectic of consciousness, the other elaborated an objective dialectic of nature and history. The neo-Hegelians were largely drawn towards the existentialists, whose roots in phenomenology provided a ready point of contact. Hence they tended to reap much of the criticism which Marxists directed against existentialism in the immediate post-war years. Association with subjective individualists of Sartre's type did not enhance the appeal of Hegel for Marxists. Consequently, the impact of the neo-Hegelian revival on French Marxism in general was diminished and delayed. But the convergence with Lefebvre in particular, on at least one point, has already been hinted at. The objective idealism of Hegel brought him nearer to materialism than the subjective idealists, and Lefebvre moved towards the neo-Hegelians on that basis.

Kojève, for example, acknowledged the objectivity of the dialectic as the structure of concrete reality, and not simply a method of thought. In so far as the dialectic exists in thought, it is because it already exists beforehand in the whole of reality. If the dialectic is the very structure of concrete reality, which thought seeks to describe, then the way is open to a dialectic of nature and of history independent of the human mind. Kojève is quite willing to agree that 'il faut qu'un monde sans homme existe avant qu'il y ait des hommes dans le monde',[16] and that Hegel's view of history includes an analysis of infrastructures and superstructures which verges on materialism.[17] His idealism intervenes at the point where nature and history are in turn based in mind, though not the individual mind. Hegel's *Phenomenology* leads philosophically, as it did historically, to his *Logic*. The exploration of experience leads to and presupposes a structure of rationality.

Decisive though the objective dialectic is as a bridge between idealism and materialism, the nature of the final transition still remains to be clarified. In attempting to propound a complete philosophical explanation of what Marx, Engels and Lenin expressed in hints and metaphors, Lefebvre was effectively crossing the bridge in the opposite direction. He moved inexorably from Marxism to neo-Hegelianism, from the *Logic* to the *Phenomenology*, to develop a theory of experience founded on the notion of alienation. This notion which had begun to assume an important role in *Le Matérialisme dialectique* (1939), comes to the centre in *Le Marxisme* (1948), gradually emerging as the motor of history. It is outside the scope of the present study to elaborate on the ramifications of the concept of alienation, but in Lefebvre's case it can be seen to arise from his truncation of the materialist dialectic. Attempting to confine the dialectic to a method, he has already been seen to give an insufficient inversion of the Hegelian dialectic, and to retain it virtually untransformed as a Marxist dialectic.

For Hegel, history is characterized by a succession of alienations, beginning with the initial self-alienation of mind and culminating in the final synthesis of the absolute idea. Lefebvre's inversion simply disclaims the start and finish, but retains the structure of the process intact. Though seeking to retain only the Hegelian method, Lefebvre might have profited by pondering on Kojève's affirmation that Hegel's dialectic, far from being a method, was the structure of reality. A method leads directly to the view of reality which produced it, and by a subtle twist, the Hegelian content of Lefebvre's inverted dialectic operates in practice to revert it back to its original idealist orientation.

References

1   Reprinted in G. Politzer, *Ecrits*, I (Paris, 1973), 315–389.

2   *Ibid.*, 363.

3   See Etienne Fajon, 'La lutte idéologique', *Cahiers du communisme*, octobre 1947, 976–988.

4   R. Garaudy, 'Les sources françaises du marxisme-léninisme', *Cahiers du communisme*, décembre 1946, 1120–1138, p. 1120.

5   See H. Wallon, 'Pour une encyclopédie dialectique', *La Pensée*, juillet–septembre 1945, 117–123; H. Mougin, 'L'esprit encyclopédique et la tradition philosophique française', *La Pensée*, octobre–décembre 1945; janvier–mars 1946; avril–juin 1946.

6   See Cécile Angrand, *Le Matérialisme dialectique* (Paris, 1946); Etienne Fajon, 'Quelques aspects théoriques du problème de l'unité', *Cahiers du communisme*, septembre 1945, 8–18; Marcel Prenant, 'Le matérialisme dialectique', *Cahiers du communisme*, octobre 1946, 934–943.

7   See Henri Mougin, *La Sainte famille existentialiste* (Paris, 1947); Henri Lefebvre, *L'Existentialisme* (Paris, 1946); Jean Kanapa, *L'Existentialisme n'est pas un humanisme* (Paris, 1947); Georges Lukács, *Existentialisme ou marxisme?* (Paris, 1948).

8   Jean Kanapa, 'Henri Lefebvre ou la philosophie vivante', *La Pensée*, novembre–decembre 1947, 66–72.

9   H. Lefebvre, *Logique formelle, logique dialectique*, 2nd edition (Paris, 1969), 11.

10 J. V. Stalin, *Dialectical and Historical Materialism* (New York, 1940), 17.

11 Lefebvre, *Logique formelle*, 34.

12 K. Marx, 'Contribution to a Critique of Hegel's Philosophy of Law', in K. Marx and F. Engels, *Collected Works*, III (London, 1975), 187.

13 Alexandre Kojève, 'Hegel, Marx et le christianisme', *Critique*, 3–4 (1946), 339–366, p. 366.

14 Sir James Baillie, Translator's introduction to G. W. F. Hegel, *The Phenomenology of Mind*, 2nd edition (London, 1931), 13.

15 V. I. Lenin, *Collected Works*, XXXVIII (Moscow, 1961), 180.

16 Kojève, 'Hegel, Marx et le christianisme', 347.

17 *Ibid.*, 356.

4

Cold War

1948–1956

Two camps

Deux camps se sont formés à travers le monde: le camp impérialiste et antidémocratique, qui voit dans la guerre dirigée contre l'Union soviétique le moyen d'instaurer l'hégémonie américaine et d'écraser les forces de la démocratie et du socialisme; et le camp anti-impérialiste et démocratique, qui veut faire échec à la guerre impérialiste, sauver la paix, renforcer la démocratie et liquider le fascisme.

Maurice Thorez, Le Fils du peuple *(Paris, 1949), 223*

Il y a des classes sociales affrontées, il y a dans le monde des forces de guerre et des forces de paix. Il n'y a pas, dans je ne sais quel pathétique arrière-monde, une 'troisième force', celle de 'l'Esprit' ni aucune autre.

Roger Garaudy, Lettre à Emmanuel Mounier *(Paris, 1950), 16*

The uneasy political honeymoon of the Liberation faded month by month. The great hopes for a new start, a new society, a second Renaissance, were slowly eroded. The expulsion of communists from government on 5 May 1947 was a significant turning point in the position of Marxism in France. At first, it was regarded as a temporary disagreement, but international events soon demonstrated that it was part of a world-scale conflict. The dismissal of communists from the Italian and Finnish governments occurred within a few days of the French expulsion, and a concerted 'roll-back' of communist advances was openly initiated by the Americans and their non-communist allies. Over the ensuing months, crisis followed crisis, setting the pattern for the Cold War which enveloped the world from the late 1940s until the early 1960s.

The effects of the intensified social and political conflict between two world systems had immediate consequences in culture and ideology.

Marxism, particularly in its communist expression, came under sustained attack. Marxists were excluded as far as possible from public life, many lost their jobs or failed to gain the posts they merited. Frédéric Joliot-Curie was dismissed as Commissioner for Atomic Energy, though he was a Nobel prize-winner and France's most famous living scientist. Many lesser known Marxist scientists suffered a similar exclusion. Henri Lefebvre was dismissed from his research post at the Conseil National des Recherches Scientifiques, August Cornu was obliged to seek a post outside the country, and other Marxist writers and intellectuals came under varying degrees of harassment. The Sorbonne was barred to Marxist lectures and conferences. Left-wing, and especially Marxist, publications, including the reviews *La Pensée* and *La Nouvelle critique*, were banned in schools, universities, public libraries, and also in many bookshops and distribution chains. Sales dropped and readership declined. It was in this context that the planned Marxist encyclopedia was abandoned in late 1948, although it was at an advanced stage of preparation.

The embattled political and ideological situation of French Marxists affected not only their relations with non-Marxists and their position in society. It also had repercussions in their internal organization and relations. The polarization of public life carved a series of rifts between communist intellectuals and their non-communist colleagues who professed belief in or sympathy with Marxism. Polemic became the predominant mode of communication, bringing with it a bitter harvest of mutual recriminations, denunciations and abuse. The French Left was riven with conflicts over a succession of national and international affairs, each one throwing up sharp controversy on fundamental principles. Berlin, Yugoslavia, Korea, Indo-China, trials, imprisonments and executions in East and West, colonial wars, Henri Martin, General Ridgeway, strikes, working conditions, paintings and a host of other *affaires* left a series of scars which have not soon or easily been forgotten.

Among the communists themselves, the ferocious assaults on them inevitably had far-reaching consequences. The closing of ranks and stiffening of sinews was a widespread spontaneous response, but where it was not voluntary it was frequently imposed as a matter of discipline. The three years from 1949 to 1952 saw an unprecedented effort to unite intellectuals in an ideological solidarity around an agreed formulation of Marxism. Within the Communist Party, the text upon which the weight of authority was thrown was Stalin's 1938 essay, and the consistent efforts of Laurent Casanova, the secretary responsible for ideology, were directed at ensuring a maximum of conformity with that text. In his major statement, *Le Parti communiste, les intellectuels et la nation* (Paris, 1949), he stressed that intellectuals should adopt a strict *esprit de parti* and place themselves unreservedly on the political and ideological positions of the working class, as expressed by the party. While the political and class partisanship of ideology is indisputably a principle of Marxism, Casanova interpreted the principle in a narrow, exclusive sense which drastically reduced the exploration of new formulations, and the diversity of permitted interpretations.

The fruits of this policy in human terms were painful retractions, embarrassed silences, expulsions and resignations among intellectuals. In philosophical terms, perhaps the worst consequence was the notorious, sectarian theory of the 'two sciences'. For some eighteen months from the beginning of 1950 it was held as party policy that science, natural and social, was an 'idéologie historiquement relative'.[1] On this view, science was a superstructure and therefore essentially a class-determined ideology. Hence, in the modern world there were two sciences, one bourgeois, the other proletarian, of which the latter, expressing the progressive interests of the rising class, was objective and true. But, however pervasive the influence of bourgeois ideology in science, it soon became evident that it was absurd to deny the knowledge-value of natural sciences developed and practised in bourgeois societies. Moreover, Stalin himself, in his discussion of the status of language and linguistics in 1950, warned against an over-rigid division between base and superstructure.[2] Hence, by October 1951, the 'two sciences' theory was officially disavowed as an error, though it was stressed that the social sciences were tied to class interests in a way that the sciences of nature were not.[3] The detailed implications of this episode for the philosophy of science and the conception of society do not directly concern the present discussion of the development of the materialist dialectic. But the incident illustrates the extent to which the intense conflicts of this unhappy period were reflected in theoretical questions.

One of the principal methods by which the unanimity of communist intellectuals was ensured, at least in public, was the exercise of self-criticism. At the crudest level it was a device for eliminating differences of opinion which might be exploited by opponents to damage Marxism in general and the Communist Party in particular. At a higher level it was a means of encouraging people to reconsider their position on questions where they were clearly divergent from agreed principles or policy. There was of course nothing new in the phenomenon of people expressing their rejection or correction of views previously held by them: among philosophers especially it has always been a common practice. Nor was there anything new in the obligation of individuals to retract views running counter to those of the ideology or organization to which they owe allegiance. What was new was the introduction of self-criticism as a regular exercise to be done regardless of whether any urgent current controversy was involved. The recently founded communist monthly *La Nouvelle critique* even instituted a regular rubric, 'Autocritique', in 1949 to cater for the new genre. Material was not lacking, for in the few short post-war years a wide range of explorations had been initiated, leading to a variety of different positions in areas as diverse as psychology, philosophy, economics, literature, the visual arts, politics, and natural science among others. The attempt to bring these within the defensive fortifications of an orthodoxy could not fail to produce a series of tactical retreats.

The subjective relationship between a writer and his self-criticism varied considerably. In some cases it was written in a spirit of genuine reappraisal, in others a spirit of expediency approaching cynicism. More often than not, both types of response were involved. Retrospective appreciations in later years often reflect this complexity, though the constructions placed on self-criticisms in subsequent changed circumstances must necessarily be regarded with a degree of caution. But the major significance of these essays lay in their public rather than private dimension. Those of Cornu, Lefebvre and Garaudy in particular contributed to forming the conditions in which the materialist dialectic continued to be developed.

Cornu's self-criticism came in response to a critical review by Félix Armand in *La Pensée*.[4] Armand had words of praise for Cornu's *Karl Marx et la pensée moderne*, but regretted the 'défauts flagrants et insuffisances regrettables',[5] primarily connected to the excessive attention to Hegel, the lack of an historical dimension and the decision to stop at *The German Ideology* as though it represented the completion of Marx's development. Cornu agreed that there was too little historical or class content to his analysis and that he had portrayed Marx's development predominantly as the solution of theoretical problems. In particular, he recognized that he had understated the complete break between Marxism and all forms of idealism. This fault, he conceded, had been reinforced by his concentration on the formative years, which inevitably presented a more strongly Hegelian picture of Marx himself.

It is an earnest of Cornu's sincerity that he endeavoured in subsequent works to present a more fully rounded view of Marx's early years, integrating not only a broader intellectual range but also a deeper social and political understanding of the developments he described. In his case, at least, the process of self-criticism had the effect of stimulating a renewed and enlarged perspective on his work. The same is also true of

Roger Garaudy who was obliged to admit to comparable errors in his work on *Les Sources françaises du socialisme scientifique* (Paris, 1948).

Garaudy's faults arose from the excessive zeal with which he linked Marx to French philosophy, particularly eighteenth-century materialism. He admitted in his self-criticism that he had virtually presented Marxism as the 'fruit d'une expérience nationale française' and Marx virtually as French.[6] In so doing he had neglected to emphasize the proletarian nature of Marxist philosophy as against the bourgeois basis of the previous French tradition. He had also neglected the dialectical nature of Marxism as against the metaphysical, or mechanical, materialism of the Enlightenment. Behind these mistakes, he accepted that he had tended to overemphasize ideological factors in historical development, coming near to idealism in his neglect of social and material factors. Garaudy shared Cornu's determination to correct his mistakes, and his subsequent study on Hegel and German philosophy is proof of the reorientation of his researches. The social and political circumstances figure prominently in many of his later studies in intellectual history though the charge of ignoring class factors has often been levelled against them, and his ultimate return to an avowed idealism is evidence of the constant dangers which attended his position. In the medium term at least, though, his efforts to implement the resolutions of his self-criticism were considerably more whole-hearted and successful than those of his comrade and mentor, Henri Lefebvre.

In a long and tortuous essay Lefebvre presented his self-criticism as more of an ideological clarification, on the grounds that he had not taken an erroneous position as such, but that he had fallen into certain hesitations and uncertainties which might be misconstrued.[7] Discussing his analysis of the materialist dialectic, he accepted that he had been guilty of 'une certaine surestimation de l'hégélianisme' but criticized those of his comrades who seemed to want to throw Hegel out altogether.[8] He felt it necessary to retain Hegel's dialectical method and his concept of the movement of the natural, social and intellectual world. On the other hand, he admitted that he had strayed into a certain formalism, particularly in *Le Matérialisme dialectique*, by seeking to derive philosophical materialism from the internal necessity for thought to have a content.[9] This, he acknowledged, was a speculative illusion which tried to make materialism a product of knowledge whereas in fact it is a class position proved true by human praxis.

Unlike Cornu or Garaudy, Lefebvre did not accept that he had committed the mistake of idealism. It might be thought that his recognition of formalism and speculation amount to the same thing, but it should be remembered that he nourished the project of reconciling or overcoming both materialism and idealism. In agreeing that materialism could not be proved philosophically, he was not necessarily strengthening his materialism, but was expelling it from philosophical discourse, outside definition or rational demonstration. His 'formalist' and 'speculative' errors may be traced to his attempts to incorporate the materialist postulate in some way into a system which was not essentially dependent on it. In recognizing them, Lefebvre was implicitly severing whatever inadequate links still bound his position to materialism. On the other hand, he did recognize the dangers of cutting thought from history, the natural sciences, society and practice. His repudiation of formalism was aimed at obviating such dangers, but it was not accompanied by any reformulation of his general account. Hence the repudiation remained a verbal gesture without significant effect on his philosophy.

Lefebvre realized that fundamental divergences remained between his position and that of his party comrades. His 'clarification' on the materialist dialectic contained only the bare minimum acknowledgement of them. For the following half dozen years he avoided any major work on the question, preferring to direct his attention rather to sociology and aesthetics than philosophy as such. When he returned to philosophy it was evident that the divergences were, if anything, greater than ever, confirming the impression that his disavowal was an obligatory submission to political necessities. More than anyone Lefebvre illustrates how self-criticism could be an empty gesture, going through the motions with no conviction and no constructive effect.

Nadir of philosophy

Nous croyons aujourd'hui que la cause bourgeoise de Hegel n'est que la mise en cause de Marx. Ce Grand Retour à Hegel n'est qu'un recours désespéré contre Marx, dans la forme spécifique que prend le révisionnisme dans la crise finale de l'impérialisme: un révisionnisme de caractère fasciste.

'Le retour à Hegel', La Nouvelle critique, novembre 1950, 54

Where the Second World War inflicted grievous physical losses on French Marxism, the Cold War took a dire ideological toll. The deterioration of intellectual life was, each in its way, as severe in both cases. The harsh polarizations of the late 1940s and early 1950s almost robbed science, let alone philosophy, of the margin of freedom and autonomy necessary for growth. On both sides of the divide, immediate political considerations increasingly dictated what might be thought and said. Debate rapidly became polemic, and polemic often degenerated into abuse. The polemical mode is an ever-present form of philosophical expression, but it is directed at gaining ideological victory rather than exploring the truth, and presupposes fixed positions which are respectively attacked and defended. Polemic has a legitimate and historically hallowed place in philosophy. But if philosophy is reduced to polemic as its only mode of expression, it begins to lose its cognitive value and becomes no more than another weapon in the class struggle. Moreover, without the leeway to maintain and extend its value as knowledge, its cutting edge is soon dulled and it becomes even a poor weapon. French philosophy of the Cold War period suffered greatly from this polemical reduction, and Marxists, as much as their opponents, found their conceptual swords becoming bludgeons. The consequences were felt in many fields, among them the matter of Marxism's relation to its antecedents, not least the Hegelian dialectic.

The post-war Hegel revival aroused mixed feelings among Marxists from its earliest days. They could rightly claim a degree of responsibility for the phenomenon, but they could also feel legitimate apprehension at the possible consequences. Whereas the materialist dialectic had much to gain from the renewed interest in Hegelian philosophy, an excess of enthusiasm might rehabilitate the idealist dialectic which Marx had struggled so hard to overcome. It has been seen how far Lefebvre and Cornu went in their attempts to incorporate the Hegelian dialectic into Marxism. With the intensifying Cold War, the danger of creeping idealism within Marxism itself gradually came to represent a serious internal ideological threat. Sharp reaction against Hegelianization was embodied in a series of attacks in the Marxist press. Prominent among them was the review *La Nouvelle critique* which specialized in pungent polemics on cultural and ideological issues. The review, subtitled *Revue du marxisme militant*, was conceived as an ideological arm of the Communist Party, and adopted a characteristically aggressive tone, which it maintained for the first few years of its existence. A product of the Cold War, its approach was well typified by the controversy over Hegel.

In November 1950 the journal printed a collective article signed by an *ad hoc* body, 'La commission de critique du cercle des philosophes communistes'.[10] Noting that bourgeois philosophy had returned to Hegel in the last twenty years, after a century of scorn and igorance, the article suggested that Hegel had been too reactionary and too revolutionary for the nineteenth-century liberal bourgeoisie. While Marxism had recognized and adopted the revolutionary aspects, the bourgeoisie had only turned to the reactionary aspects when capitalism entered the stage of imperialism. This stage required a justification for extreme repression and war, inherent in imperialism, but also a tragic conception of life to universalize the experience of the doomed bourgeois class. This article went on to suggest that a crucial political objective of the Hegelian revival was to undermine the rational and revolutionary materialist dialectic, revising it in terms of a mystified and idealist dialectic. In this way Marxism could be presented as a misunderstanding, and concrete class struggle could be reduced to the tragic eternal human struggle. Ultimately, as the passage quoted suggests, Hegel could be invoked, and had been invoked, to the defence of fascism.

As with so much Cold War polemic, the article tends to undermine its own validity by schematism and exaggeration. The central idea, that Hegel was used as a means of eroding Marxism, is undoubtedly true. The materialist inversion which gives the Marxist dialectic its cutting edge was consistently challenged by the neo-Hegelians. And Lefebvre in particular came increasingly near to rejecting it in his Hegelianized Marxism. It was certainly a crux of ideological struggle. The view that the concept of tragic, universal and eternal conflict articulates the bourgeoisie's social consciousness of its historical position, that view, too, has ample basis in social reality. The rendering of practical and historical developments into abstract and eternal principles is a primary mechanism of ideological mystification.

However, the notion that the Hegelian revival was inherently bound to fascism is exaggerated and excessive. If any German philosopher was implicated in fascism it was surely Nietzsche rather than Hegel. Admittedly, Kojève's assertion that the Master-Slave relation implied a necessity for bloodshed lent itself to the charge of fascist tendencies. Likewise, it is undeniable that Gentile and other Italian neo-Hegelians became involved with Mussolini. But both logically and historically, Right-Hegelianism has always been associated with conservative, even authoritarian, politics in defence of the *status quo*, rather than the aggressive radical terrorism of fascist rule. The article's simplified view of the bourgeoisie and its ideology similarly fails to carry historical conviction. The passage from Kant to Hegel cannot be schematically tied to the passage from liberalism to imperialism, or from rationalism to irrationalism.

These crude identifications are of a piece with the blanket anathema which was pronounced against most of the non-communist ideologists during the three worst Cold War years. It was lamentably common to find extreme polarizations of view which assimilated all shades of opponents to the darkest and most detested. It is little excuse to point out that symmetrical excesses were committed on the other side. But at least there were other Marxists less lacking in nuance.

The Marx scholar and translator Emile Bottigelli shared the general thrust of his colleagues' article, but disagreed with the simple historical identification of Hegel with the worst forms of reaction, pointing out that his dialectic, even in a mystified form, had contributed to the rise of the radical German bourgeoisie before 1848.[11] His value for the bourgeoisie today was indirect, Bottigelli contended. The contradictions of capitalism had become so acute that even petty bourgeois intellectuals were aware of them, and the availability of a mystified dialectic was therefore a valuable expedient for the bourgeoisie. The return to Hegel was thus two-edged. Marxists had prepared the ground with the materialist dialectic, and the theory of contradiction was powerful and seductive for intellectuals. But in its idealist Hegelian form the dialectic effectively assisted the bourgeoisie and prevented the development of revolutionary consciousness and action among intellectuals. It was clear, he concluded in a pointed reference, that some Marxists had fallen under the spell of the Hegelian dialectic, and it was an urgent matter to root out the mystification.

Bottigelli's contribution dwelt lengthily on the historical complexities of Hegel's influence, showing the inadequacy of simple schematic assertions. He employed the distinction between Hegel's system and method to demonstrate the problems posed by such assertions, but was careful to distinguish further between the materialist and idealist methods. Though he did not undertake a comprehensive restatement of the materialist dialectic, inappropriate in the context, he articulated the concerns of his colleagues in a more restrained and considered way. His intervention, without breaking any new ground, bears witness to the possibility of less sectarian responses by Marxist philosophers even at the height of the Cold War, in the context of the same basic political and ideological conclusions.

Among the comrades suffering from the 'engouement hégélien', Henri Lefebvre, rightly feeling himself under fire, attempted a defence.[12] He denied that the return to Hegel was necessarily linked to fascism, pointed to the considerable esteem in which Marx, Engels and Lenin had held Hegel, and noted the complexity of his historical influence. The pseudo-dialectic put forward by contemporary neo-Hegelians, he argued, made the mistake of ignoring the historical content and regarding contradictions as absolute. The materialist dialectic, on the other hand, reflected the movement of nature and history and did not seek to deduce movement from concepts.

Like Bottigelli, Lefebvre identified the worst excesses of the earlier article and attempted to make necessary allowance for the full intricacy of the Hegel question. He pertinently referred to Lenin's regard for the philosopher, but in defining his own understanding of the materialist dialectic he pointedly spoke in terms of the primacy of content, the precise notion he had conceded to be insufficient only a few months previously in his self-criticism. Equally pointedly, he avoided referring to any class basis for philosophy in general and Hegel in particular, and offered no general analysis of why the current revival should be taking place, much less what the social basis or implications of his own position might be. He was in effect fighting a rearguard action to preserve his freedom to hold, as Marxist, a view which he recognized was considered generally to be neo-Hegelian. The disfavour with which his position was regarded is reflected by the decision of *La Nouvelle critique* to publish his article as a letter, thereby dissociating the editorial board from his views.

The coarsened and debased quality of Marxist thought at this nadir is well illustrated in this polemic, in the abuse of self-criticism, and in the 'two sciences' theory. The damage was, however, more general. Creative and innovative reappraisal, the lifeblood of Marxism, almost came to a standstill. Even work which was not directly polemical in intention was largely confined to the tired reiteration of well-known texts from the classics of Marxism, or worse, the laborious amplification of Stalin's 'crude digest'. One of the most typical products of the time, though by no means the worst, is the 390-page doctoral thesis which Roger Garaudy submitted to the Sorbonne Faculty of Letters in 1953, published under the title *La Théorie matérialiste de la connaissance* (Paris, 1953). Though it was supervised by the eminent philosopher and critic Gaston Bachelard, and though it was awarded the top grade, *très honorable*, by the distinguished jury composed of Maurice de Gandillac, Etienne Souriau and Pierre-Maxime Schuhl, the thesis combines the worst faults of the academic *doctorat d'état* and the doctrinal compendium.

Within three years, Garaudy disowned his *Théorie matérialiste de la connaissance*, refusing to permit any reprinting of it, on grounds of its dogmatism. His reaction is easily understood in view of the destalinizing context of the later 1950s, but the fact that for a few short months it was widely thought of as a major addition to Marxist philosophy must be regarded as reflecting the general paucity of French Marxist writing. It sets in perspective the considerable effort of thought represented by the pre-war work of Marxists like Politzer, Nizan, Lefebvre, Maublanc and Cornu, and their attempted reappraisals of the materialist dialectic. Even more, it highlights the theoretical development of French Marxism which took place during the following two decades.

There can be no doubt that the quality of thought and analysis deteriorated seriously among Marxists during the early 1950s. But, distressing though it may be, it is entirely consistent with the Marxist analysis that this should happen. Since it is a fundamental tenet of Marxism that thought is determined by social being, it would almost be more disturbing if Marxist philosophy had flourished in the Cold War. Economically and socially, the working class was subjected to a sustained and often violent assault on its working and living conditions: politically, the communists were systematically isolated, and the socialists subordinated to right-wing interests and alliances; ideologically, Marxism was anathematized and excluded as far as possible from cultural and intellectual life. In these circumstances, a siege mentality, breeding sectarianism, could hardly fail to be generated, and the evidence of its ravages among Marxist philosophers is not hard to find. What is surprising is rather that its effects did not run deeper or last longer.

Stirrings of recovery

On falsifie Hegel lui-même. Ce n'est pas *La Logique* en tant qu'expression des catégories fondamentales de l'Etre que l'on met au premier plan, mais *La Phénoménologie de l'Esprit*, interprétée comme l'histoire dramatique de la conscience qui se cherche. La dialectique ainsi n'apparaît plus comme une méthode scientifique, expression des exigences propres du concept rationnel de l'être, mais comme une aventure intérieure à la conscience proprement humaine, et que Hegel aurait idéalisée à tort. La méthode dialectique n'est plus alors le noyau rational du hégélianisme.

Jean-T. Desanti, 'Intervention du Cercle des Philosophes', La Nouvelle critique, avril–mai 1953, 140

The mediocrity of the Marxist philosophical effort during the early Cold War years was no secret for the Marxists themselves. As the worst of the crisis passed, they began to look more closely at their mode of expression. Interrogations and reassessments began to appear and within the Communist Party in particular there were moves towards a more collective practice of reflection. Contrary to the widely accepted stereotype, these developments did not await the revelations of 1956.

Already in 1953, French Marxists were taking the initiative to seek new organizational forms and new theoretical formulations of philosophy. Two collective events in the spring of that year marked the turning point: a national meeting of intellectuals called by the PCF, and a colloquium organized by the review *La Pensée*.

Nominally marking the seventieth anniversary of Marx's death, the 'journées nationales d'études des intellectuels communistes' was called by the PCF's central committee and held in Ivry over the weekend of 29 and 30 March 1953. During the two months of preparatory discussion the death of Stalin occurred, but the two central themes were nonetheless related to his last work, *The Economic Problems of Socialism in the USSR* (1952), and focused on questions of socialist humanism and the objectivity of the laws of nature and society.[13] The aim of the meeting was to give a new impetus to intellectual work, in the criticism of bourgeois ideology, in the elaboration of Marxist theory, and in the extension of the influence of Marxism. To a large extent it was a discussion of what work needed to be done and how it should be approached, ranging over philosophy, physics, chemistry, biology, geology, medicine, psychology, sociology, history, geography, literature and linguistics. Over 600 intellectuals attended the conference. Henri Lefebvre was present, but took charge of the sociology section, leaving philosophy to Jean-T. Desanti, who, with Roger Garaudy was coming to the fore among the leading Marxist philosophers of the post-war generation.

Characteristic of the entire conference, Desanti's report was largely devoted to criticizing bourgeois theories.[14] Attacking in passing thomism, pragmatism and logical positivism, he singled out phenomenology and neo-Hegelianism as the avantgarde of reaction, with Merleau-Ponty and Hyppolite as their main proponents. Phenomenology, he pointed out, put forward the view of freedom as unconditioned, history as unintelligible, and nature as a collection of human interpretations. Neo-Hegelianism, he said, was a more subtle attack on the notion of objective laws, first falsifying Hegel and then identifying Marx with his early writings interpreted in the light of falsified Hegel. As the above quoted passage suggests, Desanti saw the primacy accorded to the *Phenomenology* as a preliminary to discounting the rational dialectic in favour of a dramatic vision of the adventure of consciousness. With Hyppolite, he argued, the dialectic became simply an envelope in which the drama of life was wrapped.

It was significant that Desanti should attack Merleau-Ponty, who was rapidly moving towards a violent anti-communist position, rather than Sartre, who had effected a *rapprochement* with the PCF. Hyppolite was attacked as the militant leader of neo-Hegelianism, while Kojève was passed over in silence because he had practically withdrawn from public philosophical activity. The criticism outlined by Desanti succinctly expressed the view generally held by his comrades. It reflected the growing inclination for Hyppolite and his followers to assimilate their Hegelian views to the existentialism of the *Temps modernes*, run by Sartre, Merleau-Ponty and Simone de Beauvoir. The result, a shift from objective to subjective idealism, could only be detrimental to Marxism and materialism generally, making it more difficult to comprehend the rational dialectic which Marx took from Hegel.

What was at stake in the question was science and the claim of Marxism to be scientific. Successive reports to the conference, from scientists, emphasized that while the bourgeoisie was usually content to permit the spontaneous materialism necessary to immediate scientific research, it resisted any attempt to incorporate consistent materialism in a general world view. The consequence, in natural science, was a contradiction which hampered fundamental research and the long-term development of knowledge. In social science, bourgeois ideology was on the contrary anxious to deny any notion of an objective material basis for laws of society, and consequently to deprive Marxism or any other social theory of scientific status. The resulting debate over the objectivity of laws of nature and society became a central focus of controversy for the next decade, providing a major framework in which the materialist dialectic was challenged and defended.

Though it offered a series of critical attacks and an appearance of militancy, Desanti's exposé was a defensive position which added little to the development of Marxist theory on a positive level. PCF philosopher Guy Besse noted the fact in a review of the event,[15] but it was also clearly articulated in the conference's concluding address by Georges Cogniot.[16] While calling for a general raising of the level of activity and the sharpness of critical responses to hostile doctrines, Cogniot spoke of the need for more research on Marxist philosophy. He called for work on the categories of the dialectic: internal links, interaction, the old and the new, contradiction, development by leaps, form and content, essence and phenomenon, virtuality and act, freedom and necessity, laws and contingency. 'En étudiant ces problèmes', he declared, 'vous aurez l'occasion de vous expliquer une bonne fois à propos de l'hégélianisme.'[17] As an example of the work that needed to be done he mentioned the revision of Hegelian concepts being undertaken by Soviet philosophers, including an examination of the concept of the identity of opposites, and whether it did not run the risk of obscuring the struggle of opposites. He recognized that many other problems remained to be solved, some of which he listed. But emphasizing the need to construct philosophy on the basis of concrete scientific knowledge, he issued the call which in many respects summed up the conference: 'Au travail, camarades philosophes.'[18]

Although it was a call to action, Cogniot's discourse was also an indication of the direction to be taken by Marxist philosophers, and it is evident that a reassessment of Hegel and the philosophical concepts he formulated was high on the agenda. For Cogniot, unlike Zhdanov, the question of Hegel was not closed, rather it was through a reworking of his dialectic that Marxist philosophy might be expected to advance most effectively. Though he considered that Wahl, Hyppolite and their supporters were purveying a reactionary Hegelianism, he did not share the earlier tendency to reject Hegel completely. And as a *député* and member of the PCF's central committee, he can reasonably be taken to represent the view of the party leadership.

From aspiration to implementation is often a long step, particularly in the elaboration of philosophy, where the rhythm of development may be slow. But the Ivry days mark the beginning of a mobilization of philosophical resources among the Marxists of the Communist Party, and among their sympathizers. Mobilization did not necessarily mean regimentation, as the continuing presence of diverse interpretations confirms. The party's commitment to promote Marxist philosophy in a planned and organized way implied the imparting of a certain direction, and many of the implicit limits of Cold War discipline were still observed. But in a tangible way limitations began to be removed: intellectuals were encouraged to seek bourgeois publishers for their work, to write for bourgeois reviews, to be active in non-communist circles, professional organizations, public debates and so forth. They were encouraged to deploy their invention and creativity rather than producing dull compilations and reiterations of classical texts. The tone of Georges Cogniot's address is in contrast to the earlier stern admonitions of Laurent Casanova. Where Casanova tried to keep the intellectuals in line, Cogniot told them, as one intellectual to another, to roll up their sleeves and give of their best. There was a great deal of ground to be made up, but Ivry was undoubtedly a start.

On a more technical basis than Ivry, the review *La Pensée* organized a colloquium of university intellectuals to mark the same anniversary. It took place the following Whitsun weekend, 24 and 25 May 1953. Although the review was run largely by communists, it attracted many sympathetic intellectuals who, without being communist, or even Marxist, shared the journal's commitment to the values of rationalism and scientific enquiry. Its colloquium drew some 500 participants, of whom many were eminent academics in their own field. The topics chosen dealt with the role of Marxism in economics, science and philosophy, natural sciences, French history and education. In some respects it was more important than the Ivry meeting, because it involved many of the leading Marxist intellectuals, because it dealt in detail with complex theoretical questions, and because it focused on the development of Marxist concepts rather than on polemic against third parties or on matters of organization. In philosophy, it was as yet a long way from achieving the aspiration of freshness and creative reappraisal, but the proceedings reflected a renewed affirmation of the intellectual value and power of Marxism along with a determination to apply it at the highest theoretical level.

Even in the immediate sense, the 1953 colloquium was more than a dull ritual. Among other things, it was the scene of a sharp confrontation over the views of Henry Lefebvre on Hegel's place in Marxism. Lefebvre was present and delivered a paper tracing the categories of dialectical logic at work in Marx's *Capital*.[19] Though Hegel was not explicitly invoked Lefebvre was careful to emphasize the continuity between Marx's early philosphical writings and *Capital*. It enabled him to incorporate the entire system of Hegelian categories into Marxist economics, and although he might be said to be following Cogniot's call to work on the categories of Hegel's dialectic, it is clear that his position was in more perfect continuity with his own development since *Le Matérialisme dialectique*.

Emile Bottigelli, following Lefebvre's paper, delivered a direct attack on his stance.[20] He rejected the interpretation of Marx as essentially the greatest disciple of Hegel. Such a view, he considered, placed Marxism within the idealist and speculative tradition, calling into question its materialism. Though Lefebvre was not named directly, the project of giving a concrete content to the Hegelian dialectic indicted by Bottigelli was an unmistakable identifying feature which lay at the heart of Lefebvre's position. Its non-materialist implications, Bottigelli suggested, were ultimately aimed at setting Marx the philosopher against Marx the scientist, emasculating his thought and reducing him to an epigone of Hegel. He accepted that philosophical categories derived from Hegel are present in *Capital*, but argued that their presence stems from the dialectical relationship between philosophy and science. The initial philosophical idea designates an area of reality which is subjected to scientific examination, after which the results are generalized in the form of philosophical concepts which may be related to the earlier idea. In addition to this form of transition between early and later Marx, Bottigelli points to a hiatus between the early Marx and Hegel, based on

Marx's awareness of social realities and rejection of abstract speculation. Hence a double distance is proposed between Hegel and Marxism.

Bottigelli's critique is pertinent in introducing scientific considerations where Lefebvre bases his account purely in philosophy. Philosophy's role in generalizing scientific conclusions is partly recognized by Lefebvre, who sees science as enriching philosophy, and vice versa, but it does not undermine the essential continuity of philosophy. Bottigelli, on the other hand, conceives science as playing a disjunctive role within philosophy. The importance of the disjunction is not confined simply to ensuring recognition of the originality of Marxism. It also relates to the cognitive value of philosophy, which is primarily dependent on its correspondence with the conclusions of science, and only secondarily derived from its own internal procedures of development. If it is accepted that the first major achievement of Marx and Engels was to found the science of society and history, and subsequently to develop a scientific economic theory, then it follows that philosophical generalizations made before that occurrence stand in need of reformulation in the light of the new science. On the other hand, Bottigelli ought to acknowledge a measure of continuity to the extent that the former philosophical synthesis incorporated generalizations of the natural sciences, of the structures of rationality developed slowly over centuries and of the elements of Marxist social science already existing in a pre-scientific form. To the extent that science changes, Bottigelli is surely correct in attributing to it a disjunctive role in philosophy. Hence it might further be concluded that the more closely Marxist philosophy integrates the results of modern scientific enquiry, the less dominance its Hegelian ancestry will exercise in its formulation.

The early Althusser

Les thèses du matérialisme ne font donc qu'exprimer et développer consciemment les implications de la 'practique spontanée' des sciences, cas particulier de la pratique humaine. Cette pratique implique la confrontation de deux termes, unis dans une unité profonde: *l'idée (ou la conscience)* du savant (ou des hommes) – *et la réalité extérieure*. Cette confrontation comporte la reconnaissance du *primat de la réalité extérieure* sur l'idée ou la conscience, qui, dans la pratique, se règlent sur elle, et la reconnaissance de l'objectivité des lois établies, dans cette pratique, par la science.

Louis Althusser, 'Note sur le matérialisme dialectique', Revue de l'enseignement philosophique, *octobre – novembre 1953 14*
(italics his)

The same year, 1953, saw a little-noticed but significant attempt to draw up a clear exposition of the materialist dialectic. Distinguished more by its clarity than its originality, it is principally of interest because its author, Louis Althusser, went on to develop the same basic principles in an influential and controversial form during the 1960s. Writing for the professional journal of a philosophy teachers' association, he offered two articles during the year with the aim of providing a brief exposition, with bibliographical information, of the main points of Marxist philosophy. A young philosopher, teaching at the Ecole normale supérieure, Althusser had been a member of the Communist Party for five years, and was a committee member of the association (Association des Professeurs de Philosophie de l'Enseignement public).

Presenting the Marxist conception of the dialectic as the most advanced form of the scientific method, he notes the relation of opposition and inversion between it and the Hegelian dialectic. [21] In the first instance, he says, Marx rejected the schematic and dogmatic use of the dialectic, which tries to impose it on every aspect of reality, and which stems from Hegel's idealism. He accepts that some of Hegel's analyses correspond to reality: for example, his view of history as a process, and his critiques of the abstract ideas and the 'beautiful soul'. But it is the rational kernel which is primarily adopted by Marxism, he affirms. Its components – interaction, development, qualitative 'leaps', and contradiction – offer, in his view, a remarkable approximation of the most advanced method of positive science, and are validated by scientific use. This, he argues, is the precise meaning of the famous 'inversion', and its further consequence is that scientific use develops and refines the dialectic. He proposes two examples of such development: Stalin's elimination of the negation of the negation, and Mao Tse-tung's introduction of the notions of principle contradiction and principal aspect of a contradiction. How far they may be described as scientific is questionable, but Althusser's later work constantly returns to these points as a basis for his own re-elaboration of Marxist philosophy. Certainly the two points, whatever their value, do constitute major philosophical modifications which Mao and Stalin introduced into Marxism. Finally, overcoming the gap between the two aspects of dialectical materialism, Althusser presents the dialectic as both a method of discovery and as an expression of the structure of reality, thereby relating it directly to Marxist materialism.

Though they have not reached a state of full elaboration, the premises of Althusser's later anti-Hegelian assault are visible within the traditional framework of his 1953 essay. He articulates the two-stage view of Marx's development from Hegel: an inversion followed by a reworking; and he subordinates the reworked dialectic to positive science. As opposed to Lefebvre he emphasizes that 'ce n'est ni par référence à un système philosophique quelconque, ni par une sorte du vertu intrinsèque, par une nécessité "logique" absolue, que la dialectique s'impose à eux'.[22] Marxism does not therefore grow out of Hegel, it adopts his dialectic for its scientific value. In a footnote, Althusser mentions Hegel's economic, historical and scientific background as a possible explanation for the scientific value. Implicitly, rather than explicitly, he situates Marx and Engels outside the Hegelian system, and even outside philosophy, though within theory.

In his discussion of the controversial early writings of Marx, Althusser emphasizes the discontinuity between Marx's Hegelian period and his mature theory. He discounts any organic link with Hegel, depicting the relationship as a purely external one of borrowing ideas. He also limits the rational kernel to Stalin's four principal features. Though he refers briefly to Lenin's notebooks, there is no acknowledgement of the extent to which either Lenin or Engels studied and respected Hegel's enormous philosophical achievement in later years. His position is therefore substantially the same as Bottigelli's. However, he does recognize the intimate link between the structure of the method and the structure of reality. This enables him to some extent to overcome the schematic separation of the dialectic and materialism for which Stalin was largely responsible.

Turning to the question of materialism, Althusser rapidly dismisses the misunderstandings which conceive it as a denial of the reality of thought, or as the replacement of science by some metaphysic of substance. Materialism is simply the assertion of the primacy of existence over consciousness, enshrined in all scientific practice. The theses of materialism, he argues, simply express and develop on a conscious level the implications of all human practice, science in particular, which presupposes the recognition of a prior external reality. Matter cannot therefore be defined dogmatically, since it is merely a category to designate objective reality. The materialist theory of knowledge is neither a science of the sciences nor a theory from which sciences can be deduced, but it is a theory which is confirmed in practice and embodied in theory within the sciences, entailing the rejection of idealist illusions, the criticism of dogmatic fixism and the refusal of abstract formalism.

To a large extent, Althusser's exposition of materialism follows Engels and Lenin. He avoids using Stalin's presentation in terms of three principal features, and attempts to convey the scientific and theoretical power of materialism as a response to the fundamental question of philosophy and as a theory of knowledge. The fact that he spends twice as long discussing materialism as he does the dialectic is an indication of the ideological conflicts of the time as well as of the deep antipathy he bears to Hegel. It is also evidence of his overriding concern to define Marxist materialism in terms of scientific practice. In terms of his later development, Althusser's emphasis is entirely consistent with his recurrent preoccupations, but the role of external reality is acknowledged explicitly in a way which was subsequently resisted. As the quoted passage shows, the familiar Althusserian vision of human activity in terms of practices is supplemented by the notion of a confrontation between idea and reality, in which the former 'models itself' on the latter, and in which the objectivity of scientific laws is ensured. The extent to which the notion of this confrontation subsists in his later theoretical position is open to question. What is significant is the way his exposition in 1953 takes up the view of materialism as a defence of science and scientificity, implicitly using physics as the model of science, emphasizing the primacy of external reality over consciousness, and therefore acknowledging the decisive role of the raw material of reality in the production of knowledge. It is a view which his later writings could not continue to accommodate, but equally one which the philosophical environment of 1953 imposed.

Read retrospectively, Althusser's articles are an unadorned presentation of the sources from which his well-known essays of the 1960s sprang. Read in the context of their date, they are an attempt to state coherently and in academic form the central philosophical preoccupations of Marxism in the year of Stalin's death. When they appeared, their importance lay less in the specific ideas put forward than in the fact of demonstrating that Marxism could be, and was increasingly being, taken seriously by recognized academic philosophers. It is not always easy to contextualize in this way the early writings of someone who later achieves fame. But the articles belong just as much to the picture of French Marxism in 1953 as they do to the development of Louis Althusser.

Critiques of the existentialist dialectic

Tout interprète de Hegel est, au fond condamné au choix suivant: ou bien il renonce à tirer bénéfice de la Logique, ou bien il comprend le concept de l'être comme celui de la matière en mouvement. Ou bien il falsifie Hegel, ou bien il le dépasse dans le matérialisme dialectique.

Jean-T. Desanti, 'Hegel, est-il le père de l'existentialisme?', La Nouvelle critique, juin 1954, 109

The spreading popularity of Hegel, particularly in the existentialist interpretation, posed a serious ideological challenge to Marxism, in addition to the political ramifications it engendered. The initial reaction against Hegel was, however, neither unanimous, nor long-lived. The deep resistance, characterized by the polemics of La Nouvelle critique in late 1950 and the positions of Bottigelli and Althusser, was rapidly superseded by a more nuanced response which aimed to distinguish a genuine Marxist view of Hegel from a distorted existentialist reading. The philosophical objective was a sharp differentiation between the rational dialectic which could be adopted from Hegel's Logic into Marxism, and the phenomenological dialectic which confined its attention to the movement of consciousness.

The French Marxists were assisted in their efforts by the important study on the young Hegel which George Lukács published in 1948.[23] Laying heavy stress on Hegel's early interest in political economy, it provided the elements of a historical account of how the Hegelian dialectic developed in contact with the leading contemporary scientific theorists. Though not immediately available in translation, Lukács's work was widely echoed in the French periodical press. More immediately influential was the publication of a full translation of Lenin's philosophical notebooks in 1955.[24] The 1938 partial edition by Lefebvre and Guterman had long been unavailable, and a scholarly edition of the full text, prepared by Emile Bottigelli and Lida Vernant, gave considerable impetus to the reappraisal of Hegel's dialectic by Marxists. Announcing the publication in 1954, Bottigelli emphasized that Hegel could still be valuable to Marxist theory provided he was read with the vigour and intransigence of Lenin's approach.[25]

At the same time, the thirtieth anniversary of Lenin's death provoked a variety of commemorations, including a colloquium which La Pensée organized in the spring of 1954 on the theme of Lenin as a philosopher and scientist. Henri Lefebvre, presenting the philosophical address, emphasized Lenin's recognition of the importance of Hegel in the formation of Marxism.[26] Dialectical materialism, he said, was both a negation and a realization, a transformation and a fulfilment of Hegelian philosophy. Lefebvre took the opportunity to criticize Merleau-Ponty's inaugural lecture at the Collège de France, in which the existentialist philosopher implicitly attacked Lenin, and Engels, for replacing the brilliant intuition of the dialectic of consciousness with an objective dialectic of things and matter. The result, Lefebvre argued, was an ironical and ambiguous philosophy of detachment within every commitment: a non-conformist conformity. Whatever the difficulties of his own view of Hegel, he was at least in agreement with his comrades

that the existentialist dialectic was a deformation of the Hegelian and
Marxist dialectics.

Lefebvre pointed to the resemblance between Merleau-Ponty's
position and that of the turn-of-the-century empirio-criticists, attacked
in Lenin's *Materialism and Empirio-criticism* (1908). What the
existentialists sought, he argued, was a third way, between materialism
and idealism. Their insistence on the complementarity of consciousness
and its object attempted to evade an answer to the question of which
had priority. Lenin's materialist dialectic, he said, asserted the
reciprocity of contact between consciousness and its object, but rejected
the isolation of this moment of the knowledge process from its overall
context. Merleau-Ponty's interpretation of Marx's notion of praxis, he
claimed, reduced practice to the organization of relations between men,
and with nature, failing to acknowledge the dimension of contact and
penetration in a reality whose essence and laws are gradually discerned.
'S'il y a une dialectique des idées', he concluded, 'c'est parce qu'il y a une
dialectique de la nature, hors de la conscience, avant la conscience, et
ensuite dans l'homme et sa conscience, *avant qu'il le sache*.'[27]

At the very least, Lefebvre's position was an affirmation of the
objective as opposed to the subjective dialectic. There can be little doubt
that his position was closer to Hegel's than Merleau-Ponty's at least in
that respect. On the other hand, it is arguable that the existentialists do
safeguard the idealism and therefore the religious dimension of the
Hegelian dialectic, even if it is at the price of its objectivity. Specifically,
the Absolute Idea which Hegel sought to elucidate was closely
dependent on the notion of God, which in some form underlies any
system of objective idealism. If the notion of an objectively existing God
is abandoned, as it is by the existentialists of Sartre's and Merleau-
Ponty's persuasion, then the basis for objective idealism effectively
collapses. In its place they argue for either a non-commital agnosticism
in which anything is possible or a subjective idealism which provides a
dimension of transcendence into which God may be inserted as a
guarantor of individual experience, or as an optional extension to it.

The debt of the existentialists to the mystified dialectic of Jean Wahl
and neo-Hegelians like Kojève and Hyppolite is evident in so far as they
embrace subjective idealism. The question of whether this or Marxism is
more faithful to Hegel is by no means as clear as Lefebvre suggests, not
least because his own version of Marxism was more heavily Hegelian
than most Marxists might be prepared to allow. However, it was a
question which exercised many of his contemporaries, and which
played an important role in the developing ideological struggle of the
mid-1950s.

Jean Desanti, a leading figure among PCF philosophers of the period, devoted two articles to the question 'Hegel, est-il père de l'existentialisme?'[28] He recalled his own pre-war contact with Kojève's seminar, which had only three other members when he attended in 1936, but had since attracted such attention that the master and slave analysis was on the *agrégation* programme. Kojève himself owed more to Heidegger than to Hegel, he said, and interpreted the *Phenomenology of Mind* in terms of *Sein und Zeit*, abstracting man from the totality as a negative absolute, and reducing the Hegelian dialectic to an 'orgeilleux travestissement du malheur', a subjective dialectic divorced from the objective dialectic.[29] Desanti, following Lenin, argued that the essence of Hegel was his notion of being as movement and self-development. Marxism, he continued, took this notion, defining being as matter in movement. Being and thought were necessarily united but being had priority whereas thought was its highest form of development. He concluded, in the passage cited above, that the identification of being with matter in motion was the only way in which the value of Hegel's *Logic* could be preserved. The alternative was a falsification of Hegel.

Desanti had, of course, no difficulty in quoting passages from Hegel demonstrating the latter's belief in the dialectical movement of the natural world, and therefore his belief in the objective existence of the dialectic throughout the totality of things. On the other hand, Hegel's totality was conceived in terms of the movement of idea. Both existentialism and Marxism operate an 'inversion' of Hegel: one a subordination of the objective to the subjective, the other a subordination of the ideal to the material. Desanti describes his inversion as a 'dépassement' and the other as a falsification of Hegel. This distinction rests on the existentialists' obligation to ignore the *Logic*. But his own view can equally be taxed with ignoring the *Phenomenology*.

Given the consistency and circularity of Hegel's philosophy, it seems futile to judge either existentialism or Marxism in terms of its fidelity to Hegel. Each takes what it conceives to be the most valuable part, considering that to be the essence of Hegel's thought. In the case of Marxism, the structures of rationality, reflecting the movement of reality, constitute the rational kernel of Hegelianism. In the case of existentialism, the movement of consciousness, generating the structures of experience, constitutes the phenomenological core of Hegel. Either side may theoretically claim superiority by seeking to encompass the other's ground within its own perspective, but, at least in the 1950s neither chose in practice to do so. At all events, each was certainly right to deny the other a monopoly of Hegel's succession, but equally certainly wrong to claim it for their own. Ultimately, the arbitrator is practice. It is what they succeed in doing with Hegel that decides who is keeping his thought alive, and therefore who is his best successor. And the judgment is made in history, not in textual analysis.

It was in response to Merleau-Ponty's book, *Les Aventures de la dialectique* that the sharpest criticism of the existentialist dialectic was formulated by Marxists. Not surprisingly perhaps in view of the political and ideological threat which his position represented, he was vigorously attacked as an anti-Marxist as well as an anti-communist. The most comprehensive riposte took the form of a well-attended public symposium held in November 1955, with the general title 'Mésaventures de l'anti-marxisme: Les malheurs de M. Merleau-Ponty'. Rapidly published in book form, it brought together leading PCF intellectuals, including Roger Garaudy, Henri Lefebvre, Jean-T. Desanti, Maurice Caveing, Victor Leduc, Jean Kanapa and Georges Cogniot.[30] Their contributions ranged over many aspects of Merleau-Ponty's political and philosophical position. Lefebvre satirized the idealist basis of his philosophy of ambiguity. Desanti developed the same criticism, demonstrating how Merleau-Ponty was ultimately faced with the choice of either solipsism or theology. Maurice Caveing accused him of reducing practice to pure pragmatism in which success or failure retrospectively determine the legitimacy of an activity. Leduc, Kanapa and Cogniot attacked the reactionary political implications of his stance. But the most extensive philosophical analysis was provided by Roger Garaudy in the opening paper.

Garaudy argued that Merleau-Ponty was attacking the central Marxist tradition, replacing its dialectic with relativism and its materialism with phenomenology. Garaudy rejected the Weberian view of history on the grounds that historical knowledge consequently became subjectivized. He suggested that Merleau-Ponty's ambiguous dialectic gave such a privileged role to consciousness and to choosing that they replaced any practical or constructive activity. As a result, he pointed out, Merleau-Ponty's interpretation of revolutionary politics ultimately meant a vague commitment to go forward into the unknown with a questioning attitude, not a very rousing perspective for the toiling and oppressed masses.

The *Mésaventures* was a deliberate and organized attack on Merleau-Ponty, and the essays in it were sought and written as a matter of political necessity. The problems attendant on a debate conducted at the level of polemic have already been noted. But although they were commissioned, the conceptual content of the essays is not thereby abolished, nor did the essence of their criticisms disappear with the changing political situation. The immediate political and ideological issues were intensified in the Cold War climate which was only beginning to pass its peak. Five years later the confrontation between Marxism and existentialism was able to take place face to face in a spirit of dialogue, where in 1955 it happened at a distance and in a spirit of mutual denunciations. It is true that the mainstream existentialist current led by Jean-Paul Sartre did not share Merleau-Ponty's political position at this time. Indeed the *Aventures* were in large measure a virulent attack on Sartre's sympathy for the communists, designated by Merleau-Ponty as 'ultra-bolshevism'. But the conditions for Sartre's fellow-travelling included a tacit agreement to avoid confrontations on the level of philosophy or social theory with his Marxist colleagues. When confrontations subsequently did take place, the circumstances were much more congenial to the comradely recognition of differences.

References

1   See Jean-T. Desanti *et al.*, *Science bourgeoise et science prolétarienne* (Paris, 1950).

2   J. V. Stalin, *Marxism and Problems of Linguistics* (Moscow, 1954).

3   J.-T. Desanti, 'La science, forme de la conscience sociale', *Cahiers du communisme*, octobre 1951, 1188–1204.

4   F. Armand and A. Cornu, 'Critique et autocritique', *La Pensée*, septembre–octobre 1949, 84–88.

5   *Ibid.*, 86.

6   R. Garaudy, 'Autocritique: Jdanov est passé par là. . .' *La Nouvelle critique*, avril 1949, 37–44.

7   H. Lefebvre, 'Autocritique', *La Nouvelle critique*, mars 1949, 41–57.

8   *Ibid.*, 51.'

9   See quotation at the head of this section.

10 'Le retour à Hegel', *La Nouvelle critique*, novembre 1950, 43–54.

11 E. Bottigelli, 'A propos du retour à Hegel', *La Nouvelle critique*, décembre 1950, 73–81.

12 H. Lefebvre, 'Lettre sur Hegel', *La Nouvelle critique*, janvier 1951, 99–104.

13 The proceedings are substantially reproduced in *La Nouvelle critique*, avril–mai 1953, 125–368.

14 Jean-T. Desanti, 'Intervention du cercle des philosophes', *ibid.*, 138–145.

15 G. Besse, 'Les journées nationales d'étude des intellectuels communistes', *Cahiers du communisme*, juin–juillet 1953, 776–780.

16 G. Cogniot, 'Conclusions', *La Nouvelle critique*, avril–mai 1953, 324–357.

17 *Ibid.*, 354.

18 *Ibid.*

19 H. Lefebvre, 'Des phénomènes aux lois dans *Le Capital*', *La Pensée*, novembre 1953, 58–63.

20   E. Bottigelli, untitled paper, *La Pensée*, novembre 1953, 65–71.
21   Louis Althusser, 'Note sur le matérialisme dialectique', *Revue de l'enseignement philosophique*, octobre–novembre 1953, 11–17.
22   *Ibid.*, 12.
23   G. Lukács, *Der Junge Hegel* (Zurich and Vienna, 1948).
24   V. I. Lénine, *Cahiers philosophiques* (Paris, 1955).
25   E. Bottigelli, 'Comment Lénine lit Hegel', *La Pensée*, septembre–octobre 1954, 110–114.
26   H. Lefebvre, 'Lénine philosophe', *La Pensée*, septembre–octobre 1954, 18–36.
27   *Ibid.*, 35, his italics.
28   J.-T. Desanti, 'Hegel, est-il le père de l'existentialisme?', *La Nouvelle critique* juin 1954, 91–109; juillet–août 1954, 163–187.
29   *Ibid.*, juin 1954, 97.
30   *Mésaventures de l'anti-marxisme* (Paris, 1956).

5

New Beginnings

1956–1962

1956 and its aftermath

Les marxistes avaient parfaitement conscience à l'époque
(1956–1958) . . . de la menace de stérilisation que le dogmatisme
de naguère avait fait peser sur le marxisme, en partie sinon en
totalité. La volonté de redresser la barre, de réactiver la théorie
sans rien abandonner de ses principes ni de sa nécessité vitale pour
le mouvement ouvrier était manifeste.

Jacques Milhau, Chroniques philosophiques *(Paris, 1972), 15–16*

The year 1956 was a historical turning point for Marxism and for
France. Nationally and internationally dramatic changes took place
which intensified the complexities and contradictions of their
development, and sowed the seeds of subsequent crises. The rising
economic prosperity which France enjoyed was in sharp contrast to the
political confusion which prevailed. The January parliamentary
elections saw important advances by the parties of the Left. Had the
communists, radicals and socialists enjoyed a Popular Front agreement
they would have commanded a comfortable majority with 56 per cent of
the vote between them. The Guy Mollet administration, however,
pursuing a resolutely anti-communist policy, stumbled pragmatically
from one debacle to another, from the opening hostilities in the
Algerian war to the abortive Anglo-French expedition to wrest the Suez
canal from the Egyptians. The growing prestige enjoyed by Marxism
politically and ideologically was also in sharp contrast to the dramatic
international events which had profound repercussions on its
development. The 20th Congress of the Soviet Communist Party
(CPSU) witnessed the unexpected denunciation of Stalin and the
recognition of the crimes, abuses and mistakes which were committed
during the period of his 'personality cult'. The beginning of
destalinization was followed closely by an uprising in Hungary during
the same autumn, which was put down firmly with the intervention of
the Soviet army.

The effect of these events on world history and on French history was
far-reaching. The internal relations and organization of the world
communist movement were thrown into uncertainty. The abolition of
its information bureau (Cominform) signalled the end of any centralized
organization, and the major split led by the Chinese can in part be
traced to the problems which arose out of these and accompanying
changes. The revulsion and shock provoked by Khrushchev's
revelations undermined the confidence which many communists and
sympathizers had loyally accorded to the Soviet Union, a confidence
which was further shaken by the Hungarian events. The resulting
disillusionment and division were reflected in varying degrees in every
communist party, precipitating political upheavals and disorientation.
In Western Europe, parties were all weakened, and the different
attempts to chart new and independent directions spring at least in part
from the rude awakening of 1956.

In France the implications of destalinization were not lost, but their
effect was less immediate and less dramatic by virtue of the conditions in
which they were received. The close historical identification of the
French Communist Party with the Soviets had produced an affinity
which was hard to shake. The position of Maurice Thorez, General
Secretary since 1930, was so firmly assured as to preclude any challenge
to his leadership, and he was sufficiently flexible to preside over a degree
of change without provoking unnecessary conflict. Moreover, the
political uncertainties and polarizations within France provided ample
urgent work for the party in a national framework without its energies
being dissipated in internal dissension over long-term perspectives and
international problems. The crises of decolonization, Suez, and the
threat of extreme right-wing Gaullist and Poujadist movements posed
more immediate problems than the CPSU Congress or Hungary. But
the long-term questions remained, and slowly made their way, to the
point that they formed an essential component of the dynamic of the
PCF's development over the following decades.

Philosophically, there was no immediate or dramatic change among
the communist intellectuals. Stalin was discreetly dropped from the
canon of classical texts which were regarded as authoritative. But then
his works had, since his death, been somewhat less used, as the French
Marxists came to grips with their domestic friends and enemies, and
began to develop their own formulations of Marxist theory based on
newly available material of Marx, Engels and Lenin. The impetus given
to the growth of Marxist philosophy in 1953 had gradually gathered
momentum, and a new generation of Marxists had developed their
principles to a much more sophisticated level than the schematic

exposition offered by Stalin's short essay. Many explorations were already in train when the 20th Congress burst on the theoretical scene, and the result was an acceleration in their progress rather than a change in their nature.

The intensified movement of reappraisal and diversification was accompanied and supported by important social and political changes, which acted to extend the implantation of Marxist ideas and modify their intellectual configuration. The period inaugurated by 1956 presents an originality and complexity in the nature of Marxism which for most practical purposes did exist before: it was the rapid growth of schools of Marxist thought which would not accept the designation of dialectical materialism. The new situation corresponds to the spread of Marxist ideas far beyond the confines of the communist movement, and the consequent end of the simple equation of Marxism and communism.

The equation had, in fact, never been simple. Even during Marx's lifetime serious divergences existed over the interpretation of his ideas, and their practical implications. And every period since then has had its share of differences. But in the forty years following the October Revolution, Marxism was largely synonymous with communism, and those who disputed the identification were either minority currents with negligible influence, or broader movements whose first allegiance was to another, non-Marxist, tradition. In France they were the small handful of Trotskyists and anarchists, or the more numerous Proudhonist syndicalists who generally dominated the social-democratic movement, or else the progressive christians whose primary source of inspiration was Catholic social encyclicals. As Marxism penetrated more widely and deeply into all spheres of French life, it was tailored to fit the needs of those who wished to adopt one or other part of it without accepting it in its entirety. Most pervasively, these neo-Marxisms took all or most of the theory of history and society, including Marxist economics, but stopped short of accepting its philosophical generalization, particularly materialism and the objective dialectic.

To a large extent, dialectical materialism, which is in the narrow sense of the word the philosophy of Marxism, has been rejected by non-communists. It is commonly dismissed under the label 'diamat', a derisive abbreviation usually intended to convey the impression of a crude and unreflecting dogmatism, and to dispense its user from a serious appraisal at a theoretical level. Many forms of dialectic have been advanced and discussed by non-communists, but a materialist dialectic remains characteristic of the communist understanding of

Marxism. Wherever it has been invoked for discussion, communist Marxism is ultimately in question, and with it the nature of a fully integrated and consistent Marxist synthesis. The widespread efforts to replace the materialist dialectic, either by some non-materialist dialectic or, more rarely, by some non-dialectical materialism, or even by something which is neither materialist nor dialectical, all represent attempts to graft Marxism onto some other philosophical outlook. The fruits and fortune of these various attempts require separate assessment. The problems of enriching and developing Marxism without undermining its coherence and power are complex and many-sided. In the post-1956 world many approaches have been made with differing success, some of the most ambitious being the work of French Marxists.

In taking the materialist dialectic as the focus of attention, and the touchstone for the development of Marxist philosophy, the present study therefore deliberately keeps communist Marxism at the centre of its concern. In France and in the world as a whole, communism and its ideas have assumed such historical importance that no apology need be offered for their study. But also on a conceptual level the theoretical debates they have engendered offer a richness and complexity which, with some limited exceptions, have not been sufficiently recognized. Other studies have focused on Christian, Freudian, existentialist or structuralist reworkings of Marxism, and on ephemeral 'New Left' interpretations such as those of the greatly overestimated 'Arguments' and 'Socialisme ou Barbarie' groups. The communist positions they were discussing, attacking or assimilating have, on the contrary, received little study. The imbalance needs at least to be rectified.

In focusing hereafter on communist theorists, this study is not making any judgements of legitimacy, or suggesting that only those studied are really Marxist. Such scholasticism would be among the least productive of approaches to the problems in question, as is often evidenced by theoretical debates which degenerate into squabbles over whether this or that group has a right to be called Marxist. To avoid these sterile controversies, writers are described here as Marxist where they do, as far as can be ascertained, claim to be such. In this sense, 1956 provoked far-reaching changes among French Marxist philosophers. For most of them, the consequences were worked out within the terms of communist Marxism, though for some they involved leaving the Communist Party and even in some cases Marxism as such. Others again gravitated towards the periphery, remaining on the margins of the party and often of Marxism.

Among the philosophers who left communism, one or two examples will illustrate the pattern of their itinerary. The young anthropologist

Lucien Sebag was active in the party from 1953, joining the editorial board of La Nouvelle critique. He wrote for the journal on Marxist philosophy, which he saw as a 'synthèse du matérialisme mécaniste et de l'humanisme'.[1] His political support for an internal opposition and his philosophical attraction towards Freudian psychoanalysis combined to set him at odds with the party and with basic principles of Marxism. The events of 1956 intensified the contradictions of his position and he was in due course excluded from the party and La Nouvelle critique (November 1957). He subsequently sought to elaborate a synthesis of Hegelianized Marxism with Lacanian psychoanalysis, existentialist phenomenology, and the structural anthropology of Lévi-Strauss, a project cut short by his untimely death, by his own hand, in 1965 at the age of 31.[2] Another philosopher belonging to an older generation, Pierre Fougeyrollas, followed a similar intellectual path. A communist since the war, he had also been active in an internal opposition group but philosophically attracted to an existentialist, almost religious, interpretation of Marxism as a theory of alienation. Leaving the party in the aftermath of 1956 he went on to develop an anguished, mystical notion of eternal alienation, which was directed against technology as the prime enemy, and for which the pursuit of philosophy was seen as providing the only consolation.[3]

Characteristic of those who slipped into the periphery of Marxism without altogether leaving it was Jean-Toussaint Desanti. One of the leading young PCF philosophers of the post-war period, he was prominent in debates and polemics on a variety of issues, notably in La Nouvelle critique, including dialogue with Catholics and the philosophy of science; he also contributed philosophical papers to several learned journals. Early in 1956 he published an Introduction à l'histoire de la philosophie, which sought to define a scientific Marxist method for the history of philosophy, taking the concrete example of Spinoza. The book was highly praised in the communist press and elsewhere. But in the wake of the 20th Congress, Desanti found himself increasingly out of harmony with his colleagues at La Nouvelle critique, who were not prepared to move as far nor as quickly as he in abandoning their former philosophical positions. He resigned from the editorial board in late 1957 and ceased most of his involvement in party activities. His later researches into the relations between Marxism and phenomenology were published by the PCF house Editions sociales in 1963. They, and his researches into the philosophy of mathematics, fell outside the perspective and main preoccupations of the Marxist debate at the time and were treated with some reserve by his former colleagues.

The casualties of 1956 were serious, but not disastrous. With the exception of Lefebvre, whose case will be studied in more detail, and with the partial exception of Desanti, none of those who left the PCF could be regarded as having made a major contribution to Marxist philosophy. Writers like Sebag and Fougeyrollas represented a loss of potential rather than actual importance. Other second and third rank thinkers left with them, but young intellectuals like Victor Leduc, Pierre Meren, Claude Roy, Emile Baulieu and Annie Kriegel were not difficult to replace. Young writers like Jacques Milhau, Michel Verret, Lucien Sève, François Hincker and Jacques Chambaz stepped into their places, and made effective and even distinguished contributions in due course. Perhaps the most lasting consequence was the bitterness of certain ex-Marxists: virulent anti-communism is stitched into every page of Claude Roy's personal memoirs of the period, and into Annie Kriegel's various accounts of the history of French communism.

Of the philosophers who stayed with the PCF, and those who came to it after 1956, most felt the need for change. The dominant figure of the later 1950s was unquestionably Roger Garaudy, who for a decade was chief philosophical spokesman of the party: 1956 is a key date in his development. He repudiated the doctrinaire defence of a pre-established, Stalinist viewpoint represented by his thesis of 1953, and sought a new standpoint from which to develop a comprehensive Marxist philosophy open to the positive features of non-Marxist thought. Garaudy put himself to the school of Hegel and the young Marx and proposed a humanist view which found its first expression in his *Humanisme marxiste* of 1957. The search for a new synthesis to replace the constricting and defensive positions of Cold War polemic took many other forms than Garaudy's, but it is part of his tragedy that he was, or felt himself to be, rushed into supplying an urgent replacement. What he achieved was a hastily rigged eclecticism which ultimately led him outside Marxism, as will be seen. But other younger philosophers, less pressed to produce a public position, worked in relative obscurity to fashion more durable and more coherent restatements of Marxist principles. They built on the patient work of reappraisal which had already been set in train since 1953, and it is to them that the high moments of Marxist philosophy in the 1960s and 1970s are largely owed. In the meantime, the public face of Marxism was still dominated by old differences, centred mainly on Lefebvre and Garaudy.

Lefebvre's problems with Marxism

Chaque affirmation déterminée fige le concept de matière, le transforme en collection de choses immobiles, c'est-à-dire en

concept non-philosophique en même temps que non-dialectique
. . . . Pourquoi donc ne pas déléguer expressément à la poésié ou à
la musique la charge – et le pouvoir – des affirmations
'cosmologiques' ou 'ontologiques' sur le monde, la nature, la
matière et sur l'homme en tant que s'insérant dans l'univers?

Henri Lefebvre, Problèmes actuels du marxisme (Paris, 1958), 4th
edition, 1970, 31

Lefebvre admet qu'en philosophie il y a deux postulats qu'on ne
peut prouver et entre lesquels il faut opter: le postulat matérialiste
et le postulat idéaliste . . . . on peut admettre ce que Lefebvre
entend par 'matière' sans être 'matérialiste'.

Jean Lacroix, 'La pensée de Lénine', Le Monde, 17 août 1957, 7

The individual itineraries of Marxist philosophers during this period are
complex and at times tragic. Their contours are often hidden under a
discreet silence or a hail of bad-tempered recriminations, and it is
difficult to reach a balanced assessment of the overall picture. The
interplay of personal, political and philosophical factors offers a rich,
but tangled, skein. The importance of these itineraries for the present
study lies in the effect they had on the development of the materialist
dialectic and the way the central concepts of Marxist philosophy are
understood in France as a result. The evolution of those who remained
Marxists, their divergences, and their relations with those who were
not, or were no longer Marxists, these are the points of focus.

The theorist whose efforts had dominated French Marxism for most
of twenty years, in some respects followed the pattern of Sebag and
Fougeyrollas, or perhaps they followed his. Henri Lefebvre's growing
divergences with the other communist philosophers had already
occasioned at least one public controversy.[4] The effect of 1956 on him
was to exacerbate the differences driving him to consider Marxism to
have entered a profound crisis, his own questionings being ignored or
misunderstood by Marxists generally. His first expression of this view
was in a Polish review, Twórczość, reprinted in part in France
Observateur, then in full in the existentialist journal Les Temps modernes;
soon afterwards appeared an article of similar import in the De Monzie
encyclopedia.[5] Lefebvre's jaundiced appraisal of the parlous state of
French Marxism was not appreciated by his comrades, who did not
hesitate to object to his haughty dismissal of their efforts.[6] However, the
immediate occasion of the final break was the publication by Lefebvre
in early 1958 of a short book in the 'Initiation philosophique' collection:

Problèmes actuels du marxisme (Paris, 1958). There he drew up, in some 130 short pages, a catalogue of the criticisms and grievances he held against what he called 'official' Marxism.

It might be thought that with the change in the intellectual climate, a spirit of reappraisal and a renewed interest in Hegel, Lefebvre's hour of triumph had surely come. But the changes were neither quick enough nor radical enough to satisfy him, and his reaction was a deliberate and bitter attack on the PCF philosophers, naming them individually in terms of deep scorn. Moreover, on the theoretical level, his position was getting further away from materialism and constantly reducing the scope of the dialectic. Ironically, his loathing of Stalin did not prevent him from adopting the same separation of the dialectic from materialism, albeit turned in an opposite sense. He viewed the dialectic essentially as a method, not intrinsically bound to either materialism or idealism, and developed a theory of inversion to secure a maximum of separation.

Already in *Le Matérialisme dialectique* (1939), Lefebvre had taken a view of Marx's life which had him rediscovering Hegel at a late date in his development. His later book *La Pensée de Karl Marx* (1947) described Marx's complete rejection and elimination of the dialectic as such in 1846, followed by a period of purely empirical, almost positivist studies until his rediscovery of the dialectic in 1858, at which time he integrated it into his thought purely as a method. The methodological status is clearly associated with Lefebvre's account of the inversion of Hegel. Adopting the 'two-stage' position, Lefebvre considered the initial rejection of the idealist dialectic to have been followed by its readoption in a form from which had been evacuated any implications concerning the relation between thought and being. Hence, in his controversial article of 1957 in the De Monzie encyclopedia he dismissed as 'thèse peu satisfaisante' the view that the Marxist dialectic reflected the laws of reality.[7] His implicit stance was that Lenin's acceptance of such a reflection in his notebooks was indicative that only the first stage of the inversion had been carried out, and that a further purge of idealist elements was necessary.

The *Problèmes actuels du marxisme* went a stage further in the analysis. Lefebvre devoted considerable space to defining his understanding of materialism. It was, he said, an unprovable philosophical postulate, and therefore bound to disappear, along with idealism, when philosophy itself was superseded, and 'il ne saurait donc être question d'une vérité absolue, définitive – et acquise – du matérialisme'.[8] Alternately it was 'une sorte d'x (d'inconnue)', an ill-defined and strictly undefinable concept, which was distorted by any attempt to determine it.[9] Ultimately, he suggested, the ideas of being or matter would be much better left to music or poetry to express. This latter idea, expressed in the passage quoted earlier, was deliberately provocative and Lefebvre fully (and correctly) expected that it would arouse 'des protestations presque unanimes', but felt that the fact was part and parcel of the crisis of Marxism and of philosophy in general.[10]

The protests were not long in appearing. A number of hard-hitting articles appeared in communist journals during the spring of 1958. Though directed against the newly appeared book, they unanimously traced Lefebvre's latest and most explicit revision of Marxism to its roots in his previous work. The leading Africanist, Jean Suret-Canale attacked the reduction of materialism to an unproved postulate.[11] Proof, he argued, was not confined to logic; the materialist postulate was amply proven in practice; and its truth was at the basis of the Marxist claim to give scientific knowledge. The young philosopher Lucien Sève challenged Lefebvre's account of Marx's development, arguing that there was no period during which Marx had rejected the dialectic, and consequently there was no sudden rediscovery in 1858.[12] Lefebvre's view, he argued, reduced the dialectic to a method, implicitly denied its scientific reflection of the objective laws of development, and minimized the inversion of the Hegelian dialectic. Roger Garaudy, writing in the PCF's theoretical monthly, denounced the revisionist nature of Lefebvre's enterprise.[13] Lefebvre, he said, separated philosophy radically from politics, and within the resulting abstract sphere rejected materialism in favour of an agnostic position. He subsequently refused to accept the notion that thought reflects reality and could not countenance a dialectic of nature. What followed, Garaudy concluded, was an erosion of historical materialism, rejection of the Marxist theory of the state and eventually a defeatism which disarmed the working class and the revolutionary movement.

Among these and other criticisms levelled against Lefebvre, there was broad agreement that the dialectic was more than a method, and that it also reflected the structure of objective reality. Marx's inversion of Hegel, it was felt, had included a reversal of the priority of thought over being, but had not rejected the dialectical character of their relations. It was accepted that materialism was a premise which could not be proved on purely philosophical grounds. But it was urged against Lefebvre that Lenin's point in saying that was to stress that materialism was a premise or starting point for philosophy, but that it was substantiated by everyday experience, by social practice and by science. Obviously, if materialism could be proved philosophically it would have to be dependent on some prior more fundamental principle. However, the whole point of materialism is that thought depends on being, rather than on itself, and rather than the reverse. Thus the grounds on which the basic principle rests must lie outside philosophy if materialism is to be consistent.

Lefebvre's apparently radical purge of idealism from the dialectic is the price of his equally radical refusal to integrate materialism into it. But in his consequent project, the search for a supersession of philosophy in a form of thought which is neither idealist nor materialist, he is thoroughly Hegelian. Although he argues for the objectivity of the material world, his position is quite consistent with an objective idealism of Hegel's type. *Le Monde's* philosophy columnist, the Catholic personalist Jean Lacroix, drew attention to this convergence in a review of Lefebvre's short study on Lenin, suggesting that Lefebvre's attack on idealism only challenged the subjective idealist position. And there is no doubt that Lacroix was quite right to point out that one could very well accept what Lefebvre understood by 'matter' without being a materialist. [14]

Lefebvre's dissolution of materialism was already implicit in *Le Matérialisme dialectique*, but it was reaffirmed with increasing vigour during the 1950s. Its main philosophical consequence is to confine the dialectic within the field of human activity, excluding a dialectic of nature and rendering the objective world more submissive to voluntary intervention. In this respect Lefebvre's position approaches that of Merleau-Ponty. Ultimately the notion of laws of objective reality is replaced by an arbitrary methodological approach to reality. And reality itself becomes a shifting flux upon which no sure or lasting purchase can be gained.

The philosophical relativism thus reached was matched in the political sphere by Lefebvre's gradual rejection of the strategic and tactical objectives of PCF in favour of a looser, more spontaneous and open-ended project. Though not directly expressed in his theoretical writings, he favoured a broad unity of left-wing forces on a programme of common objectives. While it coincided in principle with the declared policy of the party, Lefebvre's project differed in terms of means, organizational forms and specific aims. Impatient with the PCF's commitment to a Leninist party organization, at variance with its conception of the stages necessary in the transition to socialism, and sharply opposed to its view of the state's function under socialism, Lefebvre sought alternative ways of building Left unity. The Algerian crisis, coming to a head in 1958, found the Left divided, weak and unable to offer a viable alternative to General de Gaulle's takeover of power. Lefebvre joined the newly founded 'Club de la Gauche' and began writing for the review 'Voies nouvelles', both set up by elements of an internal opposition within the PCF. Their aim was to set up some form of broad left alliance independent of any institutional or party frameworks. It was this political initiative as much as his philosophical evolution which precipitated his expulsion from the PCF in June 1958, a month after de Gaulle's assumption of power.

The French Communist Party seldom, if ever, terminates membership on grounds of philosophical divergences. Expulsions, which have become increasingly rare, are almost invariably either for political reasons or, less usually, on grounds of party discipline. So it was with Henri Lefebvre. The revisionist positions of his *Problèmes actuels* were quoted as factors in the announcement of his exclusion, but the main grounds were his 'agissements anti-Parti' and his 'activité fractionnelle'.[15] The precipitation of his political break was, however, squarely in the logic of his philosophical differences, for in philosophy the parting of the ways had long been reached. In many respects his position in 1958 was substantially that of twenty years earlier, at least on fundamental principles. In the conception of the dialectic, in the view of materialism, and in the account of Marx's relation to Hegel, his *Problèmes actuels* do little more than echo *Le Matérialisme dialectique*, albeit expressed more sharply. The main change between the two is the way that the implications of his anti-materialism have spread throughout his entire position, to the extent that the later book perceives mainly problems, and tends to a disintegration of the Marxist synthesis.

That twenty years should elapse before Lefebvre's break with the PCF is indicative of the range of divergent opinion which coexisted, and continues to exist, within the party. It is also indicative of the complex and indirect but nonetheless inescapable relation between philosophy and politics. Historical circumstances and political options constitute a concrete content of philosophy. Hence, Lefebvre's abstract and over-Hegelian account operated as a potent defence of Marxist ideas in 1939–40 and throughout the war period, when communists were being shot and Marxism was the main constituent of the Otto list of banned and burnt books. But twenty years later the same abstract and Hegelian position operated to undermine and weaken Marxism in its rapid expansion, as it increasingly permeated the political and cultural life of the country.

The dependent posture of ideas in relation to history is reflected in the political options with which they are associated. In Lefebvre's case his neo-Hegelian dialectic was politically expressed in the aspiration to a broad, non-party movement of the Left. But such a project was one thing when, under Nazi occupation, existing parties were repressed and driven into clandestinity. It was quite another thing when parties were openly contending for power on specific programmes in the middle of a colonial war which was almost a civil war. The all-embracing dialectic which promoted national unity against the foreign invader and his collaborators took on quite a different meaning when the same unity was being directed against the national liberation movement of a colonized country and its French supporters. The shifting network of historical interconnection and change needs a materialistic dialectic to grasp and, where possible, lead its sinuous developments. An idealist dialectic can at best follow, and at worst retard the forward movement of history. Lefebvre thought ideas led the world; he increasingly forgot that they must first reflect it. If ideas do not begin by submitting to the world's harsh discipline, they invariably fall victim to it later in their course.

Dialectics and dialogue

En tous les domaines, quand une grandeur a suffisamment grandi, elle change brusquement d'aspect, d'état ou de nature. La courbe se rebrousse; la surface se réduit à un point; le solide s'écroule; le liquide bout; l'oeuf se segmente; l'intuition éclate sur les faits amoncelés. . . . Points critiques, changements d'états, paliers sur la pente, – sautes de toutes espèces *en cours de* développement: encore, pour la Science, de concevoir et de surprendre 'un premier instant'.

Pierre Teilhard de Chardin, Le Phénomène humain *(Paris, 1955), 78*

The movement to open meaningful exchanges with the various contending ideologies of contemporary France was the most immediately productive result of the destalinization process in French Marxism. The polarization of non-Marxists into friends (who were left well alone ideologically) and enemies (who were vigorously attacked) gradually gave way to the more flexible approach of dialogue. Even at the height of 'rapprochement' with other movements in the 1930s and mid-1940s, Marxists had had only limited opportunity or inclination to discuss theoretical questions in a spirit of reciprocity. As the political climate made such exchanges more possible and desirable, so dialogue became gradually established as a new structure of relationship.

On a practical level, the benefits were obvious. Increased understanding led to increased co-operation. Both parties to dialogue stood to gain assistance and support in working towards objectives that were broadly shared. On a theoretical level, the benefits were less easy to define. At the lowest level, dialogue should serve at least to remove the worst misunderstandings, and enable each side to present its point of view in temperate language and with conceptual clarity. At a higher level, it should provide an opportunity for each to develop its analysis in relation to the specific preoccupations of the other, especially where one party is strongly concerned with matters the other tends to neglect. Beyond that lie the spiny thickets of change, mutual or unilateral, whether either side might learn from the other, assimilate the other's views and even be brought to shift its ground.

The most controversial and also most enduring dialogue is between Marxism and Christianity, generally between communists and Catholics. It is by no means the only dialogue, but historically the term 'dialogue', when unspecified, has tended to indicate discussions between Marxists and Christians. Internationally the currents of change within both movements have led to a mutual desire for understanding and co-operation. Though they date in France from as far back as the 1930s, talks between the two were given fresh impetus by the almost contemporaneous occurrence of destalinization and the reforming papacy of John XXIII. In France the wide implantation of Christian belief gave Marxists a strong incentive to establish relations with the institution which reflected the ideas of a large part of the population. Conversely, the strong influence of the Communist Party, especially among working people, gave Catholics many reasons to find a working relationship with Marxists.

Practical questions like peace and social justice provide fertile soil for fruitful exchange. But on the level of philosophy it is less easy to see how the materialist dialectic can find any accommodation with the tenets of Christian faith. Both sides were, naturally, aware of this difficulty: no amount of discussion can dissolve the incompatibility between belief in God and a thoroughgoing materialism. For the most part therefore, dialogue has tended to concentrate on problems of a moral and social nature. These problems cannot be isolated from philosophical positions in the long term, but on a medium term there is considerable scope for agreement on them. The very popular notion of alienation, for example, provided a frequent point of encounter on which limited agreement could be reached without confronting the question of its ultimate source and extent. Closely bound up in the same nexus was the concept of humanism which also enabled common cause to be found on a range of moral and social issues without the ultimate origin, nature and status of man being viewed in identical ways.

The chief exponent of dialogue on this basis in the late 1950s and early 1960s was Roger Garaudy, at that time a member of the PCF's political bureau and leading philosophical spokesman for the party. His book of 1957, *Humanisme marxiste*, was a first statement, and his subsequent *Perspectives de l'homme* (Paris, 1959) was a remarkable contribution. The latter work not only discussed the major Marxist, Catholic and existentialist thinkers of the period, but also included letters from several of them commenting variously on Garaudy's analysis. Discussing Catholic thinkers, he focused on three of the currents which had been denounced in Pius XII's 1950 encyclical *Humani generis*: the existentialism of Gabriel Marcel, the personalism of Emmanuel Mounier, and the thought of Teilhard de Chardin. Only in relation to the latter did he broach the question of the dialectic.

The Jesuit paleontologist was in 1959 beginning to enjoy a posthumous popularity despite the anathema which Pius XII had pronounced on his ideas. Analysing his central work *Le Phénomène humain* (Paris, 1955), Garaudy criticized the implicit finalism of Teilhard's conception and his tendency to view all development in terms of a biological model. However, he felt that Teilhard came close to a Marxist notion of the dialectic of nature in his cosmic vision of the unity of the universe and its historical development. In particular Garaudy pointed to Teilhard's use of the dialectical law of the transformation of quantitative change into qualitative change. His concept of thresholds or nodal points in the 'orthogenesis' of man embodies this law as a means of explaining human development from earlier life forms, and in particular the advent of reflexive consciousness. Garaudy conceded that Teilhard included a possible divine intervention, but suggested that it added nothing to his basic account and was probably a saving clause inserted in the vain hope of avoiding the wrath of the Catholic censorship. Teilhard foresaw a future in which human development would reach a further threshold, the 'Omega' point leading to the end of the world and the generation of a new, possibly divine mode of existence. Garaudy was forced to accept that the Teilhardian and Marxist conceptions parted company at this point, but not before drawing a comparison between the former's vision of a scientifico-religious utopia and Marx's vision of the realm of freedom inaugurated by a classless, communist society.

It is undoubtedly true that Teilhard de Chardin's formulation of the dialectical law of quantity and quality is close to that given by Engels in his *Dialectics of Nature*. The occurrence of qualitative changes at certain threshold points in the process of quantitative change is an observable characteristic of all phenomena. However, Garaudy is unduly hasty in assimilating Teilhard's view to that of Engels. Too rapid an assimilation holds the danger of projecting on to Engels the kind of 'finalist' and 'pan-biologist' view he rightly criticizes in Teilhard. Not only is the

Omega point posited in complete isolation from social organization, conceived in its qualitative difference from biology: so also is the ontogenesis of man in the first instance. The accumulation of brain cells is not an adequate explanation for the production of reflective thought, any more than reflection is the sole defining characteristic of man. Engels himself pointed to the vital role of social activity and especially labour in effecting the transition from ape to man, an observation which a century of anthropology has consistently confirmed.[16]

The use of a biological model in the analysis of human development as a whole is a specific case of a more general error. Teilhard's dialectic of nature is strongest in the analysis of the natural world and the forms of development which are to be found in it. Where he consistently errs is in projecting those forms on to the social world. Hence, discussing the accumulation of human energy, he argues that the outcome may be a more regimented mode of organization rather than an organically new level of development, 'le cristal au lieu de la cellule'.[17] A chemical concept is applied to human evolution. Whatever the analogical value of the concept, it is clearly not sufficient as a serious analysis in the absence of any scientific study of society. In Teilhard's vision, analogies with the natural sciences replace a specifically social science, and a law such as the transformation of quantity into quality is interpreted in a natural scientific form, assumed to be valid for human history. However, the essence of the materialist dialectic is that it is a guide to research and action, not an *a priori* model of the universe. The general laws of the dialectic do not enable any detailed prediction of the concrete forms they will take in a specific case: that is, they do not pre-empt the scientific study of reality. Hence, it is permissible to declare that every process of development has a threshold point, but when, how and in what circumstances it is reached, and what lies beyond it, can be determined only by specific study of the process in question. Caution is all the more necessary because of the crucial distinction between nature and society. There is more difference between the natural and social sciences than, for example, between chemistry and biology.

Garaudy criticizes Teilhard's 'méconnaissance du caractère spécifique du social et de ses lois par rapport au biologique et à ses lois'.[18] But his willingness to compare classless society with the Omega point, and to draw lessons for humanism and morality from Teilhard's view, tend to obscure the essential distinctions. Unlike Omega, the advent of communist society is not taken to signal the end of history, nor the production of some superhuman consciousness, nor the fusion of science and religion, nor an apotheosis to which everything in nature and in man aspires and converges, nor an autonomous spiritual force which draws all historical development towards itself. Teilhard's finalist utopia is a compound of the kingdom of Heaven and Science City, by no means coterminous with Marx's realm of freedom. To confuse them is also to confuse the means of attaining them. The generalized humanism in which Garaudy envelops the two conceptions can only serve to obscure the vital practical and political elements of Marxism. The socialist revolution gives way to the reconciliation of science and religion; class struggle yields to the assertion of life against entropy.

In pursuing his dialogue at the theoretical level, Garaudy constantly walks a tightrope. In overstating convergences he risks distorting his Marxism to the point where he can no longer speak for Marxists. But in overemphasizing the differences he risks losing the point of contact which distinguishes dialogue from monologue. The thirty or so pages of his dialogue with Teilhard wobble precariously between the two dangers; if he appears more often to stress convergences it is perhaps because they are less familiar and more fruitful. Garaudy's own later development illustrates the lurking dangers of losing one's theoretical balance in the process, but his study of 1959 does not in itself make such an outcome inevitable. It is better taken to indicate that the exercise is a difficult one, rather than that it is necessarily doomed to failure.

Existentialism and the dialectic

Du reste, on peut dire que, d'une façon générale, il y a une vérité dialectique au niveau humain qui a son intelligibilité plénière, et bien entendu se détermine en fonction d'un milieu naturel connu, mais qui n'a nul besoin par *elle-même* d'affirmer la dialectique de la Nature. Au niveau de la société humaine et pour comprendre celle-ci, il n'est pas nécessaire de considérer les forces naturelles . . . autrement que comme des forces d'extériorité passive.

Jean-Paul Sartre, in Marxisme et existentialisme *(Paris, 1962), 9 – 10*

In the wake of 1958, moves began on the Left to initiate contact in a wide range of areas. The intellectual area was an important part of this process, and discussions between communists, socialists, liberals, Christians, existentialists and others were slowly developed. Of course, such contact was by no means novel. But in the early stages of the Fifth Republic it took place in an atmosphere of greater urgency and correspondingly greater openness. The bitter polemic and recriminations of the 1950s slowly gave way to the spirit of dialogue in the quest for Left unity. Apart from domestic considerations, this movement was encouraged by the gradual easing of international relations. As the Cold War began to thaw out, political and ideological polarizations began to soften, a process further encouraged by the accelerating destalinization of the world communist movement.

The political upheavals had a profound effect on the relations between Marxists and existentialists. The question of the dialectic, which lay at the heart of the dispute with Merleau-Ponty, rapidly surfaced as the central theoretical question at issue with his erstwhile colleague Jean-Paul Sartre. Paradoxically, the theoretical debate arose only after political relations had first deteriorated, a fact which can in part be ascribed to the ideological truce which communists had in the past offered as part of their political co-operation with non-Marxists. From 1952 to 1956 Sartre was one of the PCF's staunchest supporters. Though not a member of the party he was energetic in its defence and proclaimed his acceptance of the Marxist analysis of social and historical development. Taking his distance as a result of the 20th CPSU Congress and the events in Hungary, he became increasingly critical of the PCF. On a theoretical level he reopened his investigation of basic philosophical concepts and attempted to achieve a reconciliation between his existentialist principles and Marxism.

In a well-known essay written in 1957, 'Marxisme et existentialisme', Sartre declared that Marxism was the indispensable framework of all contemporary knowledge.[19] He affirmed that his existentialism was now an ideology within Marxism and parasitic on it. However, he did not, for all that, simply dissolve his thought into the greater Marxist synthesis. This would only be possible, he thought, when Marxism had assimilated the essential lessons of existentialism on the decisive role of human subjectivity. His conception was basically that which he had presented in La Nausée (Paris, 1938) and l'Etre et le néant (Paris, 1943). There, the world appeared as a contingent, formless mass of inert being out of which meaning, structure and movement were carved by the dynamic negating activity of the free human consciousness. The consequent order observed in the world was sustained only by the human project of meaning-making, a position which applied as much to social as to natural being.

Embracing Marxism, for Sartre, meant accepting the general principles of the materialist theory of history and Marx's economics. But even within this field, he felt that many Marxist concepts had become rigid and dogmatic. In particular he rejected the Marxist theory of knowledge as a reflection of reality. He insisted that human consciousness, as a negative moment in human activity, actually constituted the relationship with and between things. Consciousness, he held, was the methodological foundation of all knowledge and therefore of history as a process of totalization. Traditional Marxist theory, he said, removed human subjectivity from its key position and reduced man and knowledge to a purely objective status which was quite illusory, and moreover anti-dialectical.

Like Merleau-Ponty, Sartre saw the dialectic as a relation between a human subject and an external object, between knower and known. He claimed Marx's authority for a radical separation between being and knowledge, and on this ground dismissed the dialectic of nature as a dogmatic and metaphysical foundation for knowledge. Unlike Merleau-Ponty, however, he accepted the rationality and intelligibility of history and society. The rationality moreover was not limited to Merleau-Ponty's reluctant acknowledgement that some limited and precarious meanings could be provisionally ascribed to it. Sartre believed that history was a totalization in process and that Marxism broadly provided the framework of knowledge wherein it could be rationally understood.

In the very process of adopting Marxism, Sartre implicitly confirmed the Marxist rather than the existentialist concept of development. His own evolution was not provoked by any internal or logical necessity of his former theoretical position. On the contrary, it was his practical and political experience of communism which led him to accept the Marxist theory of history. More generally, the 'force de choses' imposed itself increasingly as a major limitation on the free development of subjectivity. The inertia and contingency of pure being was a poor description for the reality which exercised constant intervention and constraint. Being-for-itself, the human consciousness, was so evidently not master of a docile world of being-in-itself that Sartre was obliged to modify his initial account. Some centre of dynamism and activity must necessarily be posited outside the human mind. In the Marxist conception of dialectical materialism, all matter is in motion. Changes occur in various regular forms which in general terms correspond to the laws of dialectics, operational in and between nature, society and thought. All of being is therefore dynamic, with thought as one of its later manifestations, in which the rest is reflected. Short of adopting this account, Sartre attempted to constitute a sphere of dynamism which would be ultimately sustained by the power of subjectivity. Provided the question of its origins could be set aside, this sphere would, he hoped, correspond roughly in structure and development to the account of history and society offered by Marxism.

Consequently Sartre set himself the demanding task of showing how the operation of human freedom is transformed into intelligible structures which nonetheless resist the initiatives of human choice. The bulky result of his labours was the *Critique de la raison dialectique* (Paris, 1960) in which he undertook to explore the complex set of interrelations which led from the free activity of the individual human consciousness to the ponderous workings of large-scale social structures. The premise for this exploration was that the individual's experience of his own freedom was the starting point and the ultimate active principle, both in the development of history, and in the creation of the rationality by which history was to be understood.

The dialectic, in Sartre's view, was a product of men's historical activity, but it was also the intelligibility of that activity. It was the living logic of action which appeared as a moment of 'praxis' and was created anew in each action. Hence, he suggested, it could not be discovered from an external viewpoint, but only by an observer situated within the process in question who saw his own experience both as a contribution to an overall understanding of the process, and as a freely chosen individual course of action. In this way, Sartre argued, the dialectic was rooted in the free activity of each individual, which was inherently dialectical. But he added that since every other individual was also freely generating his own dialectical activity, the dialectic as a whole escaped everyone. As a result, he pointed out, the dialectic appeared to each as the transparency of his own activity, and as the opacity of everyone else's products, therefore both as freedom and as necessity.

Sartre shared Merleau-Ponty's rejection of a dialectic of nature. In his view it could be nothing other than a projection of the human dialectic into a natural world where it did not belong. He understood that the projection arose from the wish for a unified world view. But the consequences, he argued, were that the dialectic was dehumanized and made to appear as an objective, external and blind necessity. Man thus became part of Nature, History became a particular form of Nature, and, he protested, man's own nature was seen as lying outside himself. It was irrational, he suggested, to discover dialectics in human praxis, project it on to the inorganic world, and then claim it as a law of nature which governed society. Sartre concluded that the dialectic of nature was a form of alienation which made lived thinking appear to be an object of some universal consciousness, and fixed it as the thought of the Other, suppressing its relation to the Self.

The differences between Sartre's conception of the dialectic and that held by Marxists were clearly brought out in a celebrated public debate of December 1961 at the Mutualité, attended by over 6,000 people.[20] Held under the auspices of the PCF's Centre d'Etudes et de Recherches Marxistes, the meeting brought together Sartre and Jean Hyppolite to discuss with Roger Garaudy and Jean-Pierre Vigier, a Marxist physicist, whether the dialectic was only a law of history or whether it was also a law of nature.

Responding to Sartre, Roger Garaudy proposed to demonstrate that an acceptance of historical materialism necessarily implied recognition of a dialectics of nature. In rejecting idealism, he argued, Sartre held that from the beginning human consciousness and activity have to face a non-human realm of being, the 'être-en-soi', which precedes man's existence. Man experienced this material realm as a negation of his activity in terms, for example, of a denial of invention, a threat, a resistance, or a limitation. However, he pointed out that the 'en-soi' was not an abstract negation, but a negation of specific human desires or projects. And therefore in some cases it confirmed rather than rejected hypotheses formed in relation to it, thereby giving man the power to manipulate it. The differentiated responses of the 'en-soi', he suggested, led man to formulate successive hypotheses which gradually increased his practical grasp over the material world. These hypotheses represented the known limitations of human activity, he concluded, and revealed 'en creux', in counterposition, the outline of the structure of the world, which in the course of time and experiment became more precisely delineated.

Having established that the 'en-soi' must at least be structured, Garaudy agreed that the exact nature of the structure, dialectical or otherwise, was a matter for the history of science to determine. Since the end of the eighteenth century, he argued, science had established that everything is in motion, all inertia being relative; that motion is not simple repetition, but is able to produce novelty; and that the production of novelty gives things age and date, therefore conferring upon nature a history. With the development of science, old forms of thinking had had to be replaced by new ones more adequate to account for the newly discovered complexities of the world. The dialectic was a product of this process, he asserted: the structure and movement of reality were such that only dialectical thought could make things intelligible and manageable. It would, he thought, be absurd to deny that the structure of nature itself was at least to some extent dialectical, since some relationship must exist between scientific thought and its object.

Garaudy noted that Sartre conceded some degree of dialectical structure in nature and recognized that science could in principle establish it. So, he asked, why not see the dialectic of nature as pre-human stages of the dialectic from which the human dialectic emerged? If the answer was that science had not yet developed enough, Sartre had surely given away his principle. To the point that nature was not a totality, he answered that dialectical materialism did not imply any dogmatic or theological conception of totality, but only required the existence of some totalities. After all, he said, the dialectical model was basically a provisional working hypothesis, whether in history or in nature, and not some closed, immutable, *a priori* schema projected on to the world.

In this classical confrontation between the two schools of thought which descended from Hegel, it is noteworthy that no agreed concept of the dialectic was established. Though both used the same terminology it was clear that they had quite a different content. Whereas Sartre understood it as a relation between a subject and an object, Garaudy took it to mean certain forms of movement and interconnection. For one, it was inseparable from subjectivity; for the other, subjectivity was but one part of the total dialectic. From these positions it is understandable that Sartre should be bewildered at the insistence on a dialectic of nature, whereas Garaudy was hard pressed to understand his reticence. In so far as the Marxist conception includes a subject–object dialectic as a particular case of dialectical movement in general, it is clearly the wider, more comprehensive view. Conversely, in so far as Sartre is prepared to generalize from the subject–object relation, he can with difficulty resist the Marxist argument for the broader conception. In this sense, an adaptation of historical materialism to existentialist premises holds the constant danger of drawing Sartre into a recognition of dialectical developments in which no clearly definable subject is present.

At the end of the debate, the two sides remained divided on the central point. Although the existentialists were led to accept a limited extension of the dialectic to nature, the concession was a practical rather than a principled one since they recognized only an analogical basis for it. Sartre and Hyppolite continued to maintain a conception of the dialectic constituted by human subjectivity and founded in the individual consciousness. Vigier and Garaudy on the other hand saw it as the reflection, in thought, of the objective dialectical movement of external reality, natural and historical. They conceded the relative importance of subjectivity in history, but their conception of subjectivity was collective, not individual, and ultimately referred to the theory and practice of organized political movements.

The refusal of the existentialists to acknowledge a natural basis for the dialectic was also an assertion of political pluralism. As long as man, and particularly the individual, was held to be constitutive of the dialectic, there was room within Marxism for a variety of different viewpoints, none of which was inherently more true than the other. Such a variety in turn legitimized and required the existence of a multiplicity of political organizations, none of which could lay claim to any special pre-eminence. Moreover it implied a preference for spontaneous movements with limited immediate objectives, a minimum of formal structures, an intense level of activity and a brief span of existence. On the other hand, an objectively based dialectic suggested that the truth value of any standpoint was definitely measurable. Consequently one political organization could attain a better grasp of reality than others and exercise a leading role. It followed that a leading party needed breadth, strength, continuity and a high level of organization.

Beyond the intricacies of the philosophical interchange, the status of science was one of the key questions at issue in the debate. The scientific and technological revolution which burst upon the post-war world was making itself acutely felt in the late 1950s and early 1960s. The antinomies of its effect were perhaps most evident in the development and application of physics, where the long-term promise of atomic power for peaceful purposes was dramatically counterbalanced by the imminent threat of annihilation through nuclear warfare. The immediacy of the threat was underlined by the explosion of France's first nuclear weapon in 1960. But in all spheres of their advance, science and technology were daily proving to be a double-edged sword. In this context, Sartre was articulating a widespread pessimism when he resisted the claims of science in the name of human values. Science, he implied, was a Frankenstein's monster which should not be allowed to get out of hand. There can be no doubt as to the emotional strength of his appeal.

Against this tendency, the Marxists' pro-scientific stance was based on an optimistic assessment of the same developments, which saw the increase of human knowledge as essentially progressive. They suggested that, despite the dangers, science was man's means of enhancing his mastery over his environment and his own nature. Undoubtedly the attraction of such a position lay in its rational rather than its emotional appeal. The accelerating tempo of scientific advance, with its dramatic impact on all aspects of human life, calls into question with growing acuteness the relationship between man and the natural world. Fundamental human values are challenged in radical and often unforeseen ways, not only by discoveries of the traditional natural sciences and their associated technology, but also by the developing social and human sciences. It therefore becomes a matter of growing urgency to achieve a general and synthetic understanding of the laws of the natural world, the laws of the human world and the relation between them.

References

1   L. Sebag, 'Marx, Feuerbach et la critique de la religion', *La Nouvelle critique*, avril 1955, 17–38, p. 19.

2   See L. Sebag, *Marxisme et structuralisme* (Paris, 1964).

3   See P. Fougeyrollas, *La Philosophie en question* (Paris, 1960).

4   'Une lettre de Henri Lefebvre à Roger Garaudy', *Cahiers du communisme*, octobre 1955, 1207–1215; Roger Garaudy, 'Sur les fondements idéologiques du parti et les problèmes de l'unité: Réponse à Henri Lefebvre', *Cahiers du communisme*, octobre 1955, 1216–1237.

5   See H. Lefebvre, 'Le marxisme et la pensée française', *Les Temps modernes*, juillet–août 1957, 104–137; article in *Encyclopédie française*, XIX (Paris, 1957), section 19.16.

6   See Jean Kanapa, 'Sur un bulletin de santé du marxisme', *La Nouvelle critique*, juillet–août 1957, 228–247.

7   *Encyclopédie française*, XIX, p. 19.16.6.

8   H. Lefebvre, *Problèmes actuels du marxisme* (Paris, 1958), 97.

9   *Ibid.*, 108.

10 *Ibid.*, 32.

11 J. Suret-Canale, 'Notes sur la méthode d'Henri Lefebvre devant les problèmes actuels du marxisme', *La Nouvelle critique*, avril 1958, 100–113.

12 L. Sève, 'Henri Lefebvre et la dialectique chez Marx', *La Nouvelle critique*, mars 1958, 55–89.

13 R. Garaudy, 'Initiation au marxisme ou initiation au révisionnisme?', *Cahiers du communisme*, avril 1958, 557–574.

14 See quotation at the head of this section.

15 See the announcement in *France Nouvelle*, 19 juin 1958, 5.

16 See F. Engels, *Dialectics of Nature* (London, 1954), 170–183.

17 P. Teilhard de Chardin, *Le Phénomène humain* (Paris, 1955), 285.

18 R. Garaudy, *Les Perspectives de l'homme* (Paris, 1959), 192.

19 First published in French as 'Marxisme et existentialisme', *Les Temps modernes*, 139, septembre 1957, 338–417; and 140, octobre 1957, 658–698; reprinted in revised form in Sartre's *Critique de la raison dialectique* (Paris, 1960).

20 The proceedings were published as *Marxisme et existentialisme: controverse sur la dialectique* (Paris, 1962).

6

Innovations

1962 – 1968   PART 1

Althusser: against inversion

Enfin s'il ne s'agit vraiment *que d'un renversement*, d'une remise à l'endroit de ce qui était à l'envers, il est clair que faire basculer un objet tout entier ne change ni sa nature, ni son contenu par la vertu d'une simple rotation! L'homme sur la tête, quand il marche enfin sur ses pieds, c'est le même homme! Et une philosophie ainsi *renversée* ne peut être considérée comme tout autre que la philosophie *inversée*, que par une métaphore théorique: en vérité sa structure, ses problèmes, le sens de ses problèmes continuent d'être hantés par la *même problématique*.

Louis Althusser, Pour Marx *(Paris, 1965), 70*

The precipitate return to Hegel by thinkers like Roger Garaudy may to some extent be ascribed to the new climate of intellectual exploration within the communist movement after 1956. In the case of Garaudy and some of his contemporaries, the return to intellectual origins was also a search for alternatives to the shaken certainties of harsher but simpler times. But an adequate explanation cannot rest primarily on subjective factors. More important are the objective historical movements which determine them. The late 1950s in particular posed difficult political problems to which the purely negative position of destalinization offered no obvious answers. The new authoritarian Fifth Republic of General de Gaulle easily withstood the limp challenges of a divided and demoralized Left. The PCF, like the SFIO, was electorally at its lowest ebb since the war, and still without any strong ally on the Left. The urgent search for political allies found a philosophical reflex in the conciliatory ecumenism of Garaudy's dialogistic Marxism, as it had earlier in Lefebvre's all-reconciling Left-Hegelianism.

There was, however, an alternative strategy already being suggested. It looked towards a resurgence of political militancy by the people, organized around a pure and uncompromising programme of Marxism-

Leninism. And it found its reflex in the newly emergent philosophy of rigour and sharp distinctions put forward by Louis Althusser and the group of young philosophers who gathered round him. Strongly marked by the teachings of Mao Tse-tung, both philosophically and politically, Althusser's work was influential in the formation of a Maoist student group within the PCF, though he dissociated himself from it when it began openly attacking the party. The precise political implications of his thought are consequently complex and often equivocal. But his philosophical position proposed major innovations of a fundamental nature to Marxist theory, and has been extremely influential both in France and internationally. By virtue of the novelty and the importance of Althusser's challenging reformulation of Marxist philosophy, his writings demand an extensive and detailed discussion. This enterprise will therefore form the substance of the present chapter.

Since the question of Hegel occupies a central place in the discussion of materialist dialectics, in the Marxism of the post-1956 period, and in Althusser's own work, it provides an excellent strategic approach to the development of the latter's conception of the materialist dialectic and of Marxism generally. Stated briefly, he was strenuously opposed to the rehabilitation of Hegel, and sought to construct a formulation of Marxism entirely purged of its Hegelian references. In the first instance, his position was in a direct line of descent from that put forward in the articles he wrote in 1953 for the *Revue de l'enseignement philosophique*. As has already been seen, he there rejected the notion of the organic link between Marx and Hegel, though he acknowledged the Hegelian content of the early writings.[1] The interest of his viewpoint is, however, less in its anti-Hegelianism than in the conceptual apparatus he deployed to consolidate it.

After his articles of 1953, Louis Althusser made no major written interventions on Marxist philosophy until 1960. In the meantime he had acquired a growing reputation as a philosopher and scholar by virtue of his professional activity as a teacher at the Ecole normale supérieure, his interpretative study of Montesquieu, and his translation of selected works by Feuerbach from the period 1839–45.[2] In his presentation of Feuerbach, he argued that Marx substantially rejected Hegel after his student days, passing to a Feuerbachian viewpoint which effectively inverted the Hegelian edifice. Subsequently Marx realized that although Feuerbach inverted them, he retained Hegel's principles in substance. Marx therefore went on to replace the Hegelian frame of reference by a new one of his own.

His work on Feuerbach made Althusser a competent person to prepare for *La Pensée* a substantial review article on the important volume of *Recherches internationales* devoted to 'Le jeune Marx'.[3] The article, later collected in his *Pour Marx* (Paris, 1965), is the first extensive statement of his new interpretation of Marxism, and inaugurates his attack on the notion that Marx is related to Hegel through a process of inversion.[4]

Althusser develops the view that 'inversion' is most apt to describe Feuerbach's relation to Hegel. But since the Hegelian system is a 'sphere of spheres' such a process does not offer a means of escaping it. He points out that whether a man walks on his head or his feet he is the same man; the same applies to a philosophy which is not changed, except metaphorically, by being inverted or reversed.[5] He regards it as obvious that neither the nature nor the content of an object is changed by mere rotation, though he concedes that the metaphor may have a limited pedagogical value. He also rejects the view that Hegel is 'superseded' by Marx, since 'supersession', a Hegelian notion, presupposes that what was true in Hegel is retained by Marx. Althusser resists the view that Hegelian philosophy survives in Marxism in any form, and proposes the notion of a 'retreat' from Hegelian illusions, establishing Marx in a different domain and territory, in some ways pre-Hegelian (in politics and economics). The retreat, he suggests, made it possible to make discoveries which classical German philosophy obstructed, and Marx retained from Hegel only a training in theoretical intelligence rather than any elements of theory as such.

Though pregnant with consequences, Althusser's remarks largely constitute a clearing of the ground. The legacy of Hegel is denounced without immediately being replaced: an omission which was soon to be remedied. But as far as it goes, his critique of Hegelianism remains substantially within traditional terms of reference. Its originality lies in undermining the accepted view that the young Marx was dominated by Hegel, and in challenging the notion of inversion.

Althusser's attempt to cast Feuerbach, rather than Hegel, as the mentor of Marx's early development is only partially new. Engels extensively acknowledged the debt which he and Marx owed to Feuerbach in his well-known study *Feuerbach and the End of Classical German Philosophy*. In Engels' view the birth of Marxism proper is located in Marx's celebrated *Theses on Feuerbach*, suggesting that the mature doctrine emerged from a critique of that philosopher rather than of Hegel himself. However, it is Hegel and the neo-Hegelians who loom large in *The German Ideology* which Marx and Engels wrote at the same period as the *Theses*. Moreover, Feuerbach was a neo-Hegelian thinker and Althusser considers that he was basically a prisoner of the Hegelian system. Consequently the promotion of Feuerbach does not entirely displace Hegel, even if it does bring a greater complexity to the emergence of Marxism.

More fundamental is Althusser's attack on the notion of inversion. Perceiving the strategic importance of Marx's relation to Hegel within the Marxist synthesis, he adopts the issue as a fulcrum with which to redirect the theoretical development of Marxism. By eliminating inversion he seeks to cut off at source the entire panoply of concepts and categories which have passed into Marxism from the Hegelian inheritance. This done, he finds a vast freedom to redefine the basic principles in terms drawn from quite different philosophical traditions and from scientific disciplines which have developed in more recent times. The breathtaking prospects opened up, and the exhilarating sense of intellectual adventure which they generated, have undoubtedly played a large part in the enormous success which Althusser's conceptions have enjoyed. Moreover, the consequent assimilation of analyses originating in cybernetics, linguistics, anthropology, psychology and other modern disciplines has been accelerated in large measure by the freedom of innovation thus created. Although in some respects the results served mainly to whet the voracious appetite for novelty endemic in the intelligentsia, in other respects they have permitted a much-needed renovation of Marxist thought which has extended to many of those who would strongly criticize Althusser's positions on any given question. Whatever theoretical conclusions may be reached about his work, its practical effects have been powerful and far-reaching.

The assault on inversion was not an enterprise to be embarked upon lightly. It struck at a deeply rooted notion in Marxist thought. Both Marx and Engels repeatedly used it to describe their relation to Hegel, and Lenin's *Philosophical Notebooks* contain many specific confirmations of it. Can it be that the classics of Marxism are in error on such an important point? Althusser does not shrink from this conclusion. He admits that as a loose, metaphorical expression, 'inverting Hegel' conveys some acceptable meaning, but insists that it is without theoretical value as a concept. The literal effect of his position is to distinguish between scientific and pre-scientific analyses. The pre-scientific analysis, functioning by means of metaphors, may point to problems and their solution in a very general way, but falls short of providing the specific concepts and categories in which they can be grasped scientifically. The pre-scientific component of Marxist analysis is a provisional substitute for the scientific within an otherwise scientific account. It functions as a stopgap solution until a suitable permanent solution can be generated. But when a correct scientific account becomes possible the stopgap, however well it had served, becomes an obstacle to progress and must be discarded. Hence, the 'error' of Marx, Engels and Lenin is not a stupid or culpable blunder, but a historically inevitable approximation which has done valiant service but is now obsolete and should be pensioned off.

The boldness of Althusser's conception is undeniable, but at the same time well supported by the Marxist recognition that thought must develop to accommodate changes in the world, and the growing resources of science and philosophy. Marx, Engels and Lenin may be found to have been mistaken on this and other issues. Certainly their work calls for continual reappraisal and reformulation. But before accepting that 'inversion' is no longer an appropriate way to describe Marx's relation to Hegel, it is useful to recall what place the notion occupies within the Marxist synthesis, and what the effects of its replacement would be.

Inversion expresses (metaphorically or theoretically) the relationship between idealism and materialism in philosophy. Whereas idealism considers that mind, spirit or ideas determine being, matter or the world, materialism holds that the reverse is true. Inversion is therefore a rational term to describe the relation between the two opposed positions at the most general level, in their most fundamental principles. Hence, to reject the term 'inversion' implies the view that Marxism is not materialist or that idealism and materialism are not opposite philosophical positions. Various conclusions might follow from, or be compatible with, such a view: that materialism (or indeed, logically, idealism) is not a philosophical position; that Marxism does not take up a philosophical position; that the relation between consciousness and being is not the basic question of philosophy; that if it is the basic question there are more than two answers; that Marxism is either idealist or occupies some other non-materialist position. The clue to what Althusser means is given in his warning that 'ce qui est en cause dans cette double rupture avec Hegel d'abord, avec Feuerbach ensuite, c'est le sens du terme même de *philosophie*. Que peut être, comparée aux modèles classiques de la philosophie, la "philosophie" marxiste?'[6] His answer to his own question will emerge in the course of this chapter. Meanwhile it is sufficient to note the fundamental nature of the question.

If inversion were allowed to represent conceptually the most general relation of idealism and materialism, the question would still remain open as to whether more particular Hegelian analyses could meaningfully be 'inverted'. If it were found that almost none of them could be so appropriated into Marxism, then it might reasonably be argued that the notion of inversion was misleading in having no application beyond the most general. Even in its attenuated form, the rejection of inversion runs counter to express declarations of the founders of Marxism, who indicated by it a degree of continuity between their dialectic and the Hegelian one. To challenge this continuity is Althusser's explicit objective, based on the notion of a radical break between the ideological pre-Marxist problematic of Hegel, Feuerbach and Marx's own early writings, and the scientific problematic of mature Marxism.

His major premise is that the pre-Marxist works are ideological in the narrow sense that they contain a coherent set of ideas related to a particular historical situation, but have no truth value. In this respect they are diametrically opposed to the scientific writings which followed and which provide the means for understanding the ideological writings scientifically. He therefore sharpens the distinction between ideology and science to the point of total dichotomy, emphasizing that the errors and illusions of ideology must be escaped from and dissipated before a scientific Marxism can be established.

Althusser rejects even the suggestion that 'elements' of the previous ideology are retained in Marxism. Ideologies, he argues, are characterized by their internal unity, constituted by a determinate unitary structure which underlies each one, and gives it the qualities of a coherent system. The underlying structure, which he calls the 'problematic', so determines the unity of an ideology that it is impossible to extract an individual element without altering its meaning. To extract elements retrospectively is, in Althusser's view, to distort historical truth; to extract them at the time was logically impossible since they could not exist independently of their system of reference and therefore belonged either to an ideological problematic, or to a totally different scientific problematic, but not to both. For similar reasons he excludes any Hegelian 'supersession' (*Aufhebung*) which would seek to include part of the superseded position in the eventual synthesis.

Though his position is comparable to the one he offered in 1953, there is one significant difference. The philosophical sphere, in which Hegel and the young Marx floundered, was previously characterized as a realm of contradictions. Its 1961 successor, ideology, on the contrary appears as a realm of self-contained and wholly consistent systems devoid of internal contradictions between their component ideas, systems so isolated as to lack even external contradictions with each other. This 'ideology' has no better status than the earlier 'philosophy', however: whereas the latter was contradictory, the former lacks truth value.

Even admitting Althusser's contentious definitions of science and ideology, it may be objected that in taking the ideological nature of pre-Marxist philosophy as a premise he is assuming that which is to be proved. Once they are accepted as ideological they can be dismissed by definition as having no truth value. Hence, the question of whether they *can* have truth value precedes and excludes the question of whether they *do* have truth value. In like fashion, the Italian theologians deduced theoretically that Jupiter could have no moons and therefore refused to look at the planet through Galileo's telescope. Of course, if Hegel were ascribed any degree of truth value, it would follow either that he was not ideological in Althusser's terms, or that the latter's concept of ideology was defective.

Althusser holds that Hegelian philosophy was vitiated by an enormous burden of ideological illusion such that Marx only achieved his eventual position at the price of a 'prodigious break with his origins'.[7] Hegel's importance is then solely that his philosophy gave Marx experience in handling complex theoretical material. As for its content, Marx had to repudiate it and retreat from it in order to discover Marxism. It therefore becomes almost inconceivable how any transition could have been historically possible. From the murky gloom of ideology to the bright day of science appears a short but mysterious step. What then of the successive discoveries of key insights and the gradual elaboration of a conceptual framework? Did Marx (and presumably Engels) experience an illumination on the road to some Damascus? And if so where did he (they) speak of it, and when did it occur? And what of the later survivals of which the 1953 article spoke: how could erroneous ideological notions be accommodated into a theory ruled by the iron hand of an unseen scientific problematic?

The concept of the problematic is a key to Althusser's attack on inversion. It is a rich and suggestive notion which articulates the view that the significance and unity of an intellectual position lies not in the answers it gives but in the questions it asks. A problematic comprises the objective internal reference system of a body of thought: the system of questions, or problems, which determines the answers an ideology can offer. It is therefore an underlying structure, not to be identified with the public declarations in which it is expressed. Moreover, a problematic is itself a response to real problems. But though it responds to reality, it does not necessarily correspond to it. A comparison between the real problems of an era and those suggested in a given problematic reveals how far the latter is mystified and deformed. It is, of course, axiomatic that such a comparison can be, and is, based on a scientific and therefore true understanding of the real problems.

As a means of exploring the inner coherence of intellectual movements, and of identifying the kinship between them, the notion of problematic is a potent analytical tool. Althusser declares that the essence of a problematic lies not in its internal functioning but in its relation to real problems. In the case of an ideology the relation is one of deformation. But that view embodies Althusser's characteristically Manichaean approach to knowledge: if ideology is necessarily deforming then it can contain no truth, however partial or attenuated. It replaces the more flexible notion of reflection, where the truth value of a more or less deformed reflection of reality is determined not by the mode of reflection but by the correspondence of the end-product to the reality it purports to reflect. This notion by no means excludes the existence of a variety of processes by which a reflection is produced, some of which may be inherently deforming. But it does allow and account for true, helpful or progressive aspects in an otherwise distorted conception, and enables the passage from one viewpoint to another to be conceptualized.

Althusser has the tendency, which he develops much further, in his later work *Lire le Capital* (Paris, 1965), to accord an absolute dominance to the problematic within a body of thought, as its organizing and originating principle. Unless a determining role is given to extra-mental reality (the real problems) in the formation and verification of the problematic, and unless some relative autonomy is given to the themes and concepts it governs, then the problematic becomes a kind of conceptual absolute destined to railroad Marxism into a new idealism. An excessively rigid notion of the problematic underlies Althusser's total rejection of inversion. The rejection of any continuity between ideology and science, between Hegel and Marx, leads to the total denial of Hegel's paternity in the conception of Marxism. In its stead is an intellectual Virgin Birth, which, however appealing it may seem, can only mystify the origins and present status of the materialist dialectic.

Contradiction and overdetermination

La 'contradiction' est inséparable de la structure du corps social tout entier, dans lequel elle s'exerce, inséparable de ses *conditions* formelles d'existence, et des *instances* même qu'elle gouverne, ... elle est donc elle-même, en son coeur, *affectée par elles*, déterminante mais aussi déterminée dans un seul et même mouvement, et déterminée par les divers *niveaux* et les divers instances de la formation sociale qu'elle anime: nous pourrions la dire *surdéterminée dans son principe*.

Louis Althusser, Pour Marx (Paris, 1965), 99–100 (italics his)

The rejection of inversion was a new and original step for a Marxist theorist to take. Many writers before and since the 1960s have variously evaded the notion even to the point of ignoring it altogether, but the explicit refusal of a concept embodied in one of Marx's most celebrated passages was a bolder, more open step. It was not a simple denial but rather an integral part of the reformulation of Marxism in terms of a new theoretical framework which Althusser elaborated with growing sharpness during the early 1960s. The articles in which the new ideas took shape appeared in *La Pensée* and other Marxist reviews, before being collected in the volume *Pour Marx* (Paris, 1965). Together they constitute an innovatory reinterpretation of Marxism, at the centre of which lay a translation of the materialist dialectic and its characteristics into an unfamiliar terminology which challenged Marxists to define more precisely the basic concepts of their philosophy.

In a major article of 1962, Althusser looks more closely at the relationship between inversion and Marx's image of the 'rational kernel' and the 'mystical shell', suggesting that it too raises as many questions as it answers.[8] He rejects the view that the shell is speculative philosophy or the Hegelian system as opposed to the method. It is, he says, unthinkable that the place of the dialectic in Hegel's system could be conceived as that of a kernel in a nut. It is the dialectic that is mystified, he argues, and the 'shell' is an element internal to it. In his view, the 'extraction' of the 'kernel' is the same process as the 'inversion' already referred to. Consequently, he asserts that the problem of inversion does not relate to the nature of the object to which the dialectic is applied, but rather to the specific structures of the dialectic. Moreover, he adds, 'il est à peine utile d'indiquer que, dans le premier cas, l'extériorité de la dialectique à ses objets possibles, c'est-à-dire la question de l'application d'une méthode, pose une *question pré-dialectique*, c'est-à-dire une question, qui, en toute rigueur, ne peut avoir de sens pour Marx.'[9] The inversion, or extraction, of the Marxist dialectic, he claims, means simply that the basic structures of the Hegelian dialectic, insofar as Marx takes them over at all, have for him a structure different from the one they have for Hegel.

The coalescence of 'inversion' and 'extracting the kernel' into a single process of transformation marks Althusser's abandonment of the two-stage view of Marx's development from Hegel. His position is the exact reverse of Henri Lefebvre's. Where Lefebvre took the inversion for the transformation, Althusser takes the transformation for the inversion. He rejects the notion that the dialectic is a method, and is idealist or materialist according to whether it is applied to thought or life. On the contrary, he argues, the crucial difference between the Marxist and

Hegelian dialectic is internal, the one being rational where the other is mystical. Paradoxically, Lefebvre and Althusser reach similar conclusions about materialism and idealism, albeit from different directions. For Lefebvre the philosophical opposition is transcended or superseded; for Althusser it becomes meaningless and dissolves. Both thinkers see philosophy replaced by thought reaching out to grasp the world: in one case the dialectic is reorientated, in the other case it is reorganized. In both cases the dialectic is grounded and generated within thought and is internally self-validating. The mechanisms of generation and validation proposed by Althusser will require further examination, but before this is undertaken it is important to develop this analysis of the changed structures of the dialectic.

Lenin declared in his *Philosophical Notebooks* that 'dialectics can be defined as the doctrine of the unity of opposites',[10] and again that 'dialectics in the proper sense is the study of contradiction in the very essence of objects'.[11] It is therefore appropriate that Althusser should address himself first to the concept of contradiction in his programme of defining how the structure of the Marxist dialectic differs from the Hegelian dialectic. Taking the October Revolution of 1917 as his example, Althusser quotes Lenin's view that Russia was the weakest link in the imperialist system, and comments that it was because 'elle cumulait la plus grande somme de contradictions alors possibles'.[12] The basic contradiction between forces and relations of production, embodied in the struggle of antagonistic classes, is not in itself sufficient to provoke revolution, he argues. What is necessary is that it should 'fuse' (*fusionner*) with other contradictions in a unity which provokes radical change. This unity of fused contradictions, he suggests, reveals its own nature, which is that contradiction is inseparable from its conditions of existence and from the moments, or instances, it governs. Determining and determined by the various levels and moments of the social formation, contradiction is therefore 'overdetermined'.

Extending this analysis of a given revolutionary situation to explain the workings of societies in general, Althusser argues that all contradictions in a social formation are overdetermined (*surdéterminé*) in this way. In other words, a society itself and all the various levels of its activity are intimately affected by the state of relations within and between all those levels. Althusser contrasts the complex overdetermination of Marxist contradiction to the simplicity of Hegelian contradiction. He agrees that Hegel may at times appear to permit complexity in his dialectic, but points out that it is only ever a cumulative internalization of superseded stages which invariably resolves into a simple relation of consciousness to itself. For Hegel, he says, the essence of every historical period is contained in a simple internal principle, and the complexity of any society is reducible to this principle, which in turn is only a form of the world's self-consciousness, culminating in its supreme expression: Hegelian idealism.

Hence, Althusser pursues, Hegel's 'system' is inseparable from his dialectic, which reduces all to a simple contradiction. He contrasts it with Marx's dialectic which recognizes that the basic contradiction between Capital and Labour is always specified by the concrete historical forms and circumstances in which it occurs, including political, ideological and religious superstructures, and national and international historical developments. If the Hegelian view were simply 'inverted', Althusser argues, the result would be a reduction of all social activities to the status of pure phenomena of the economic base which would be their 'truth': an economistic caricature of Marxism. He accepts that Marx could be said to 'invert' Hegel's relation of the State and Civil Society, but since Marx's analysis of the state and of the social formation bears little or no resemblance to Hegel's, he feels that the notion of 'inversion' is highly misleading. Even the relation is quite changed, he says, from that of one level being the truth of another, to that of the economic level determining the others in the last instance, while they retain their relative autonomy. In sum, he suggests, there is a need for a more rigorous theoretical approach to Marxism, aimed at a casting out of the shades of earlier philosophies. He concludes: 'plus que jamais il importe de voir aujourd'hui qu'un des premiers fantômes est l'ombre de Hegel. Il faut *un peu plus de lumière sur Marx*, pour que ce fantôme retourne à la nuit.'[13] The exorcism of Hegel is therefore presented as the essential condition of Marxism's true development.

Althusser's close analysis of the relation between contradictions goes some way towards clarifying the difference between Marx and Hegel. His argument that Marxism does not conceive one sphere of social life as the 'truth' of another is a salutary critique of reductionism. Whereas in the domain of pure thought one idea may perhaps be the truth of another, the logical relation of implication cannot be transplanted into society. Althusser is right to insist that the notion of determination be used to designate the relations existing between different levels of activity in society. Only relations of determination can safeguard the relative autonomy of such levels, recognizing that they develop according to their own internal mechanisms and do not necessarily march in step with other levels, even though they are affected by them in various degrees. His account also explains why the concurrence of contradictions to produce a revolutionary situation is more exceptional than the rule. In so doing he is advancing a view which permits a more sophisticated understanding of the mechanism of change, and one which finds ready confirmation in the relatively rare occurrence of successful revolutions. An economic reductionism, on the contrary, is hard-pressed to explain why revolution, or even political change, does not regularly accompany economic crisis.

On the other hand, Althusser's notion of overdetermination contains a number of dangers. The term, taken from Freud's analysis of dream-images, is not crucial in itself. It is frankly imported into Marxism, and Althusser declares that he is not especially wedded to it. The problems stem from what it designates: an interpretation of the relations between different levels of society. If economism cannot account for lack of change, Althusser falls into the opposite difficulty, since his concept of overdetermination makes it difficult to show how change can occur at all. His is a static account, representing a state of affairs from which the dynamic element has been removed. Economism, which Althusser correctly attacks, arises from an oversimplification of the determining role of the economy. But in combating economism, Althusser stands in danger of denying the economy its determining role altogether. Thorough discussion of this point belongs to a more extensive examination of historical materialism. Nevertheless it is important to point out that whereas Hegel saw mind as the dynamic factor in the world's development, Marx located the motor of development in the material production of the means of existence. Althusser, on the other hand, sees the existence of superstructures as 'en grande partie spécifique et autonome'.[14] While he accepts the economy as determining in the last instance, he also insists that 'l'heure solitaire de la "dernière instance" ne sonne jamais'.[15]

Without prejudging Althusser's view of historical materialism, it is clear that the overdetermined structure of the social formation has no internal principle of change. At any given moment the existing structure of society, consisting of the play of relations between *instances* and *niveaux*, is internally reproduced within each part of that society. The parts and the whole therefore combine to reinforce and perpetuate the *status quo*. With the economy duly neutralized by the superstructures, how can change ever take place? In a subsequent essay, Althusser attempts to surmount the problem by introducing a concept of dominance, but it is fraught with similar difficulties, as will emerge. The Hegelian dialectic contained a principle of change, was indeed a logic of motion. Marx's was also a dialectic of motion and change. The concept of inversion maintains that common characteristic by reversing the direction in which change proceeds: from the world rather than from thought. What can be drawn from the discussion of overdetermination is that any redefinition of the Marxist dialectic must incorporate an account of how change occurs, and that Althusser's redefinition fails to do that. In laying the ghost of Hegel he comes near to throwing out the rational kernel with the mystified shell – the Marxist baby with the Hegelian bathwater.

The new model dialectic

La différence spécifique de la contradiction marxiste est son 'inégalité', ou 'surdétermination', qui réfléchit en elle sa condition d'existence, savoir: la structure d'inégalité (à dominante) spécifique du tout complexe toujours-déjà-donné, qui en est l'existence. Ainsi comprise, la contradiction est le moteur de tout développement . . . .

Si la dialectique est bien, comme le dit Lénine, la conception dans l'essence même des choses, de la contradiction, principe de leur développement, et de leur non-développement, de leur apparition, de leurs mutations, et de leur disparition, alors nous devrions atteindre dans cette définition de la spécificité de la contradiction marxiste, la dialectique marxiste elle-même.

Louis Althusser, Pour Marx *(Paris, 1965), 223 (italics his)*

Although Althusser's essay of 1962 sets out to deal with contradiction, it must be evident that it in fact deals with relations between levels of social activity but does not confront the nature of contradictions within the different levels. The one contradiction he specifies is the basic one between Capital and Labour, but he is concerned primarily to show how it is overdetermined by the superstructures, and does not examine its intrinsic nature. He does not therefore examine the concepts of negation, negation of the negation, unity of opposites or the transformation of quantity into quality, all of which are explicitly Hegelian notions closely linked to the concept of contradiction. Similarly, he does not pronounce upon the nature of Marxist philosophy, which he had so portentously declared to be at stake in the discussion. These omissions were, however, temporary. No writer can reasonably expect to present an exhaustive exposition of his philosophy in one short essay, particularly when it is largely new and unfamiliar to his readers. Moreover, Althusser's views were as yet incompletely formulated and much of his analysis was still couched in the traditional Marxist terms he wished to discard. The process of elaboration was rapid though, partly driven by the logic of a radical de-Hegelianization, partly spurred by the sharp opposition his views encountered within some sections of the PCF, partly fuelled by the rich deposits of structural analysis which were beginning to mark French intellectual life. Within a few months of 'Contradiction et surdétermination' he produced a second, longer essay with the programmatic title 'Sur la dialectique matérialiste' which substantially set out his general reformulation of Marxist philosophy, grounded in a new theory of knowledge, and settled his account with Hegel. [16]

Althusser suggests that the difference between the Marxist and Hegelian dialectic has already been solved in practice and only remains to be elaborated at a theoretical level. He defines practice as any process of transformation of particular raw material into a particular product by specific human labour using some definite means. Any society, he says, contains a large number of such 'practices', the main ones being economic production, politics, ideology and theory. Theory is therefore seen as a specific form of practice which works on a raw material of representations, concepts and facts to produce knowledge by means of a conceptual apparatus. Althusser distinguishes three types of theory: *theory* as any theoretical practice of a scientific nature; 'theory' as the conceptual system of a science; and Theory as the theory of theoretical practice and hence of practice in general, corresponding to the materialist dialectic. [17] He argues that Theory is the principal defence of science against ideology, and that therefore an inexact Hegelian approximation is inadequate, particularly for the development of new scientific domains. He agrees that a theoretical practice may proceed effectively for a time on the basis of its 'theory' without a Theory of its own practice, but in the longer term, he feels, Theory is essential. This is the crux of his argument as to why Marx, Engels and Lenin did not, and did not need to, produce a *Logic* or a *Dialectics*, setting out the theoretical foundations of their work, and explaining clearly how their dialectic differed from Hegel's. Most of the 'famous quotations', he claims, simply point to the Marxist dialectic, recognizing it without giving theoretical knowledge of it. This is true of the repeated statement that Marx 'inverted' Hegel's dialectic, he says, since, if taken literally, an inversion of Hegel would lead to a *reductio ad absurdum*.

Althusser admits of three texts, however, which do offer a methodological approach to Marxist Theory: Marx's unpublished 1857 Introduction to his *Critique of Political Economy* (1859); certain passages of Lenin's *Philosophical Notebooks* (1914–16); and Mao Tse-tung's pamphlet *On Contradiction* (1937). Drawing on these sources, he outlines his view of the process of theoretical practice, in which generalities, the raw material drawn from mainly ideological conceptions (Generality I), are transformed into specified concepts, valid as knowledge (Generality III), by a corpus of concepts, its 'theory' (Generality II). On this basis, he asserts, it is obvious that Generality I is different in essence from both II and III, contrary to Hegel's view, and that the process of transformation takes place entirely within knowledge. He draws a sharp distinction between the concrete reality which is the object of knowledge, but exists quite autonomously outside thought, and the concrete in thought, which is entirely a product of the process of knowledge in thought. Consequently the difference between abstract and concrete is between two types of Generality, not between thought and reality. Hegel's error, criticized by Marx, is in Althusser's view twofold. First, he mistakes the production of the concrete in thought for that of the concrete reality. Second, Hegel takes the general concept (Generality I), from which he begins, to be the active element in its own transformation, whereas the 'theory' (Generality II) is in fact the active principle. To repair these errors, says Althusser, it is not sufficient to 'invert' the idea that the general concept produces the concrete reality, giving the result that reality produces the concept. For science, he argues, the starting point is always a Generality (I), not a reality; and even Generality I is a product not of reality but of other practices, mainly ideological. To deny this, he affirms, is to deny the reality of theoretical practice, which produces scientific knowledge by stripping ideas of their ideological context and content.

Althusser's account of the production of knowledge is fundamental to the further development of his notion of contradiction. Since it relates primarily to the materialism of the Marxist dialectic, it is appropriate to pause in the exposition to consider the theoretical ramifications of his analysis. In a broad sense, he provides a social content for the principle that thought, while determined by being, is also a manifestation of being, and is the highest form of organization of matter. It prevents any crude 'mechanical' materialism in which thought is reduced to matter, without its own specific characteristics. The conception of *theory* as one of the constituents of social practice ensures its recognition as a practical activity. And the division of society into 'practices' lays valuable emphasis on the fact that society is a moving, changing process made up of processes of transformation arising from human activity. Again, the relative scarcity of pure philosophy in the writings of Marxism's major figures is accounted for and justified by presenting Theory as an end-product of valid 'theory', a 'general' theory reached by working on 'regional' theories. The interpenetration of theory and practice, a central Marxist principle, is safeguarded by the presentation of theory as a practice, and practice as theoretically grounded, although the grounding of practice in theory raises the fundamental problem of idealism. Any consistent theory must have an account of practice, but if it is to remain materialist it cannot admit that theory precedes or constitutes practice, a danger Althusser does not always avoid. These strengths of his analysis have found widespread recognition and advocacy in the English-speaking world and internationally. However, his analysis is also open to serious question, both for its general implications and on questions of specific detail.

The interpretation of Hegel's relation to Marxism is flawed by a misunderstanding of Marx's 1857 *Introduction*.[18] Althusser is correct in saying that Hegel regards concrete reality as the end-product of the labour of mind, and that Marx criticizes him for confusing the reproduction of the concrete in mind with the process of emergence of the concrete reality.[19] He is also correct to say that Marx rejects Feuerbach's 'inversion', which simply designates Hegel's concrete as 'real' rather than 'real – ideal', reversing the order of production. But he is wrong to suggest that Marx views knowledge purely as the production of the concrete in mind, while breaking off any link with the real concrete. On the contrary, Marx insists that whereas the concrete appears as the result in the process of thinking, 'it is the point of departure in reality and hence also the point of departure for observation and conception'. Furthermore, he warns that 'the real subject retains its autonomous existence outside the head. . . as long as the head's conduct is merely speculative, merely theoretical. Hence in the theoretical method, too, the subject, society, must always be kept in mind as the presupposition'.[20] Marx's text is awkward, sometimes obscure, and difficult to interpret. It was not revised, not offered for publication, and does not necessarily represent Marx's final position on the matters it raises. Nevertheless, it does not support Althusser's interpretation which introduces a radical discontinuity between the real – concrete and the process of knowledge. Where Marx sees concrete reality as the point of departure for observation and conception ('Ausgangspunkt der Anschauung und der Vorstellung'),[21] Althusser asserts that 'pour ce qui est du travail scientifique: il ne part pas des "sujets concrets", mais des Généralités I'.[22] Whereas Marx accepts a starting point, or presupposition, outside thought, Althusser clearly does not.

The argument of 'Sur la dialectique matérialiste' continues with the assertion that what is specific about Marxist contradiction is that it is a Generality III, a theoretically elaborated piece of knowledge. He finds the most satisfactory definition of it in Mao Tse-tung's essay *On Contradiction*, particularly in the concepts of principal and secondary contradictions, principal and secondary aspects of a contradiction, and the uneven development of contradiction. These concepts, he says, presuppose that any process is complex, containing several contradictions, each of which reflects the complexity of the whole. They therefore radically exclude the Hegelian model of contradiction, in which a simple whole is split into two contradictory parts.

Marxist analysis, Althusser argues, never envisages the reduction of a complex process to a simple origin either in principle or in fact. Where simple categories are defined, he suggests, it is only by virtue of their development within a complex whole, or for reasons of simple exposition of a complex problem. With Hegel, on the contrary, he asserts, the logic of his model moves from an original simple whole, through a series of self-alienations and negations, to an eventual reconstitution of a simple totality. Marxism, he says, does not 'invert', but eliminates simplicity as a philosophical myth. The Hegelian categories of alienation, fission, unity of opposites, negation of the negation, and supersession (*Aufhebung*), are removed from Marxist theory, he claims, occurring only in an ideological context where the rigour of theory is not applied.

Since, as Mao puts it, 'nothing in this world develops absolutely evenly', a complex whole necessarily implies relations of domination in Althusser's view. The domination of one contradiction over the others and of one aspect within a contradiction, he argues, distinguishes the Marxist totality from the Hegelian totality, in which the whole is the development of one essential contradiction and no domination is possible between its alienated phenomena. For Marx, he says, secondary contradictions and aspects are not phenomena dependent on the principal one, but are the principal's indispensable conditions of existence, and are therefore reflected in it. This characteristic, previously named overdetermination, is, he suggests, absent from Hegel. In a final step, he announces that the 'dominated' structure and its reflection in each 'dominated' component IS contradiction, the invariant structure of every totality. He offers on this basis an explanation of how contradiction can be a 'motor of development'. He rejects the Hegelian notion that negativity is the motive principle of contradiction, since it presupposes a negation of the negation, restoring the original unity of the Idea, and therefore running counter to the Marxist principle of complexity. Marxist contradiction, he says, is a real struggle located within the complex whole and conditioned by the configuration of relations subsisting between its components.

Examining first Althusser's assessment of the Hegelian dialectic, it is apparent that he allows it only an ideological value, not a theoretical value. But this distinction, consistent with his radical separation of science and ideology, raises serious problems of how Marxism can combine two quite dissimilar conceptual systems, only one of which is theoretically valid, and how Marx, Engels and Lenin could propagate the invalid one in their writings without any apparent unease or loss of integrity. Leaving these problems aside, it may be questioned whether Althusser is wholly just in his assessment of Hegel's dialectic, and of Marx's and Engels' adaptation of it. Certainly he is correct in affirming the essential simplicity of Hegel's system, where each science has a circular structure. Hegel describes his own science of logic as 'a circle returning upon itself, the end being wound into the beginning, the simple ground, by the mediation; this circle is moreover a circle of circles, for each individual member as ensouled by the method is reflected into itself, so that in returning into the beginning it is at the same time the beginning of a new member'.[23] The initial Hegelian Notion passes through mediations before eventually reaching its own truth in the Absolute Idea, and Althusser is right to point out that Marxist contradiction does not envisage a totality in which everything finds its eventual resolution in one fundamental principle. There are, however, important distinctions to be made.

In the first instance, Hegel's circularity is ascribed to knowledge or science. But Althusser himself has no objection to circularity in knowledge, since he regards his own production and transformation of Marxist philosophy as taking 'la forme nécessaire d'un cercle'.[24] His circle refers to the use of Marxist concepts to draw out the full philosophical implications of Marxism from a reading of Marx's works and an expansion of his basic notions. In form at least, his circle is remarkably similar to Hegel's: both aim to advance knowledge by spinning science out of itself. Other Marxists may well find that both philosophers misconceive the nature of science and scientific advance. But in so far as Hegel's analysis describes the knowledge process, Althusser himself can have little quarrel with its circularity. However, Hegel makes a further claim, that science is 'the crowning glory of a spiritual world', that is, where spirit is reality and reality spiritual.[25] His circle is therefore also the process of production of reality. On this precise point, Marx and all subsequent Marxists oppose Hegel. Althusser shares this opposition, but takes it further, to question whether Hegel's dialectic does not imply, within its structure, his idealist conclusions. Is his concept of contradiction compatible with a material, and therefore complex, reality?

It is true that for Hegel everything ultimately returns to the simplicity of the Absolute Idea, but he was insistent that his view did not constitute a reductionism where everything is *reduced* to the one Idea. In his Preface to the *Phenomenology of Mind*, he denounced the 'monochrome formalism' of those who simply reiterate a single idea which they apply to different material, as opposed to his own view of 'the same principle taking shape in diverse ways'.[26] Reality, he argued, 'is the process of its own becoming, the circle which presupposes its end as its purpose, and has its end for its beginning; it becomes concrete and actual only by being carried out, and by the end it involves'.[27] It is clear therefore, that the process is for Hegel indispensable in the production of the end, and is also part of the end. The mediations are the conditions of existence of the resolution, and are indeed part of the resolution, or in Hegelian terminology 'a positive moment of the Absolute'.[28] It is clear then, that Hegel's simple final principle is of a complex simplicity. Between his initial immediate Notion and his eventual mediated Idea lies the whole world. As he points out, 'if we say "all animals", that does not pass for zoology'.[29] The end-product – zoology – may well provide knowledge, though not complete, of all animals, but the science of zoology is not reducible to the concept 'zoology' any more than to the concept 'all animals'. Even for Hegel the science comprises its mediations in terms of its methods, procedures, history and conclusions.

If the Absolute final end of the Hegelian system is abandoned, and if the process is construed as a reflection on the structure of knowledge and a reflection in knowledge of the development of reality, might not the Hegelian totality appear all the more as a complex structure, and Hegelian contradiction as a viable basis for its construction? Althusser may reply that Hegelian contradiction could not survive such a dismemberment of the system it belongs to. Certainly Hegel argues that if the mediations are part of the end, the end is also inherent in the mediations. His concept of contradiction, and particularly its active component, negation, is therefore in a sense teleological. But if the end and the beginning are 'wound in' with each other, and if the end is constituted by the mediations, it is arguable that the process as a whole generates its own finality. If the absolute end is excised, and thus also the absolute beginning, the process changes from one of movement towards a simple pre-established end, to one of movement of a complex totality. The teleology of negation changes from the internalization of an externally established goal to the production of an internally generated direction.

It seems clear that Althusser disregards the capacity of Hegelian contradiction to generate a complex totality. He may therefore be too precipitate in the associated matter of Marx's, Engels' and Lenin's rejection of Hegelian categories. To claim, as he does, that there are but two occasions when Hegelian terms are used in *Capital*, is a misleading and histrionic gesture. The opening analyses of commodities, labour, value, fetishism, and circulation, are heavily and deliberately Hegelian in presentation. Marx even admitted that he 'flirted' with Hegel. Althusser is inclined to dismiss the Hegelian 'flirtation' as an unfortunate lapse from seriousness, but things are not so simple. First, Marx does not simply borrow Hegel's terminology, his entire analysis is structured by the analysis of 'simple' contradictions: the twofold nature of commodities, exchange, and labour in particular. Second, the section in which the flirtation is most apparent is that in which Marx defines his own basic terms and lays his theoretical groundwork: hardly an appropriate moment for mischievous levity. Third, references to Hegel are sprinkled throughout *Capital*, even when no terminological borrowing is apparent.

The cases of Engels and Lenin are even less amenable to Althusser's de-Hegelianizing project. He needs to dismiss large sections of *Anti-Dühring*, *Dialectics of Nature* and the *Philosophical Notebooks* to support his thesis. And initially at least, he appears ready to do so, on one or other pretext. To abandon these works in favour of Mao's *On Contradiction* is particularly incongruous in the light of Mao's explicit conviction that his own pamphlet was based on them.

By contrast with the Hegelian view of totalities generated logically by a sequence of contradictions, Althusser's totality, social practice, excludes logical generation. He therefore confronts the problem of how to establish any system of priority. Although Marx, in *Capital*, presented the logical generation of the main characteristics of capitalism from an analysis of commodities, he was careful to explain that it was not an arbitrary starting point. It was determined by his conception of social dynamics. He had already resolved the question of structural priority in the basic enunciation of historical materialism that 'the mode of production of material life conditions the social, political and intellectual life process in general'.[30] Since capitalism has developed commodity production into a universal characteristic, extending it even to labour-power, the logical generation of concepts by Marx is a reflection of the historical and social generation of capitalism. For Althusser, on the other hand, refusing a generative view of society, the problem is to establish how a series of simultaneous interlinked levels can establish a structural priority.

The notion of uneven development offers an inventive and challenging solution. Althusser gives a novel twist to Mao's conception by first correlating the unevenness of individual contradictions with that of the whole, and then declaring that the individual contradiction is nothing other than the reflection of the whole in the part. Whereas Mao derives the theory of unevenness from an analysis of the development of the two opposed aspects of a contradiction, Althusser derives it from an analysis of the structured whole. Where the one sees unevenness as a product of contradiction, the other sees contradiction as a product of unevenness.

It is clear that Althusser's notion of contradiction is sharply different from Hegel's. It is, however, questionable whether his notion is consistent with Marx's, and whether it constitutes contradiction in any meaningful sense. It is hard to conceive how Althusser's 'contradiction' can be reconciled, for example, with the *Communist Manifesto*'s powerful analysis of the relations between bourgeoisie and proletariat. There, the ascendant bourgeoisie forge the weapons of their own destruction and call into being the class of men who are to wield the weapons. In due course the proletariat gains ascendancy, overthrowing the bourgeoisie and ushering in a new social order. In broad outline at least, the process strongly resembles the movement of Hegelian contradiction. The first term, the bourgeoisie, generates its own negation, and the ensuing struggle is only resolved by an upheaval in which a new order is born. Althusser's account does not permit analysis of contradiction at this high level of generality, since he cannot countenance a simple contradiction. But without it, fundamental motive forces cannot be described in their own contradictory development. They can only be seen as part of a larger process. And while they *exist* in relation to the whole, it is a theoretical limitation that they cannot be *analysed*, even partially, in their own specificity.

Nothing exists in isolation, but any attempt at conceptualization must abstract from universal interrelatedness, otherwise knowledge could scarcely advance beyond the recognition that 'all is flux'. Althusser does not dismiss the need for simpler conceptual units. For example, he examines class struggle in abstraction from the whole, finding it to be structured, like any other practice, as a process of production: raw materials (social relations) are transformed by a given means (class struggle) into a product (new social relations). However, the process is a non-contradictory one which breaks the link between social relations and class struggle. For Marx, on the contrary, class struggle is at the heart of social relations, in capitalist society, not simply a means by which change can be brought about.

Althusser's refusal of simple contradiction makes his contradiction a phenomenon of complex structures whereas his simpler units of analysis are non-contradictory in nature. How then can his description correspond to the materialist dialectic, when dialectics is the study of contradictions in the essence of all things. Althusser's contradiction is not in the essence of all things, but a product of more basic, non-contradictory processes, even, that is, if the relations between social practices, which he calls contradictions, can be accepted as contradiction at all.

Althusser and Garaudy

Si nous remplacions le marxisme vivant par ce doctrinarisme décharné, nous nous couperions totalement de la vie, de notre propre vie, de la vie du Parti, de la vie des autres aussi.

Roger Garaudy, Perspectives de l'homme, 4th edition (Paris, 1969), 366, referring to Althusser

La fin du dogmatisme a produit une réelle liberté de recherche, et aussi une fièvre, où certains sont un peu pressés de déclarer philosophie le commentaire idéologique de leur sentiment de libération et de leur goût de la liberté. Les fièvres tombent aussi sûrement que les pierres.

Louis Althusser, Pour Marx (Paris, 1965), 21, referring among others to Garaudy

This somewhat lengthy examination of Althusser's conceptual framework has been necessary for several reasons. First, Althusser has been and continues to be an influential and widely read interpreter of Marxist philosophy. The originality and appeal of his views are internationally recognized. Second, the theoretical implications of his position are far-reaching, affecting every aspect of Marxist theory. It need hardly be added that the implications extend, in very many ways, into Marxist practice. Third, Althusser's articles of 1961 – 63 represent the most thorough and sustained attempt by any Marxist philosopher to expunge Hegel from Marxism. He constructs a determined theoretical rejection which goes far beyond the efforts of previous periods when Hegel has suffered disfavour or neglect. Finally, his position, which could well be called a system, is at the centre of much of the debate which has taken place in French Marxist philosophy since the early 1960s. By presenting a cogent and self-sustaining reinterpretation of Marx, Althusser has stood for a complete alternative Marxism with which any contemporary exposition of Marxist theory has had to contend at a high level of debate.

Within the French Communist Party, Althusser has represented an aggressive and polarizing tendency which sharply counterposes itself to that represented successively by Lefebvre and Garaudy. On a philosophical level, he proposes a rigorous and sharply defined theoretical view against their woolly catch-all ecumenism. His is a professional, almost technical approach, impatient with imprecision and thoroughly convinced of its own rectitude. Theirs is a broad, humanistic approach, geared to exploring convergences with other thought systems and open to the assimilation of whatever insights they offer. The difference of approach is by no means a question of individual temperaments: both Garaudy and Lefebvre were old hands at the art of vitriolic polemic, now practised by Althusser. It was a difference in generation, in the intellectual movements with which each had affinities, in the social groups to which they appealed, and in the political strategy which they envisaged. The emergence of Althusserianism took place after the departure of Lefebvre from the PCF, so that a comparison with Garaudy is the most apposite and corresponds to the major polarization of the 1960s.

Where Garaudy was aiming to contact the Christians and existentialists, Althusser's appeal was to the structuralists. Garaudy was trying to draw together the strands of the past twenty years of philosophical discussion; Althusser was staking his claim on the next twenty. There was in part a difference of generation: Garaudy joined the PCF in 1933, and was a *député* and member of the Central Committee by the time Althusser joined in 1948, though in age Garaudy was only five years the senior. It was also a difference of social base: both appealed to intellectuals, understood in a broad sense, but while Garaudy addressed writers, artists, teachers and the liberal professions, Althusser addressed social scientists, students and the new white-collar occupations which the scientific and technological revolution was rapidly generating. Garaudy and his audience were grappling with religious questions; for Althusser and his audience, religion was no longer a personal problem. Both were concerned with what have come to be known as the 'human sciences', but one was preoccupied with their humanity, the other with their scientificity.

Politically they were also diametrically opposed, though the antithesis is easy to oversimplify. In the early 1960s it could be stated in terms of left and right. But from the middle 1960s onwards, as will be seen, Althusser's position was considerably modified and could not so readily be categorized. In basing so much of his analysis explicitly on Mao Tse-tung he nailed a left flag to the mast, whereas Garaudy was busily destalinizing and at the same time moving rapidly to the right. In terms of the international communist movement, Garaudy sympathized with the Italians, Althusser with the Chinese. In terms of practical politics, Garaudy's programme led to a policy of broad alliance, almost at any price, to the point of opportunism; Althusser's led to a policy of uncompromising independent action, almost at all costs, to the point of sectarianism. For a party recovering from the low ebb of the late 1950s, each programme held its attractions, each held its dangers. The opposition between the two thinkers and their associated schools spanned the entire range of options in politics as they did in philosophy. And if in the end, neither prevailed, they did pose the alternative extremes in sharp contrast.

Because of the polarization of the two views, it is not easy to reconstruct the debate which ensued, at least in terms of the materialist dialectic. The principal polemics took place in relation to the problem of humanism and associated issues of the early Marx and concepts of man and alienation. The great humanism debate of the mid-1960s assembled Garaudy on the one hand, proposing a redefinition of Marxism in terms of a theoretical humanism which might offer common ground in dialogue with thinkers of other traditions, and Althusser on the other hand, arguing that on a theoretical level Marxism was anti-humanist and could have no truck with ideological mystifications like the notion of man.[31] The gulf between the two positions was so wide that it might be thought there were no points of contact. Garaudy was less able to conduct dialogue with the Althusserians than with Catholics. Similarly Althusser had more conceptual affinity with Foucault and Lacan than with Garaudy. The question of man was pivotal in defining and revealing their differences. Garaudy attempted to re-centre Marxism on the notion of man, gradually abandoning the dialectics of nature and thought and even the objective dialectic of society in favour of the dialectical interaction of subject and object. Althusser re-centred Marxism on a philosophy of the concept, dissolving the notion of subject, subordinating the movement of nature and society to that of knowledge and redefining the dialectic as a mode of internal structuration of concepts.

In some respects, the Althusserian concept of the problematic is useful to describe the systematic inability of each side to communicate with the other. Certainly it is in large measure true that although both claimed to be Marxist, they were operating within different conceptual frameworks. Though they shared many terms, the weight and meaning attributed to them were widely different, and there were many more terms which were not shared. When the two sides met in discussion, a rare enough occurrence, their relations were marked by scorn, impatience and mutual denunciation. The most remarkable incident of this type took place in 1966 when the PCF's Central Committee was planning a major session on intellectual and cultural affairs. In preparation, it called a conference of philosophers which met at Choisy-le-Roi to raise and discuss the major theoretical questions. These 'journées d'étude des philosophes communistes' of January 1966 were the scene of long and vehement confrontations between Garaudy and the supporters of Althusser. For various reasons, the proceedings have never been published, but the bitterness which ran through them has been clearly echoed in later comment. [32]

Paradoxically, this type of conflict underlines the limitations of a notion of problematic based solely on concepts. Two intellectual constructs occupying different territory could hardly meet, let alone conflict. But it is clear that, politically, the two in question occupy, or aspire to occupy, the same territory: the leadership of the revolutionary movement and specifically the direction of the Communist Party. Moreover, they both stem from a common Marxist tradition, even if they seek to develop it in divergent ways, and they are both driven to articulate their position in terms which have been laid down by a century or more of previous thought. Hence, while at the philosophical level it is possible to speak of two separate problematics, they are united by a wider philosophical frame of reference, Marxism, and by a common political objective. The real problems are the same for both, even if they are articulated differently, and the general theoretical apparatus is also the same, even if it is developed and interpreted differently. The two problematics are opposed rather than simply separate, locked in a conflict which is perhaps more properly a contradiction. Their unity and struggle are material, that is, primarily social and political before being conceptual. Hence, the type of symmetrical opposition which can be observed on practical questions of political and ideological alliances is not necessarily reflected in a comparable symmetry of conceptual elaboration. The oppositions between opportunism and sectarianism, and between speculative humanism and theoretical anti-humanism, cannot be correlated with a neat series of oppositions over materialism and the dialectic, for example. Even an apparently obvious opposition such as acceptance or rejection of Hegel proves on examination to be deceptive since Garaudy is less and Althusser more indebted to Hegel than either concedes. The reformulation which each proposes of the materialist dialectic has its own coherence and internal unity. Each articulates the questions which preoccupy it and those it seeks to ignore, using concepts and procedures taken from different intellectual frameworks. Since they have a common ground in Marxist philosophy the two problematics are not entirely discrete. But since they select different aspects of Marx and adapt different non-Marxist analyses, they may be said to share one but not two parents. Half-brothers rather than full siblings, they are the *frères-ennemis* of French Marxism.

References

1 See chapter 4, 'The early Althusser', p.85.
2 L. Althusser, *Montesquieu, la politique et l'histoire* (Paris, 1959); Ludwig Feuerbach, *Manifestes philosophiques, textes choisis 1839-1845*, traduit par L. Althusser (Paris, 1960).
3 *Recherches internationales*, mai – juin 1960.
4 L. Althusser, 'Sur le jeune Marx', *La Pensée*, mars – avril 1961, 3 – 27.
5 See passage at the head of this section.
6 L. Althusser, *Pour Marx* (Paris, 1965), 42, his emphasis.
7 L. Althusser, *For Marx* (London, 1969), 84.
8 L. Althusser, 'Contradiction et surdétermination', *La Pensée*, novembre – décembre 1962, 3 – 22.
9 Althusser, *Pour Marx*, 91.
10 V. I. Lenin, *Collected Works*, XXXVIII (Moscow, 1961), 223.
11 *Ibid.*, 253 – 254.
12 Althusser, *Pour Marx*, 96.
13 *Ibid.*, 116.
14 *Ibid.*, 113.
15 *Ibid.*
16 L. Althusser, 'Sur la dialectique matérialiste', *La Pensée*, juillet – août 1963, 5 – 46.
17 The typographic distinction (*theory*, 'theory', and Theory) is Althusser's, employed in the article under discussion, but subsequently replaced by a clearer terminology.
18 The text is reproduced in K. Marx, *Grundrisse* (London, 1973), 81 – 111.
19 See *ibid.*, pp. 100 – 102.
20 *Ibid.*
21 K. Marx and F. Engels, *Textes sur la méthode de la science économique*, édition bilingue (Paris, 1974), 158.
22 Althusser, *Pour Marx*, 194.
23 G. W. F. Hegel, *Science of Logic* (London, 1969), 842.
24 L. Althusser, *Lire le Capital*, I (Paris, 1968), 37.
25 G. W. F. Hegel, *Phenomenology of Mind* (London, 1966), 76.
26 *Ibid.*, 78.
27 *Ibid.*, 81.
28 *Ibid.*, 83.
29 *Ibid.*, 82.
30 K. Marx, Preface to 'A Contribution to the Critique of Political Economy', in K. Marx and F. Engels, *Selected Works* (London, 1968), 181.

31   The present study does not enter into this very important debate, but there is a useful survey of it in Robert Geerlandt, *Garaudy et Althusser: le débat sur l'humanisme dans le Parti communiste français et son enjeu* (Paris, 1978).

32   See in particular the proceedings of the 1966 Central Committee meeting at Argenteuil, published in *Cahiers du communisme*, mai–juin 1966.

7

Explorations

1962–1968 PART 2

The destalinization of philosophy

Sur le plan philosophique proprement dit, les défauts de l'exposé de Staline peuvent être groupés en trois chapitres essentiels:
1. Le matérialisme de Marx y est assimilé au matérialisme dogmatique pré-marxiste. Un tel exposé empêche de comprendre ce qui fait du marxisme une révolution en philosophie à partir du primat de la pratique.
2. La dialectique est coupée de la science vivante en train de se faire et puise seulement des illustrations dans les sciences du siècle passé. Un tel exposé ne permet pas d'échapper au positivisme et au scientisme.
3. Le matérialisme dialectique est coupé de l'héritage philosophique. Il est ainsi appauvri et stérilisé.

Roger Garaudy, 'Les tâches des philosophes communistes et la critique des erreurs philosophiques de Staline: Rapport', Cahiers du communisme, *juillet–août 1962, 91*

After 1956 a trickle of philosophers left the Communist Party, some noisily, some quietly. Others, anxious to stay within the party, for political reasons, avoided taking issue on controversial subjects. The Algerian crisis and the serious reversals suffered by the Left made many feel that the time was inopportune for public philosophical soul-searching. Marxist philosophy did not, of course, cease to develop. On the contrary, growing numbers of young intellectuals began to make serious theoretical contributions. But it was with considerable reluctance that French Marxists faced the question of how the Stalin era had affected their philosophical work, and what needed to be rooted out. Roger Garaudy's important *Perspectives de l'homme* (Paris, 1959), for example, simply ignored Stalin, as if he had never existed. Lucien Sève's lengthy survey of French philosophy in 1960 suggested that Stalin's personality cult had had only a benign effect on French Marxism, largely based on the illusory sense of complacency his prestige encouraged.[1]

One of the first to push the analysis a little further was the young philosopher Jacques Milhau, who had joined the editorial board of *La Nouvelle critique* in 1957. Writing for the journal in late 1958, he suggested that the personality cult had led to a 'timidité dans l'initiative théorique' and a tendency to argue from authority.[2] Moreover, he outlined three major failings from which French Marxism had suffered in recent times: a philosophical sectarianism which tended to reduce philosophy to ideology, closely linked to the aberration of the two sciences theory; an arrogant dilettantism which promoted rash philosophical interventions in all manner of questions, regardless of the lessons of science and experience; and a disregard for the internal workings and epistemological value of non-Marxist currents, superficially criticized on purely political or sociological grounds.

Milhau had several specific cases in mind. The two sciences theory has already been evoked; the development of that controversy exemplifies his first two points. Philosophers neglected the cognitive dimension of science, and made various assertive proclamations on scientific matters without adequate knowledge of the real issues. The third point is particularly relevant to the hasty dismissal of new scientific developments in information theory and cybernetics during the mid-1950s, on the basis of their idealist presentation. The storm over biology and the theories of Lysenko was perhaps the most damaging example of the attitudes Milhau indicated, though even in 1958 it had not entirely abated.

The limitation of Milhau's account is that it is confined mainly to attitudes and style of work. Important theoretical questions were involved, of course, but he did not directly broach their more philosophical consequences. It was another two years or more before a serious appraisal of them was undertaken. Part of the impulse was internal. The reversals of 1958 set in train a general movement of reappraisal within the PCF once the shock had registered. A new generation of philosophers had reached maturity and did not feel bound by the habits of their predecessors. The PCF, recognizing the upsurge of interest and energy, set up a new organizational framework, the Centre d'Etudes et de Recherches Marxistes (CERM), in 1960, to co-ordinate and develop intellectual work and broaden contacts with non-Marxist intellectuals. The emergence of new problems and new ideas effectively rendered parts of Stalin's analysis inadequate if not obsolete, and the growing level of output and sophistication of Marxist philosophers required that their relation to Stalin be clarified to a greater degree.

This general movement was given an external impulse by the 22nd Congress of the CPSU in 1961, when the destalinization of the Soviet Union was given a renewed vigour.

The 14th (July 1956), 15th (June 1959) and 16th (May 1961) congresses of the PCF all acknowledged that the personality cult had been a serious obstacle to the creative development of Marxism, and the party's general secretary Waldeck Rochet made the same point in January 1962 to a gathering of philosophers who were party members.[3] But the first major attempt to define precisely what the philosophical implications were was a report to a similar gathering later in the same year by Roger Garaudy.[4]

Addressing himself to defining the tasks of communist philosophers and to a critique of Stalin's philosophical errors, Garaudy situated the problems in the context of continued attacks by bourgeois ideologists on the objectivity of science, the specificity of history, and the morality of Marxism. He acknowledged the considerable pedogogical value of Stalin's *Dialectical and Historical Materialism* (1938), his *Foundations of Leninism* (1924), and the various writings of Andrei Zhdanov, but spoke of 'les très graves et profondes erreurs contenues dans ces textes'.[5] The most fundamental, he suggested, was the separation of theory and practice. If practice is seen as the source and criterion of theory, materialism is a point of arrival rather than a point of departure, therefore dialectical rather than dogmatic; and the dialectic stems from a confrontation with nature, which it reflects in a materialist rather than a speculative manner. Stalin's errors were: to assimilate Marx's materialism to pre-Marxist, dogmatic, materialism; to cut off the dialectic from the development of modern science; and to isolate Marxism from its philosophical heritage.[6] In distinguishing materialism as a conception of the world and the dialectic as a method, Stalin obscured the fact that each is method and conception, and that both are intertwined. His view of idealism was caricatural, his theory of reflection was mechanistic, his materialism was non-dialectical and his dialectic was non-materialist.

Criticizing the dogmatic projection of the Hegelian dialectic into nature, Garaudy pointed out that the concept of negation could not be applied dogmatically, for which reason Stalin had excluded it from his closed list of four principles of the dialectic. For comparable reasons, the notion of the unity of opposites and the category of totality also disappeared from Stalin's dialectic. Moreover, he lumped together as 'features', general characteristics (e.g. movement), principles (e.g. contradiction), categories (e.g. reciprocal action), and laws (e.g. the transformation of quantity into quality). In so doing he jettisoned the major contribution of Hegel to Marx's critique of alienation and his conception of scientific laws as internal and necessary relations. Stalin's view of Marxism, he argued, was an amalgam of eighteenth-century materialism and nineteenth-century science: D'Holbach + Darwin = Marx, a mutilated and impoverished view.

Garaudy declared that Stalin's mechanistic conception of relations between the base and superstructure had led to the tendency to deduce ideologies from their social base, ignoring their role in reflecting reality, even if in a distorted way, and neglecting the importance of traditional material in their composition. He quoted the distinction between materialism and idealism, crudely regarded by Stalin as corresponding to progressive and reactionary philosophers, and pointed out that philosophers could not be simply classified as one or the other, that idealists could make progressive contributions and materialists could be reactionary. Furthermore, he argued, Stalin had applied his deductive approach to the relation of philosophy to the sciences, considering Marxism as a fixed set of principles by which the value of a science could be judged, attempting to anticipate on scientific discoveries by philosophical deduction, and being unable to distinguish the objective content of scientific theories from idealist interpretations of them. In each case, Stalin abandoned practice as the criterion of truth.

In relation to the philosophical heritage, Garaudy identified Stalin's major error as the virtual elimination of the Hegelian tradition in Marxism, even at the price of expurgating Marx's 1844 manuscripts and Lenin's philosophical notebooks from editions of their collected works. He suggested that Marx and Engels took from Hegel, in modified form, the primacy of activity, the theory of man's self-creation in work and the resulting struggle against alienation, and the dialectical method. The dogmatic neglect of these important concepts had left Marxism vulnerable to the various forms of bourgeois ideology, including personalism, existentialism, catholicism and revisionism, which borrowed Marxist notions in a mystified form and used them against Marxism itself.

From a conceptual point of view, Garaudy makes many telling points against Stalin's conception of Marxist philosophy. His analysis of the separation of theory and practice, with its damaging ramifications, is particularly powerful. As a root cause of dogmatism it demonstrably leads to a mechanistic materialism and a speculative dialectic, with all the deleterious effects that combination has on Marxism. The relentless dismantling of the 1938 essay was especially significant if, as Garaudy recognised, it had been 'une sorte de charte fondamentale' of communist philosophy.[7] In actual fact, despite its undoubted influence, the essay had never exercised quite the same exclusive domination over philosophers as it had over French communists as a whole. When Marxists examined their theory beyond the level of elementary pedagogy, they were not long in discovering the inadequacies of Stalin's outline, even if they were hesitant to declare it openly. In an important sense, the question of Stalin was one of the relation between the party and members who were specialists in some field of enquiry. In philosophy, the problem was particularly acute since the enquiry concerned basic guiding principles which to some extent affected all aspects of policy and activity. Under Stalin, the party leadership had assumed the role of arbiter, not only on general questions, but even on matters of detail in philosophy, a policy which also extended to other branches of enquiry. Destalinization meant, among other things, being content to leave specialized questions to specialists.

A far-reaching consequence of Garaudy's report is the large-scale rehabilitation of Hegel. The renewed interest among Marxists in Hegelian philosophy had not, of course, waited for 1962, or even 1956. The mid-1950s had already seen a growing interest in the Hegelian dimension of Marxism. Lefebvre's influence was extensive, but even beyond that, the confrontations with the existentialists and the increasing re-examination of their historical origins had produced among Marxists a more general acknowledgement of the significance of Hegel. Lenin's philosophical notebooks played an important role, as did the early philosophical writings of Marx and Engels. The influence of Palmiro Togliatti and Italian Marxism was also felt. As early as 1955 the General Secretary of the Italian Communist Party (the PCI) had published an article on Marx and Hegel in *La Nouvelle critique*,[8] and the Italian communists, quicker to destalinize, were regarded as philosophical pathfinders in some circles. Auguste Cornu contributed to the trend with his weighty three-volume study of Marx and Engels during their formative years, when they were both active in the German Young Hegelian movement.[9]

The stormy debates which arose in the early 1960s over the early Marx and questions of humanism and alienation stimulated a concern to define the philosophical origins of Marxism. The review *Recherches internationales* in 1960 published a collection of articles on the problem of 'Le jeune Marx', drawing largely on debates in the Soviet Union and East Germany.[10] It aroused considerable comment in the French press, sparking off a series of controversies in which it became evident that a resurgence of opposition to Hegel was arising to meet the pervasive spread of Hegelian ideas among French Marxists. More generally, a struggle was initiated in which two hostile tendencies were developing, divided on almost all aspects of Marxist philosophy. The divisions were sharpest on two questions: humanism and the materialist dialectic. The humanism debate, encompassing the development of Marx in relation to Hegel and Feuerbach, the nature and status of Marxist humanism, the concept of man, and the theory of alienation, is a complex network of problems which would need a separate study. The debate on the materialist dialectic was also centred on the relation of Marx and Hegel, and largely grew out of the philosophical developments that have already been examined. The first major protagonist was again Roger Garaudy.

Garaudy began with a legitimate attempt to restore an awareness of Hegel's importance in the origins of Marxism. It was widely accepted that Stalin's influence had generally diminished the attention paid to Hegel. The PCF's Chairman, Maurice Thorez, gave an assessment of the consequences in 1962: 'Staline . . . a considéré Hegel d'un point de vue étroit, en oubliant les recommandations de Marx, d'Engels et de Lénine sur la nécessité d'étudier sa dialectique et de la réinterpreter. Ainsi il a joué un rôle négatif; il a rendu plus difficile l'étude du matérialisme dialectique.'[11] The price of neglecting Hegel was seen to be a weakening of the dialectic, and Thorez's comments reflected both a concern at the development and a determination to rectify it. Hence, in his efforts to rehabilitate Hegel in Marxist philosophy, Garaudy was articulating the general movement of his party as well as his own personal preferences. Thorez's call to study Hegel had been anticipated by Garaudy, and though the call itself bore valuable fruit in the course of time, the first fruits were premature and unstable. The criticism of Stalin's ideas and their influence was accurate and well deserved. The charge that they impoverished Marxism was also well founded. But the remedy proposed was frequently no more than a hasty and uncritical reimportation of Hegel into Marxism: a response which marked a clear stage of Garaudy's development.

Early in 1962, Garaudy published a substantial and detailed study of Hegel under the title *Dieu est mort*, in which he tried to avoid what he saw as symmetrical excesses. On the one hand, he thought, Jean Wahl had presented Hegel as a secret Kierkegaardian existentialist; on the other, George Lukács had made Hegel a Marxist 'avant la lettre'.[12] Considering neither view to be accurate, Garaudy sought to balance the valid elements in both, recognizing the ideological and religious origins of Hegelianism but also stressing the social, political and economic conditions in which it grew. The importance of classical economists in Hegel's development were emphasized but since his understanding was limited to capitalist economics it was not surprising that he should confuse objectification with alienation and conceive materiality as an alienation of mind, thereby deducing the world speculatively. The constant presence of alienation was seen by Hegel as tragic, but also as a source of the dialectical movement of the whole. However the conception of the totality as absolute led, in Garaudy's view, to a contradiction between the system and the dialectical method with which it was constructed. Hegel's loss of confidence in the revolutionary movement led him to opt for the system, reconciling all contradictions in thought, and producing a theodicy in which an ascending dialectic of being and knowledge led to God. The rejection of the Hegelian system, Garaudy argued, could lead either to the existentialist view of contradictions as insuperable, or the Marxist view that they were rooted in the world and could therefore only be overcome by real change. He chose the latter as an inversion of idealism, which was itself an inversion of the real order of things. Practice, he suggested was beyond concepts and therefore his inversion was not a Hegelian *Aufhebung*, but a proletarian revolution in philosophy, transforming idealism into materialism, speculation into science and contemplation into action.

It was in the light of this analysis that Garaudy integrated Hegel into his programme of destalinization. The major criticisms have already been outlined: they included a rejection of Stalin's simplistic distinction of a dialectical method and a materialist world view. Both the world view and the method should be materialist and dialectical, he argued, the alternative being an uneasy marriage of mechanical materialism and idealist dialectic. Among Stalin's specific errors, he listed the omissions of the negation of the negation, of the unity of opposites, of the category of totality; the tendency towards positivism in science and therefore in philosophy; and the reduction of the dialectic to a closed list of laws. All of these errors were related by Garaudy to a neglect of Hegel, whom Stalin dismissed as an idealist, and considered to represent an aristocratic reaction against the French Revolution. Garaudy's view was that Marx and Engels borrowed three themes from Hegel: the primacy of activity, man's self-creation in work, and the dialectic. In each case, he added, the Hegelian version had to be demystified. But in not defining the process of demystification, his analysis holds the danger of not specifying how the three 'thèmes essentiels' are to be integrated into a coherent Marxist synthesis, and not posing a clear distinction between Marx and Hegel.

Garaudy is right to oppose the separation of the dialectical method from the materialist conception of the world, but their unity must also be conceived dialectically. Unless they retain some degree of distinctness, they simply merge into a single undifferentiated system which is ultimately neither dialectical nor materialist. To a large extent that was the eventual fate of Garaudy's speculative humanism, but in 1962 it was still in its early stage. His position, as it evolved, was a key point of focus for the major debates of the 1960s, drawing together both the crucial philosophical questions and the social and political movements they reflected.

The process of philosophical destalinization did not end with Garaudy, of course. Specific criticisms and self-criticisms continued to appear, aimed at liquidating the practical and theoretical consequences of the personality cult. Perhaps the most extensive analysis appeared in the form of a special number of *La Nouvelle critique*, the journal which in the early 1950s had been most closely associated with the most embarrassing theoretical excesses.[13] Many of the theoretical debates of the 1960s made implicit or explicit reference to Stalin and the criticism of his errors, but as time passed the references became less concrete and less meaningful. 'Stalinist' became a catch-all term to abuse or embarrass an opponent, regardless of what error he was charged with. Undoubtedly there were Marxists who were reluctant to abandon the comfortable certainty and simplicity of the 1938 essay, but they were not numerous among philosophers. And certainly among those who were striving to develop Marxism in a creative way, there was no question of a return to Stalin.

To analyse the debates of the 1960s and 1970s in terms of Stalinism and anti-Stalinism is a futile and impoverishing approach. What was in question was the theory and practice of Marxism. In terms of the philophical questions being examined here, the nature of the materialist dialectic continued to be a central focus of controversy. What destalinization meant was the opening up of a wide range of new options for exploration. Marxist philosophers were invited to philosophize, pushing their researches to a higher level of sophistication, and drawing on all the riches of their philosophical heritage, all the resources of their discipline, and all the mushrooming wealth of scientific enquiry.

Godelier and the cybernetic dialectic

Nous avons donc montré la nature de la méthode dialectique en la saisissant comme l'instrument d'analyse d'un certain type d'objets, 'les totalités organiques', et des rapports interstructuraux que ces derniers comportent.

> *Maurice Godelier*, Rationalité et irrationalité en économie, II,
> *(Paris, 1969), 70*

In France, as elsewhere, the basic questions of philosophy are by no means the sole prerogative of philosophers. Marxism has in particular always been sharply aware of the close link between philosophy and science. Accordingly, practitioners of both the natural and the social sciences have increasingly intervened in questions of philosophy. One of the most interesting contributions to the philosophical debates came from the economist and anthropologist Maurice Godelier, who, over a period of four or five years, developed an analysis to pin down the specific nature of the Marxist dialectic. His primary concern was to establish a dialectical rationality appropriate to the study of economics. Developing in parallel with Althusser, though independently from him, Godelier gradually moved towards a non-Hegelian statement of the dialectic.

Writing in a series of articles in 1960, Godelier first examined the method of Marx's major work of economics, *Capital*.[14] He characterized its method as an ordered conceptualization which reproduces and reflects in ideas the movement of economic reality. Marx's inversion of Hegel consists, in Godelier's view, of two parts: a critique of idealism, and a presentation of the dialectic as a 'logique du réel' rather than a 'logique du concept'.[15] He emphasizes that the method of *Capital* is to be found in the order of presentation, as distinct from the order of investigation. The exposition, he says, takes a circular form, the method and its conceptual content being mutually dependent. The criterion of its truth, however, is not a formal one internal to the method, but an external one, based on 'l'adéquation de la pensée et de son objet', established by practical verification.[16] As a preliminary distinction, he proposes to analyse the method of *Capital* as the synthetic unity of two rational methods: the hypothetico-deductive and the dialectical.

Godelier sees Marx's use of hypothesis and deduction as a feature he shares with modern non-Marxist economists, offering a complex model of basic structures of capitalism and some of its laws. But it is complemented and completed by the dialectical method, which, he argues, provides the basis for a theory of the dynamics of capitalism. The dialectic, he says, permits a description of the reciprocal interdependence of the basic structures of an economic system which is an organic totality. He shows how the dialectic is used in analysing human labour, the cyclical process of capital, particular forms of profit, production and consumption, supply and demand, and other phenomena. In each case, he suggests, 'la pensée dialectique cherche à reconnaître l'identique dans le différent, et le différent comme identique', using concepts such as opposition, identity, mediation and reciprocity.[17] However, unlike Hegel, he says, Marx refuses to attribute substance to his concepts, which are operational (*opératoires*), that is, aimed strictly at showing common relations within different determinations. Hence Marx did not regard his dialectic as more than an operational tool.

Godelier argues that the dialectic only enters into the content of theory when it enables a concrete historical relation to be analysed. Such an entry is both possible and necessary when the field of enquiry exhibits the structure of an organic totality. In other words, he conceives the dialectic as an instrument of analysis for a certain type of object, organic totalities, and the interstructural relations they contain.[18] He acknowledges that philosophy has a role in elaborating dialectics at the most abstract, general level, provided it does not fall into the danger of elevating the dialectic into a system or a general methodology. And he concludes by locating the origin of dialectical processes in the practical relation of man to nature. Man responds to the negativity of his needs by work, which constitutes the human essence.

Godelier's account of the relation between concept and reality in Marx's *Capital* is clear and cogent. It is also informed by illuminating discussions of Marx's 1857 *Introduction*, and of several analyses contained in *Capital*. There are, however, points of difficulty. On two of these, as will be seen, Godelier subsequently modified his stance; they are: the kind of synthesis effected between the hypothetico-deductive and the dialectical methods; and the nature of Marxist contradiction as distinct from Hegelian contradiction. On two other points, Godelier did not change his position. First, it is evident that his dialectic is restricted to the sphere of history, excluding both nature and, to some extent, thought. Some attention has already been paid to the controversies surrounding the dialectics of nature, and Godelier does not take it up as a central issue. But it may be noted that by locating the origin and foundation of dialectics in human work, he is effectively excluding the possibility of a general dialectic which might extend into the sphere of the natural sciences. The second related point is that his restriction also appears to exclude an account of dialectics as the generalization of the laws of thought. By placing dialectics on the same level as hypothesis and deduction, he appears to reduce thought to a collection of assorted procedures whose strictly functional role precludes any internal coherence or unity. His definition of the dialectic as 'instrument opératoire' appears to confirm the reduction. It points to a neglect of the cognitive role of thought in reflecting external reality, in favour of its operational role in manipulating concepts about reality. Unless both

roles are combined, his initial view of the relation of *Capital* to economic
reality appears difficult to sustain. To some extent, however, this
problem is attenuated in his reassessment of the two methods.

Returning the following year to his analysis, Godelier admitted that
he had insufficiently stressed the dialectical nature of Marx's
approach. [19] He now views the rationality of Marxist economics as
rooted in the 'hypothèse philosophique du matérialisme historique' and
in the dialectical method which is based on it. [20] While he feels he has
adequately characterized the different levels on which structural and
dynamic analysis operate, he asserts that 'la méthode du *Capital*,
synthèse d'une pluralité de démarches, est de part en part dialectique', a
point he had not previously emphasized sufficiently. [21] He distinguishes
two levels of use of the dialectical method. The first level is a dialectical
movement unconscious of itself, realized in rational knowledge which
develops concepts to express contradictions in reality and in historical
practice relating to it. The higher level arises when the scientist becomes
aware of the dialectical movement as such, reflects on it and enriches it,
after which it is 'reinvested' back into the particular field of knowledge
concerned. Godelier argues that the two levels describe Marx's own
development and explain on the one hand how he both took Hegel's
dialectic and moved away from Hegel, and on the other hand why his
dialectical method is so deeply buried in *Capital*. The method, Godelier
argues, is neither empiricist nor speculative since the central concept of
Capital (the commodity) is discovered by investigation; its structures
and conditions of production are unfolded by rational analysis, and the
resulting framework is a scientific guide for understanding historical
development. The entire process, in his view, is dialectical and
combines both structural and dynamic analyses.

Godelier's rectification involves a significant shift in his account of the
dialectic. Where it was previously the rational expression of dynamic
rather than structural relations, it now designates the entire knowledge
process, particularly the relations between concepts and external reality.
In one sense, he strengthens the dialectic since hypothesis, deduction,
analysis of contradiction and the construction of models are all part of
it. In another sense, the dialectic is weakened by being restricted to the
general relation of thought to being. It describes the movement between
subject (science) and object (world) but does not describe the internal
movement of either. Godelier therefore moves simultaneously closer to
Hegel, in his phenomenology, and further from Hegel, in his logic.

In describing the dialectic of knowledge Godelier elaborates the
distinction between investigation and presentation and offers a
provocative analysis of investigation. He suggests that Marx's economic

inquiry proceeds like a psychiatric inquiry, where the patient talks until one element of his discourse appears to illuminate and unify the others, and is therefore adopted by the therapist as the 'fait typique' which can be a starting point for a coherent analysis of the illness. [22]

A striking confirmation of this might be seen in comparing Marx's preparatory notebooks, the *Grundrisse* (1857 – 58), with *Capital*. The final pages of the *Grundrisse* enter into an analysis of commodities as 'the first category in which bourgeois wealth presents itself', [23] whereas the opening sentence of *Capital* (1867), echoing the *Critique of Political Economy* (1859), characterizes the wealth of capitalist societies as 'an immense accumulation of commodities'. [24] The final stage of the investigation becomes the starting point of the presentation. Godelier's analogy with psychiatry does less than justice to the precise means by which Marx reached his key concept of the commodity. But as a first approximation, developed in the absence of French translations of texts like the *Grundrisse*, it has much to recommend it.

In common with Althusser, Godelier considered that a radical discontinuity separated Marx's early philosophical writings from his mature works. But he did not seek to reduce Hegel's role in Marx's development to this discontinuity. In an article of 1963, he describes how Marx rejected Hegel's view that the state determines civil society, replacing it with the opposite view, and consequently espousing the cause of the proletariat. [25] By 1844, he says, Marx adopted a theory of alienation developed by Feuerbach, but retained Hegel's dialectical method of analysis, albeit in modified form appropriate to its new theoretical basis. Marx's subsequent shift from the theory of alienation to a theory of praxis produced, in Godelier's opinion, a partial return to Hegel, in that he once more recognized the importance of his dialectic, neglected by Feuerbach. But in another sense, Godelier argues, Marx moves away from both Feuerbach and Hegel by conceiving the dialectic as one of human practice rather than of mind. At each step the dialectic was restructured to meet the needs of the new theory, he suggests, and at the end the materialist dialectic is 'autre dans sa structure, c'est-à-dire dans ses règles opératoires'. [26] Godelier applauds Althusser's analysis on this point, though he warns that the notion of *over*determination has an ambiguous problematic, and disguises the importance of a specific order of determinations, even if it prevents a reduction of the superstructures to the base.

While emphasizing the successive transformations in Marx's thought separating him from Hegel, Godelier represents his development of the dialectic as a kind of 'rapprochement' with Hegel, even if the specific structures of the dialectic are altered. There is an element of paradox in such a picture since it is by no means clear how the changed dialectic remains 'dialectical'. If the same term is meaningfully retained, there must surely be some continuity of content. The Althusserian reconstruction scarcely meets this condition, and however much Godelier may express his approval, it cannot be simply transposed into his own account. Within the terms of this account he was unable to formulate an adequate characterization of what he conceived the Marxist dialectic to be or how it specifically differed from the Hegelian. It was not until some years later, when he had developed his analysis in the light of a structural approach to anthropology, that he was able to put forward a confident account of the central concept of the dialectic; contradiction.

Reviewing his personal development, Godelier noted that in the early 1960s 'le pas décisif fut notre rencontre avec l'Anthropologie'.[27] He might have been a little more specific were it not such common knowledge that Mr Anthropology was of course Claude Lévi-Strauss. Godelier's experience of anthropology was not, however, confined to theory, and in tandem with his growing attachment to structural anthropology he undertook extensive research in practical questions of anthropology, including field work in Papua-New Guinea. On a philosophical level he adopted the lessons of the discipline to his study of the materialist dialectic, developing in particular a new analysis of contradiction. In a well-known article of 1966, 'Système, structure et contradiction dans le Capital',[28] and in his book Rationalité et irrationalité en économie (Paris, 1966), he argued that Marx discussed two types of contradiction.

Godelier distinguishes between contradictions internal to a structure and contradictions between structures. In the case of capitalism, he points to the contradiction within the relations of production between bourgeoisie and proletariat. It is, he says, an internal contradiction, specific to capitalism, originating and ending with it. However, he argues, it is another type of contradiction which is fundamental to capitalism: the one between the relations of production and the forces of production. This grew up during the development of capitalism, he says; it is non-intentional, it sets the limits within which the production relations can remain invariant, and it thereby exercises a pervasive structural causality. The first, internal contradiction, Godelier points out, has no internal solution since the conditions for a solution lie largely with the second contradiction and, to a lesser extent, with the superstructures. On the other hand, the second contradiction, between structures in the system, is resolved by the internal development of the whole system and particularly by a restructuring of the relations of production to bring them into correspondence with the forces of production.

Godelier draws the conclusion that Marx's contradiction rests on the *unity* of opposites, but excludes the *identity* of opposites, which Hegel requires in order to demonstrate that a contradiction internal to a structure has an internal solution. For Marx, he affirms, the elements in a structure, and the structures in a system are not reducible to each other; for Hegel, on the other hand, the identity of opposites is fundamental to his idealism, which enables everything to be proved or justified. He suggests that the confusion between the two distinct types of contradiction has prevented clear analysis of the question since Marx's own time. The second type in particular, he feels, is highly pertinent to modern scientific analysis in that it explains certain objective properties of structures. It signals the existence of externally determined limits beyond which a structure cannot remain invariant, self-reproducing, and in stable relation with other structures, but must undergo structural change. Rejecting Althusser's 'overdetermination', Godelier integrates his contradiction into a conception of society as an ordered hierarchy of structures. He therefore considers that he has finally torn Marx away from Hegel.

In many respects Godelier's analysis is an attractive reformulation of the materialist dialectic. It enables him to construct a structural model of society in which the mechanisms are clearly defined. The slippery and shifting Hegelian dialectic is abandoned for a theory of structural limitations to invariance. Certainly his attack on the notion of identity serves to clarify a possible confusion. Marx undoubtedly takes opposition rather than identity to be the basic characteristic of contradiction. Unity, or interpenetration, is a preferable term to describe the relation of opposites, though at the limit it may become a provisional, circumscribed, identity. In this connection Marx offers an analysis of traditional views of the relation of production to consumption.[29] Three senses are usually suggested in which they may be called identical. Each is immediately the other, each is dependent on the other as a means, and each completes the other. Although in very general terms that is the case, Marx points out that they are not moments in a single act by a single subject, since society is not a single subject. He suggests that there are also other processes in society which step between them, notably distribution and exchange. Consequently, he prefers to speak of 'mutual interaction between the different moments', a conception which appears to confirm Godelier's analysis.[30]

On the other hand, Godelier's vision of society as a hierarchy of structures externally related to each other seems to interpret Marx in an excessively structural way. He loses much of the flexibility inherent in the notion of contradiction. To take his example of the forces and relations of production. Using this distinction he defines two, and only two, types of contradiction. Their characteristics are determined by whether they occur within or between structures. Hence, it is structure, not contradiction, which is the essential organizing principle of any process. Indeed the second type of contradiction he discusses, external contradiction, is effectively dissipated, being no longer a unity of opposites but a general boundary marker defining the limits within which a system (or structure) may remain stable. What he does not envisage is the notion that contradictions which are external to one structure may be internal to a larger structure. His view of society as a system of structures could conceivably embrace this notion, but the systemic contradiction he allows, is, like Althusser's, not a dynamic unity of opposites but a static structural relationship; that is, not a contradiction at all. If the rigid structural determinants are discarded, it is possible to consider the contradiction between forces and relations of production to constitute an intelligible whole (the economic base). The two components can then be viewed as forming an 'internal' contradiction. But since the precise nature of contradictions may vary between components and between wholes at whatever level, the restriction of contradiction to two types is unnecessary. Contradictions are both internal and external depending on the context in which they are viewed, and their precise characteristics can not be known a priori but must be established by investigation.

The charge that Godelier offers a narrowly restricted account of contradiction needs to be qualified by the recognition that he deals only with social contradictions, ignoring or rejecting the application of contradiction to logic or natural science. Moreover, he does not share the view that contradiction is 'the essence of dialectics' (Lenin).[31] Instead, he considers contradiction as one conceptual tool among others which go to make up his overall dialectic, or movement of knowledge. Diminished in status and scope, contradiction becomes a formal property of structures which are themselves formal configurations of relationship. And when more closely examined, it appears that contradiction is an inappropriate and antiquated term for a kind of structural causality. Godelier's reformulation of the 'rational kernel' of Hegel's dialectic does not reconstruct the Marxist conception of contradiction and dialectics. Rather it deconstructs it, evacuating both dialectics, 'the science of interconnections' (Engels),[32] and contradiction which is the heart of dialectics. In its place is a variety of structuralism which at best might be termed structuralo-Marxism.

The ambiguities of Godelier's analysis stem, in part at least, from an attempt to synthesize Marxism with the methods of non-Marxist economics, in particular the construction of abstract models, operations research, and the development of artificial systems of information and communication. The efficiency and sophistication with which data could be manipulated and processed by methods of formal logic was only beginning to be realized, as the power of the computer gradually revealed itself. Whatever its pitfalls, Godelier's account was attempting to marry the materialist dialectic to a logic of systems. The instrumental conception of the dialectic was a first consequence. He equated it with a systems logic, reducing it first to a method and then to a tool. In this process he came close to severing the link between the dialectic and the structure of reality. A static conception of the dialectic was a second consequence of Godelier's account, proposing contradiction as a structural limitation on invariance. The passive role of contradiction excludes an active, dynamic or constitutive function and it is effectively relegated from the essence of things to the interface between linked systems. Godelier's Marxism is excessively bound to a cybernetic model, and to that extent fails to translate the materialist dialectic adequately. But the attempt is both fruitful and necessary if the concepts of Marxist philosophy are to be relevant to and enriched by the developments of contemporary science and technology.

The more general problem of dialectics and formal logic is a recurrent one. A rationality based on identity and difference is in many respects at odds with one based on contradiction. Whereas the former cannot admit the latter, the latter can admit the former as a circumscribed aspect of its own movement. Synthesis is therefore possible, and if dialectics does not exclude formal logic it is reasonable to suppose that Marxism does not in principle exclude structural analysis. The first problem is to define the status and scope of systems and structures within the dialectic; the second is to determine the conditions and limitations within which they can be elucidated by the procedures of formal logic. But since the Marxist dialectic is materialist the precise contours of the relationship can only be determined in concrete terms, by detailed analysis of the technical problems surrounding the scientific study of history and economics. Here, as elsewhere, the truth of philosophy is eventually decided by science.

Tran Duc Thao's materialist inversion

C'est précisément parce que le contenu de la pensée hégélienne, enveloppant la presque totalité de l'histoire mondiale, tire son origine essentiellement de la réalité objective et implique en dernier analyse un matérialisme caché que Hegel a pu élaborer la conception du devenir et la méthode dialectique, qui furent les prémisses de fait de la pensée marxiste.

Tran Duc Thao, 'Le "noyau rationnel" dans la dialectique hégélienne',
La Pensée, janvier−février 1965, 4−5

It is one of the legacies of colonial conquest that France has become a centre for the activities of radical and progressive thinkers from countries under its past and present imperial domination. Forced to express themselves through the language and culture of France, these militants have repaid their tutors by enriching the literature of socialism and revolution in French. Franz Fanon, Léopold Senghor and Aimé Césaire are well-known representatives of the African and Caribbean progressive intelligentsia. But the Asian territories, less permeable to the imperialists' culture, also made significant additions to francophone culture. Indo-China, dominated by the French from the late nineteenth century until their expulsion in 1954 after the fall of Dien Bien Phu, was a point of focus for the Left as an example of successful national liberation struggles led by communist revolutionaries. On a political level, the writings of Ho Chi Minh, Vo Nguyen Giap and other Vietnamese leaders were avidly consumed. On a philosophical level, the thoughtful and consistent work of Tran Duc Thao made valuable contributions, within the French tradition, to the debates on materialist dialectics.

Author of a book on phenomenology and dialectical materialism, Tran Duc Thao was particularly concerned with questions of human consciousness, having come to Marxism from a phenomenological position.[33] He was also concerned to throw new light on the importance of Hegel in Marxist philosophy and in a seminal article of 1965 addressed the vexed question of the 'rational kernel'.[34] He suggested that Hegel's dialectic already had a rich materialist content, as it must have if its value was to be rationally explained; and that Hegel's hidden materialism was the basis on which the dialectic was formed, in contradiction with the idealism of his overall position. The Hegelian dialectic was therefore already inverted, in his view, reducing real movement to a movement of ideas, and history to its spiritual moments. Marx's task was to recreate the dialectical method on a fresh, materialist basis.

To illustrate his point, Tran Duc Thao examines three connected passages from the *Phenomenology of Mind*, showing how, in each case, Hegel analyses processes as taking place purely within consciousness, ignoring the real historical circumstances in which they arose. Hegel's analysis of desire, for example, presents the quest for satisfaction as the motor which generates biological and social relations, whereas, Tran suggests, desire can only emerge in reality on the basis of such relations preceding it. However, once it has arisen, desire appears subjectively to the individual as the source of the satisfaction process, and so in Tran's view the Hegelian account is given a foundation in reality as the subjective reflection of an objective process. Similarly, Hegel analyses human desire as the search for recognition by another consciousness, which search, Tran says, is presented as generating social relations and the struggle for life and death. In fact, he argues, Hegel has inverted the real order of historical development, but his inversion represents the dominant view in a class society, whose ruling class seeks to legitimize its exercise of power in terms of a supposed *recognition* by the ruled of the rulers' superior worth. Finally, he examines Hegel's renowned account of the Master/Slave relationship, in which the master, having conquered by virtue of his superior courage in face of death, uses the slave to obtain satisfaction, thereby confronting the slave with the fear of death and compelling him, through the creative power of work, to attain to consciousness of his own truth. Hegel, he says, ignores the historical facts of the origins and conditions of slavery, and extolls its extraordinary educative virtues. Reducing a tragic reality to the ideal movement of two consciousnesses, he points out, Hegel is able to resolve and reconcile, on a spiritual level, conflicts even as sharp as those between master and slave, without any need to change the sordid relations of material oppression and exploitation in reality. Once again, therefore, Hegel's dialectic presents real processes as they appear, inverted and idealized, in the mirror of the ruling class.

Tran Duc Thao's central argument is to give a detailed content to the concept of inversion, which Althusser strenuously tries to exorcise. Departing from the well-worn examples given in classical texts by Engels and Lenin, he attempts to show both that Hegel's dialectic reflects the movement of reality and that the reflection is in an inverted form, corresponding to the idealist conceptions of the ruling class. In so doing he gives a closer definition of Hegel's 'hidden materialism', a notion put forward by Engels and Lenin, which has been contested by some recent commentators. The Italian philosopher Lucio Colletti, for example, in his *Marxism and Hegel* (1969), suggests that the founders of dialectical materialism implied 'a materialist stance in Hegel's text' and thereby 'simply committed an error of interpretation . . . which by now lies at the basis of almost a century of theoretical Marxism'.[35] Colletti's apparently devastating conclusion is itself based on an 'error of interpretation'. Hegel's philosophy is evidently and self-avowedly idealist: the fact is banal and hardly escaped Engels and Lenin. However, within the idealist framework are analyses which, when inverted, form the basis for a materialist conception of the dialectic. It is inversion which 'reveals', or even constitutes, Hegel's materialism.

Tran Duc Thao, drawing on the *Phenomenology*, offers two types of inversion. The first type adapts Hegel's idealist description of an ostensibly universal process, restating it as a materialist description of a real, but limited, ideological process. The second type reverses the order in which Hegel presents a process occurring, showing the real order to be from material to ideal. He does not analyse the *Logic*, on which Colletti's objections are based, nor does he exhaust the types of inversion, but he does make it clear that Hegel can only be designated as materialist at the end of a work of transformation which he calls inversion. It might be argued that Tran identifies inversion with reworking, since in the second type of inversion the Hegelian forms of causality cannot survive. The identification is terminological, however, rather than conceptual, since he specifies that 'Marx n'a pas seulement transformé par un simple retournement, pour ainsi dire, la dialectique de Hegel, il a en fait complètement recréé la méthode dialectique sur une base nouvelle, matérialiste, avec un contenu nouveau'.[36] The point of keeping the term 'inversion' is to convey that there is at least some degree of continuity between the Hegelian and Marxist dialectic.

In his rich and astute analysis, Tran Duc Thao demonstrates the complexity of Marx's inversion (and reworking) of Hegel. Particular Hegelian analyses can be fruitful in different ways. They need to be assessed on the basis of an elaborated materialist dialectic which brings a critical attitude able to situate them and determine what kind of truth, if any, they will yield. In this respect Tran proves to have a more rewarding approach to Hegel than either Colletti or Althusser who reject on principle, and therefore discount, unseen, the philosopher for whom the founders of Marxism professed such esteem.

The analysis of desire is its inverted Hegelian form also has an importance beyond that of illustrating a point. It is central to the theoretical position of Freudian psychoanalysis that desire is a fundamental and constitutive component of the human psyche. The widespread penetration of Freudian ideas, and their amalgamation with notions of human experience as an autonomous realm independent of social and historical determinants has contributed to give desire the status of a primary reality to which all other human activities can be traced. The consequent psychologization of the social and human sciences tends to deny or relativize the materialist conception of history and especially the determining role of material production. Tran's two-stage argument depicts animal desire as the product of real biological relations, a 'répétition esquissée' of the content of previous experiences.[37] In human desire the animal level, having been found unsatisfactory, is superseded on the basis of human social labour, and the objective contradictions of social existence are introduced inside desire. The inadequacy of purely animal satisfactions and the desire of the human consciousness for the Other are therefore shown to have social and historical roots, even though they appear, subjectively, to be self-generating. Tran's analysis therefore offers a critical perspective on psychological theories and their unwarranted extrapolation, and a potential means of theorizing the relation between historical materialism and psychology.

Arising from this latter point, Tran's use of inversion suggests an application beyond the immediate problem of Marx's relation to Hegel. As a device for criticizing idealist conceptions and for extracting the rational content of speculative systems it is a potent and flexible instrument, the more so since it is a constant tendency of intellectual activity to regard subjective factors or conceptual constructs as more fundamental than objective factors or material reality. Hegel's is not the only speculative system which stands in need of materialist inversion. In some respects it may be compared to Jacques Derrida's inversion procedure within his strategy of deconstruction. Derrida's inversion of the usual hierarchy of speech and writing stands at the beginning of a reconceptualization of discourse; Tran's inversion of the Hegelian hierarchy of desire and its object, idea and material conditions, stands similarly at the beginning of a reformulation of psychology. But the materialist inversion has the additional characteristic that it is carried out within a materialist framework which already indicates in broad terms a social and historical order of priorities. And since 'up' and 'down' are already established, the inversion is rational rather than arbitrary.

Garaudy's pluralist dialectic

La dialectique, au contraire, tout en impliquant la nécessité d'une assimilation critique, d'une intégration de toutes les vérités partielles découvertes dans le pluralisme des hypothèses, appelle à l'effort pour le surmonter: l'hypothèse la plus vraie étant finalement celle qui se révèle capable d'intégrer toutes les autres.

Roger Garaudy, Marxisme du XXᵉ siècle, *2nd edition (Paris, 1967), 64*

The opening up of Marxism after Stalin's disgrace freed many lines of enquiry, and enabled many things to be said aloud which had previously been whispered. More important, it enabled many things to be thought which had previously been inconceivable. The richness and variety of French Marxist philosophy during the 1960s and after is ample proof of the healthy and liberating effects of destalinization. But the process also had its victims. Foremost among them was the philosopher who was most closely identified with the ideological rigidity of the Stalin era, Roger Garaudy. The frenzied quest for an alternative to his shattered orthodoxy led him into an eclectic and speculative humanism. The first stages along this path have already been traced in his *Perspectives de l'homme* of 1959, and in his work of the early 1960s. The same tendencies received a particularly clear confirmation in his very popular book *Marxisme du XX^c siècle* (Paris, 1966). In it he proposed a restatement of the major problems of Marxist philosophy in the light of a thorough-going attack on dogmatism. Much of the controversy following the book's publication focused on his discussion of ethics, religion and art, and his conception of the progressive forces. But his general perspective is amply reflected in the exposition of dialectical materialism with which the work begins.[38] It contains a number of important shifts which echo those he suggested in other fields and constitute a redefinition of the materialist dialectic.

Garaudy began by describing Marxism as a critical philosophy, in the Kantian sense, as opposed to a dogmatism. Eighteenth-century materialism was characteristically dogmatic, he suggested, and therefore was not the major philosophical source of Marxism. That honour went to German idealism, exemplified by Kant, Fichte and Hegel, he said, and only dogmatists would subordinate their importance to writers like Feuerbach, Diderot and Spinoza. Marxist materialism was simply a call for modesty, to recognize the independent existence of the world and the provisional nature of our conceptual models of it. He rejected the notion that any knowledge was ever absolute in the sense of being permanently valid in its present formulation. Whatever was true in present knowledge would be subsumed into a higher stage of knowledge, he thought, and thus Marxism was a working hypothesis like any other and could only be declared superior to others if it succeeded in integrating all the partial truths contained in the other hypotheses. The consequent pluralism of enquiry recognized the potential validity of even diametrically opposed views, and was offered as a further safeguard against dogmatism. The scientific status of Marxism, he argued, could only be protected from degenerating into speculation by virtue of criticism and the experimental method which ensure the active role of knowledge and the importance of practice as its guarantor.

Though he continued to assert the existence of a dialectic of nature, Garaudy now saw it as a statement that the structure and movement of reality are such that only dialectical thought can make phenomena intelligible and allow them to be handled. He offered it as a working hypothesis and elaborated on his view of dialectical reason as reason in the process of being formed, the art of formulating questions, a guide rather than a determinant of action, and an element in the rational construction of reality. He was especially anxious to distinguish the rational conception of matter from the 'thing-in-itself', a potential confusion which he rejected as dogmatic. He followed the Protestant theologian Paul Ricoeur in insisting that the 'horizon' of knowledge should never be reified into a thing. He outlined a view of Marxist humanism which would integrate every contribution that the twentieth century has made to the notions of reality, truth, beauty or morality. It would be totally pluralistic, and would follow structuralism in taking relation rather than being as its fundamental category, and in using the method of reasoning by analogy.

It is a curious comment on Garaudy's development that he should now disavow those French materialists which twenty years earlier he had so ardently championed. Where his *Les Sources françaises du socialisme scientifique* (Paris, 1948) had presented Marx as the philosophical heir of the eighteenth-century Enlightenment, *Le Marxisme du XXᶜ siècle* denounced those ancestors as dogmatists and replaced them with German idealists. Moreover, the German tradition he now espoused was not the fertile acres of classical German philosophy as a whole, but very much its idealist enclosures, pre-eminently represented by the subjectivist Fichte. Even Hegel no longer found the same favour as previously, being frequently rebuked for his efforts to encompass knowledge in a monistic system. The change of ancestry is more consistent with what he wished to abandon than with the position he wished to take up. Diderot, D'Holbach, Spinoza and Feuerbach are most firmly associated with materialism. Though Diderot at times achieved a near dialectical conception and Feuerbach did not wholly abandon the Hegelian dialectic, it may fairly be argued that they all held a mechanical rather than a dialectical materialism. To that extent Garaudy is right to criticize them, though the blanket label of dogmatism is not a fair or accurate description. But for all their limitations they made important and progressive contributions to the formation of Marxism. Their exclusion is a preliminary to an assault on materialism as such, which Garaudy seeks to undertake on the longer term. Conversely, the heavy overemphasis which he had given to the

French materialists in the 1940s was in response to the fierce attack under which materialism came during that period.

The rejection of Feuerbach and the eclipse of Hegel in favour of Kant and Fichte indicate the movement from an objective monism towards a subjective pluralism, from synthesis to eclecticism, and once more from materialism to idealism. While the primary victim in the change is a coherent materialist dialectic, it is not clear that Garaudy's alternative can be so easily defined. Some aspects of his analysis are consistent with Marxist philosophy, but his underlying logic is to loosen the connections between the different aspects of Marxism to enable it to incorporate the essentials of Christianity, existentialism and structuralism.

Pluralism is a key notion in this strategy, shored up by the Kantian concept of an undefinable thing-in-itself and the consequent relativisation of knowledge. Since knowledge is conceived as production rather than reflection, the initial link between thought and the world is cut. Though he retains practice as the criterion of knowledge, there is an increased emphasis on practice as the object of knowledge at the expense of a more general object: being. The notion that knowledge applies to its own shifting horizon as a human activity is almost a restatement of the Kantian view that we can never know the things themselves and that the best we can manage is a series of more or less sophisticated hypotheses. In this way Garaudy increasingly, though as yet not entirely, cuts thought off from the world and renders knowledge a collection of ingenious but unprovable guesses. This relativistic conception of knowledge opens the way for pluralism. Since there is no proof, either now or ever, that one view is better than another, and since all views, however antagonistic, contain a portion of truth, Garaudy sees the ideal position as the one which can best incorporate all the others. Openness, tolerance and liberalism are thus the cardinal virtues, and indeed may pass for a philosophy in the absence of a more closely defined synthesis.

Garaudy's catch-all ecumenism is a poor shadow of the conservative dialectic of Hegelian idealism. A shadow because it tries to encompass all contemporary thought; a poor one because it is entirely eclectic with little pretence of a coherent synthesis. He is grossly mistaken in regarding it as the duty of Marxism to include all of thought and culture. The use to which Marx put Hegel and Feuerbach, to choose but two, is ample evidence. In each case, he subjected them to far-reaching criticism, incorporating their ideas only to the extent that he could rework them and synthesize them into a unified conception. On the other hand there were many other contemporaries for whom Marx had no time and no use: he wasted no effort searching for the rational kernel of Schelling or Schopenhauer, for instance.

The political correlative of the all-embracing philosophy put forward by Garaudy is an indiscriminate and non-directional coalition of all parties and forces. The criterion of maximum incorporation transfers directly from ideas to social movements. Since no one group or movement is inherently more important than another, the ideal becomes the widest possible unity. The working class is no more privileged by Garaudy on a political level than is dialectical materialism on a philosophical level. Both are judged strictly on their ability to unify. Just as Marxism must unify all philosophical positions, so the proletariat must unify all classes and political orientations. The class struggle is substantially attenuated, and while Garaudy does not yet abandon it explicitly, it ceases to play any functional part in his conception of history. In the same way Garaudy also tends to obscure the opposition between materialism and idealism, and to erode the distinction between dialectics and other forms of rationality. His is a declining Marxism, slowly losing its distinctness and identity both as a philosophy and as a political strategy. Garaudy slips into a philosophy of that twilight, against which even Hegel warned, where all cows are grey.

Though its author was a member of the PCF's Political Bureau, Garaudy's book did not go unchallenged. A favourable review by Jacques Roux in *Les Cahiers du communisme* provoked critical responses from Jean Kanapa and Lucien Sève, to which Roux, Garaudy and Philippe Fuchsmann replied.[39] A laudatory review in *La Pensée* by Michel Brossard was answered in the same journal with an authoritative critique by the leading geologist Jean Orcel.[40] The debate covered a wide range of issues, including relations between Marxism and humanism, Christianity, existentialism, and structuralism. It dealt with philosophy, politics, economics, the natural and the human sciences. Many questions were hammered out in fine detail and many others thrown polemically about the arena. Garaudy's general orientation was causing increasing concern as he moved further along the line he had laid down. It was opposed now not only by the Althusserian wing of the PCF, whose views have already been outlined, but even by intellectuals who had tended to steer between them and Garaudy. In essence, what was taking place was a political struggle to define the political direction of the PCF. Like Lefebvre before him, Garaudy was pursuing the objective of a maximum alliance in which no principle was allowed to pose any kind of obstacle. Philosophically, he strove to define a Marxism in which the materialist dialectic would be broadened to envelop non-materialist and non-dialectical approaches, and hence would be flexible enough to be reconciled with almost any theoretical principles. The only positions Garaudy now found himself unable to tolerate were those of his own colleagues who sought to place some limits on who might be considered an ally in the struggle for socialism, and on what ideas could now pass for Marxism.

Sève and the scientific dialectic

S'en tenir au fait que Marx ne cite qu'une fois explicitement la négation de la négation par son nom dans Le Capital est une attitude étonnamment superficielle. Qu'on réfléchisse simplement au fait que tout phénomène cyclique, tout processus de forme spirale, étant movement de sortie de soi puis de retour partiel à soi, est en son essence même négation de la négation, et on constatera qu'en réalité il n'y a dans Le Capital, guère de chapitre dans lequel, du simple échange marchandise-argent-marchandise au retour périodique de la crise, cette figure fondamentale de la dialectique marxiste qu'est la négation de la négation ne soit pratiquement à l'oeuvre.

Lucien Sève, Marxisme et théorie de la personnalité,
4th edition (Paris, 1975), 567

Within the PCF, Roger Garaudy's waning influence slumped rapidly after his Marxisme du XXe siècle (1966). His most intransigent opponent, Louis Althusser, made little headway in replacing him with the contentious theoreticism of his two major works Pour Marx (1965) and Lire le Capital (1965). Thus, although it is tempting to see French Marxism of the 1960s as a battle between these two philosophers, the real picture is more complex. Speaking at the Argenteuil meeting of the PCF's Central Committee in 1966, a senior philosopher, Guy Besse, warned that there should be no question of a philosophical boxing match, pitting, as it were, the holder Garaudy against the challenger Althusser for the title of official party ideologist.[41] Even by 1968 it was clear that neither of the two opposed schools of thought was able to prevail, and that the majority of observers had serious reservations about both, whatever their acknowledged merits. Most of the philosophers on the Central Committee were in this middle position, and were concerned that the party should not be railroaded into erroneous and dangerous excesses, while at the same time remaining open to new ideas and interpretations. These writers, including philosophers Guy Besse, Jean Kanapa, Michel Simon and others with less immediately philosophical preoccupations, did not themselves for the most part offer extensive or original contributions to philosophy. It was left to another of their number, Lucien Sève, to attempt a philosophical synthesis which went beyond reiteration of the classics but steered between the Althusserian and Garaudian conceptions.

Sève was younger than Garaudy or Althusser, was based in Marseille rather than Paris, and had been a Central Committee member from 1961. He had been involved in a polemic with Henri Lefebvre before and after the latter's expulsion,[42] and had an initial skirmish with Garaudy as early as 1962.[43] His intervention at Argenteuil was directed largely against Garaudy, though he had pertinent criticisms of Althusser, and was primarily concerned to clear the ground for a renewal of Marxist thought which would build on the achievements of the two thinkers without falling into their errors, and which would better incorporate the positive developments of the whole Marxist tradition. As an educationalist, he was concerned to elaborate a coherent psychology in the light of Marxism, and applied himself to produce a bulky treatise on the subject, *Marxisme et théorie de la personnalité* (Paris, 1969), on which his national and international reputation largely rests. The major focus of the work is an analysis of anthropology in the broadest sense, understood as a theory of human existence. It therefore outlines what Sève considers to be the scientific humanism of Marxism, based on historical materialism and the materialist dialectic. Sève subjects various forms of humanism and anti-humanism to critical scrutiny before presenting his concept of psychology and his theory of human personality, both of which depend on the centrality of social relations. In the process, he elaborates on many of the contentious questions of Marxist philosophy and attempts to develop an integrated position which is directly applicable to the problems of the human sciences.

In his study, Sève offers an analysis of the Marxist conception of man, drawing out the characteristic features of Marx's own position. Concerned not to be led into neo-Hegelian speculative humanism, he sketches the development of the Marxist dialectic in its relation to the idealist Hegelian dialectic, and seeks to highlight the essential differences between the two. He locates the first and most fundamental differentiation in Marx's essay *Critique of Hegel's Philosophy of Right* (1843), where Hegel is criticized for limiting contradiction to phenomena while arguing for unity in the essence of things. Marx on the contrary conceives contradiction as essential and constructive. For Sève, then, Hegel's dialectic is mystified both in its status and in its content. Its status is mystified by virtue of Hegel's refusal to envisage a material basis for contradiction; its content is vitiated by Hegel's method of imposing the same pre-established categories on all empirical facts. Marx's method on the contrary is to grasp the particular logic of particular objects. Hegel's dialectic is therefore speculative rather than critical, abstract rather than concrete, and fundamentally conservative, says Sève, since it has no difficulty in resolving any contradictions in thought. The mystery of how it should have any value at all is solved, in Sève's view, by the fact that, contrary to Hegel's own idealist view, his dialectic originated as a reflection of objective reality. Once this fact is affirmed, he suggests, the first stage of 'inversion' is completed. The second stage, that of scientific re-elaboration, is on the contrary a long-term task, in a sense infinite, because it involves continual reappraisal in the light of scientific and political developments. 'On doit s'y garder', he suggests, 'à la fois de la tentation de conserver de façon insuffisamment critique des catégories hégéliennes, ce que conduirait partiellement à la spéculation – et de méconnaître le noyau de vérité qu'elles contiennent, c'est-à-dire de régresser du point de vue théorique.'[44]

Sève himself sets to work a variety of dialectical concepts, redefining the original Hegelian categories in terms which can be integrated into a Marxist framework. As an example of this process, the concept of 'negation of the negation', dismissed successively by Stalin and Althusser, is rehabilitated by Sève. The 'negation of the negation' is an expression normally used to denote the process by which one component of a contradiction gives rise to its contrary, or negation, which is in turn negated to restore something of the original characteristics in a different form at a higher level. Sève suggests that Marx rejected the speculative Hegelian version, in which a contradiction is 'sublated' or transcended (dépassée) in a higher unity. Instead, he says, the Marxist version states that the material conditions necessary for a contradiction, and any 'sublation', are abolished and replaced by new conditions. The resulting 'spiral' form of movement is readily found, says Sève, in all the works of Marxism, including practically every chapter of Capital. Against Althusser, he asserts that a category, such as negation of the negation, is not confined to the instances where it is explicitly named. Consequently he proposes the overcoming of alienation, the emancipatory function of socialism, the recurrence of crises, and even the simple process of commodity exchange as examples of the negation of the negation.[45]

In effect, Sève retains only the most general form of the Hegelian category: movement in 'spirals'. Its content and function is quite changed. It does not prove anything or impose a form on events, rather it is produced by certain events and perceived as a regularity inherent in certain processes. But in each case the pattern is the result of specific and highly differentiated determinants which have to be grasped in their concrete detail, and cannot be reduced to the general movement. The strength and weakness of his position is that it is a beginning rather than an end to enquiry. Strength, because it enables philosophical analysis to play a supportive role in scientific investigation without pre-empting its conclusions. Weakness, because the validity of philosophical assertions remains dependent on the development of scientific knowledge. In relation to the Althusserian account, Sève's lacks the circularity and self-containedness of self-supporting knowledge. But the resulting 'weakness' is attenuated first by the fact that philosophical generalizations are nourished by the development of science so far, and second by the need for philosophy to remain open for future scientific developments if it is to aspire to the condition of science and therefore knowledge. Fundamentally, Sève and Althusser differ in how they conceive the relation of science to philosophy, though the latter's subsequent evolution to some extent brings him closer to Sève, with a recognition of the dependence of philosophy on science.

Sève's treatise rapidly became an authoritative document, combining, as it did, extensive philosophical discussion with the elements of a new Marxist approach to psychology. The wide range of subjects dealt with makes it something of a compendium of Marxist philosophy, though its main focus, the conception of man and the theory of personality are outside the scope of the present study. While he did not replace Garaudy within the PCF, the notion of official philosopher having been abandoned, Sève undoubtedly assumed the position of leading representative of the main philosophical orientation within the party. His appointment in 1970 as director of Editions sociales confirmed the confidence he enjoyed, and he has played an important role in guiding philosophical enquiry since that time.

References

1   Lucien Sève, 'Panorama de la philosophie française contemporaine', *La Pensée*, mars – avril 1960, 75.
2   J. Milhau, 'Contribution à l'histoire de la philosophie en France', *La Nouvelle critique*, décembre 1958, 66 – 80; janvier 1959, 74 – 91; reprinted in his *Chroniques philosophiques* (Paris, 1972). The phrase quoted occurs in the *Chroniques*, p. 102.
3   W. Rochet, 'Problèmes philosophiques', *Cahiers du communisme*, février 1962, 98 – 125.
4   R. Garaudy, 'Les tâches des philosophes|communistes et la critique des erreurs philosophiques de Staline: Rapport', *Cahiers du communisme*, juillet – août 1962, 75 – 106.

5   *Ibid.*, 88.

6   See quotation at the head of this section.

7   Garaudy, 'Les tâches des philosophes communistes', 88.

8   P. Togliatti, 'De Hegel au marxisme', *La Nouvelle critique*, février 1955, 22–36.

9   A. Cornu, *Karl Marx et Friedrich Engels*, 3 vols (Paris, 1955, 1958, 1962).

10   'Sur le jeune Marx', *Recherches internationales*, 19, mai–juin 1960.

11   M. Thorez, 'Les tâches des philosophes communistes et la critique des erreurs philosophiques de Staline', *Cahiers du communisme*, juillet–août 1962, 72–74, p. 74.

12   R. Garaudy, *Dieu est mort: Etude sur Hegel* (Paris, 1962), 413. See also R. Garaudy, *Le Problème hégélien* (Paris, n.d.), published by CERM in 1963.

13   Special number, 'Réflexions sur le culte de la personnalité', *La Nouvelle critique*, décembre 1963.

14   M. Godelier, 'Les structures de la méthode du *Capital* de Karl Marx', *Economie et politique*, mai 1960, 35–52, juin 1960, 15–36; reprinted in his *Rationalité et irrationalité en économie* (Paris, 1969), II, 30–105.

15   *Rationalité*, II, 31.

16   *Ibid.*, 35.

17   *Ibid.*, 65.

18   See quotation at the head of this section.

19   M. Godelier, 'Quelques aspects de la méthode du *Capital*', *Economie et politique*, mars 1961, 49–63; reprinted in *Rationalité et irrationalité en économie*, II, 106–124.

20   *Rationalité*, II, 107–108.

21   *Ibid.*, 109.

22   *Ibid.*, 114.

23   K. Marx, *Grundrisse* (London, 1973), 881.

24   K. Marx, *Capital* (London, 1970), 35.

25   M. Godelier, 'Economie politique et philosophie', *La Pensée*, septembre–octobre 1963, 98–112; reprinted in *Rationalité et irrationalité en économie*, II, 6–29.

26   *Rationalité*, II, 18.

27   *Ibid.*, I, 120.

28   M. Godelier, 'Système, structure et contradiction dans *Le Capital*', *Les Temps modernes*, 246, novembre 1966, 828–864; reprinted in his *Horizons, trajets marxistes en anthropologie* (Paris, 1977), II, 71–113; translated in part in *Structuralism: a reader*, edited by M. Lane (London, 1970), 340–358.

29   Marx, *Grundrisse*, 93.

30   *Ibid.*, 100.

31   V. I. Lenin, *Collected Works*, XXXVIII (Moscow, 1961), 359.

32   F. Engels, *Dialectics of Nature* (Moscow, 1972), 62.

33   Tran Duc Thao, *Phénoménologie et matérialisme dialectique* (Paris, 1951); see also his *Recherches sur l'origine de la conscience* (Paris, 1973).

34   Tran Duc Thao, 'Le "noyau rationnel" dans la dialectique hégélienne', *La Pensée*, janvier–février 1965, 3–23.

35 L. Colletti, *Marxism and Hegel* (London, 1973), 27.

36 Tran Duc Thao, 'Le "noyau rationnel"', 5.

37 *Ibid.*, 8.

38 R. Garaudy, *Marxisme du XXe siècle* 2nd edition (Paris, 1967), 49 – 104.

39 J. Roux, 'Le Marxisme du XXe siècle', *Cahiers du communisme*, janvier 1967, 151 – 153; various writers, 'A propos de quelques questions de philosophie', *Cahiers du communisme*, juillet – août 1967, 107 – 137.

40 M. Brossard, 'Marxisme du XXe siècle', *La Pensée*, janvier – février 1967, 106 – 112; Jean Orcel, 'Remarques à propos du livre de Roger Garaudy', *La Pensée*, juillet – août 1967, 66 – 78.

41 G. Besse, 'Le communisme, la culture et le dialogue', *Cahiers du communisme*, mai – juin 1966, 179 – 191, p. 183.

42 L. Sève, 'Henri Lefebvre et la dialectique chez Marx', *La Nouvelle critique*, mars 1958, 55 – 89; L. Sève, *La Différence* (Paris, 1960).

43 See L. Sève, *La Philosophie française contemporaine et sa genèse de 1789 à nos jours* (Paris, 1962).

44 L. Sève, *Marxisme et théorie de la personnalité*, 4th edition (Paris, 1975), 120.

45 See quotation at the head of this section.

8

Changes

1968 – 1974

1968

On a pu constater à la faveur des journées de lutte de mai – juin que les idées socialistes ont gagné de nouvelles couches de travailleurs manuels et intellectuels, même s'il est vrai que la façon de concevoir le socialisme diffère chez les uns et les autres.

Par exemple, dans les milieux d'employés, d'intellectuels, d'étudiants, des conceptions petites-bourgeoises du socialisme se sont montrées vivaces, comme on pouvait s'y attendre. Mais le grand fait, c'est que les idées de Marx et de Lénine, loin de rester des formules d'école froides et dogmatiques, deviennent toujours davantage le bien des masses.

Waldeck Rochet, 'Rapport au comité central', Cahiers du
communisme, *janvier 1969, 145*

Philosophy does not move with the same rhythm as politics. Not that it is Minerva's owl, taking flight, as Hegel said, at dusk. Nor the crowing cock, announcing the dawn of a new day. Neither wisdom after the event, nor anticipatory vision, or rather a degree of both, philosophy has a close but mediated relationship with other forms of historical change. Thus the dramatic moments of 1968 were not immediately matched by any spectacular shifts or innovations on a theoretical level. The events of May and June in France; political assassinations, racial riots and student demonstrations in America; student and worker protests in Germany and Italy; the Tet offensive in Vietnam; and the Warsaw Pact intervention in Czechoslovakia; all these had far-reaching effects in political and social terms. But their ideological impact was complex and difficult to localize.

In France, the May events and Czechoslovakia were the focus for major political reassessments. Each has been the subject of extensive and impassioned discussion, which it is not proposed here to repeat or summarize. But in each case the effect was to intensify and accelerate the development of existing modes of thought rather than to introduce any new element of reflection. It is true that the student milieu became a seething cauldron of ideas during the intoxicating spring 'contestation'. The multiplicity of groups and the variety of opinion created a highly diversified and dynamic process of collective reflection, most of which lay within or on the margins of Marxism. Communists, Maoists, Trotskyites, anarchists, situationists, existentialists and others thrashed out their differences and agreements with vehemence and often violence. Each group claimed to see its own ideas vindicated and its opponents discredited by the process of events, but the ideas themselves were those of an earlier generation. The student neophytes seized on the texts of Marx, Lenin, Trotsky, Bakunin, Marcuse and Sartre to articulate their grievances and aspirations. Many felt that revolution was on the agenda, and even those who did not were anxious to hasten far-reaching reforms. Accordingly, the central concern was immediate social and political change. And though they were not absent, the more abstract considerations of philosophy were low in priority and subordinate to more urgent issues.

The effervescence of ideas was not confined to schools and universities. In the workplaces, the residential localities, the cultural centres, the streets and cafés, and at meetings of groups and organizations of all descriptions, similar issues were being debated in different terms and different contexts. But again the focus was on present and future social change. Existing philosophical frameworks were mobilized to elaborate strategy and tactics, forms of organization, long- and short-term demands and means of achieving them. Some gains were made: wage increases, limited democratizations and some restructuring. But in the wake of the massive right-wing election victory of June 1968, these gains were quickly eroded and the movement of May was rolled back. The overall failure of the movement to bring about significant and lasting change meant that no new social and political basis was created in France from which new ideas might grow. At best it meant that new strategic and tactical objectives might be defined, which in their turn might be reflected in a shifting configuration of theoretical positions. The intensive interchange of ideas which had occurred also contributed to modifying the philosphical views of individual thinkers as part of a generalized cross-fertilization between different currents of the Left. The effects of it were, however, at least partly counteracted by the widespread sectarianism which often degenerated into bitter recriminations as the dust subsided and the disconsolate revolutionaries licked their wounds and counted the grievous cost.

In a different sense, the Czechoslovakian crisis also left a divisive and destructive mark on the French Left. The liberalizations proposed by the Dubček government were followed with close interest in France; the PCF gave a qualified support to the new orientations, and it was widely felt that the Czech experience might hold important lessons for the development of socialism in France. The August intervention of the Warsaw Pact forces came as a severe shock to both supporters and opponents of Dubček's direction. The first saw their hopes nipped in the bud while the second saw their fears confirmed with appalling speed. For both, the outcome was a failure of catastrophic proportions. The PCF initially protested against the intervention, then withdrew its censure, before reaffirming it once more. In other words, it was divided; the polemics which followed made it clear that the affair had aggravated rather than resolved the range of problems bound up in it. Its effect was to complicate and prolong debate on the means of achieving socialism. Correspondingly, philosophical development was not immediately altered, though the contending alternatives became counterposed with increasing sharpness. In the years that followed, Garaudy's evolution accelerated to the point of his exclusion from the PCF, the Althusserians gradually became isolated as a dissident faction within the party, and a median position was slowly established between the two.

The basic orientation of the PCF was not changed by 1968. From a political point of view its policy of constructing a left alliance as an alternative to the Gaullist regime was rendered more urgent rather than undermined by the events. That, at any rate, was its own assessment. The electoral agreements between communists and socialists during the mid-1960s had already led in early 1968 to the beginning of negotiations with a view to a common programme. The manifest inability of the PCF, SFIO and the centrist Radicals to provide effective political leadership during the great class confrontation of May led to anxious reappraisals. At the end of the year the PCF produced its Champigny manifesto laying the basis for a strategy of alliances aimed at establishing a government of popular and democratic unity to take France to socialism by way of advanced democracy.[1] Tortuous and long drawn-out negotiations ensued, until eventually four years after the May events, the Common Programme was signed, providing the platform of the major forces of the political Left for the mid-1970s. The orientation was by no means uncontested, even within the parties involved, let alone among the assorted ultra-left groups which flourished in the years immediately following 1968. Nevertheless, it provided the point of focus for left-wing politics and the context within which Marxist theory developed.

The pluralist political perspective was echoed in the growing acceptance of diversity among Marxists, even within the PCF. It was not a novelty, but the range of divergences widened continually. The sharp polarization between Garaudy and Althusser dated back to the early 1960s, and no administrative measures were taken to resolve the contention. The PCF's Central Committee meeting at Argenteuil in the spring of 1966 studiously avoided defining an 'orthodox' philosophical position in its lengthy discussion of cultural and ideological questions. Its final resolution recognized the need for debate and research, and declared that 'le Parti communiste ne saurait contrarier ces débats ni apporter une vérité a priori, encore moins trancher de façon autoritaire des discussions non achevées entre spécialistes'.[2] The policy of non-interference in science, philosophy and culture did not exclude political intervention on political issues, but it formalized the substantial autonomy which intellectuals enjoyed in pursuing their specialist interests. May 1968 confirmed the need for openness and diversity if Marxists were to understand and articulate the groping and experimentation of new aspirations, ideas, forms of organization and expression. The policy of cultural and intellectual pluralism was therefore developed with increasing enthusiasm throughout the 1970s.

The most noticeable change which this evolution produced in philosophy was its increasing assimilation to scientific research. The development of the sciences, the acceleration of discoveries, and the expanding economic importance of scientific activity, contributed substantially to the process, generating a growing demand for philosophical work on questions of method, concepts, categories and general theory. The emphasis on the cognitive role of philosophy correspondingly reduced the importance accorded to social and political determinants – at least during discussions between philosophers. The class nature of ideas was rarely invoked as an argument, even if it sometimes underlay other arguments. There was greater willingness to recognize the valuable aspects of opponents' work and a reluctance to reduce differences to class or political alignments. The tone and posture of debate became more exploratory and less conflictual. These were, of course, tendencies rather than absolute changes, and did not exclude harsh polemics and even bitter antagonisms. The three dominant figures of Marxist philosophy during the late 1960s, Garaudy, Althusser and Sève, scarcely disguised their mutual hostility and even at times contempt. But as the 1970s progressed, the different schools of thought tended to reach working arrangements and even a measure of co-operation.

Profound social and political changes played an important part in producing greater consensus among philosophers. The bulk of them were state employees who had very material grounds for agreement on remuneration, living standards and working conditions, all of which deteriorated perceptibly, especially during the economic crisis of the mid-decade. Many of them, employed in schools, universities and research units, were seriously affected by the reductions in finance for science and education. Philosophy teachers in particular were directly threatened by the Haby reforms which sought to eliminate philosophy from the curriculum. Moreover, in the wake of the great upheavals, the prestige of Marxism in France, especially among students and intellectuals, had undergone another dramatic increase. The demand for Marxist writings is a token of that: Editions 10/18, Editions sociales, François Maspéro and others found an insatiable market for Marxist classics, thematic anthologies, collections of essays, symposia and theoretical studies of all descriptions. One primary motivation in French government education policy was to counteract the effects of this development. The schools and universities were generally regarded as hot-beds of Marxism and revolution; philosophy teaching, like history, attracted growing proportions of committed Marxists. The continuing struggles surrounding the teaching of the humanities in France are in large measure ideological struggles over the strength and influence of Marxism.

Concomitant with these changes, the 1970s witnessed a huge expansion of Marxist writing of all descriptions. The tendency was already visible in the late 1950s and 1960s, but the 1970s saw a multiplication of groups, journals, publishing houses and bookshops devoted to the literature of the Left. And those already existing found their operations expanding. Even a cursory survey of the wealth and diversity of these developments would be a major undertaking, but a glance at the catalogues of François Maspéro and Editions sociales, the two Marxist-oriented publishers, reveals a dramatic increase in the numbers, range and variety of books and collections published from the late 1960s onwards. Since the present study is concerned primarily with writers in the ambit of communist Marxism, it will not be possible to give close attention to the work of writers associated with the Maoist, Trotskyite, anarcho-syndicalist, revolutionary Christian, existentialist and other smaller currents of Marxism. And even within these limits a severe selection must be imposed on the volume of material available. In the nature of things, discussion of contemporary writings can scarcely hope to evade the exercise of personal taste and judgement. But in the necessarily selective presentation of post-68 Marxist philosophy, it is hoped to examine those works which from a political or conceptual point of view have the most importance and interest.

The fate of Garaudy

Si le Parti ne veut pas être une secte de doctrinaires, mais le levain
de toutes les forces qui, en France, veulent construire le socialisme,
il ne peut avoir une 'philosophie officielle', il ne peut être, en son
principe, ni idéaliste, ni matérialiste, ni religieux, ni athée.

Roger Garaudy, Le Grand tournant du socialisme *(Paris, 1969), 284*

The events of 1968 affected philosophy in the first instance by
accelerating and intensifying the development of those currents of
thought which were already established. Roger Garaudy, the major
political casualty of 1968 among communist philosophers, well
illustrates the process. In the same way as Henri Lefebvre's
philosophical and political development was accelerated by 1956, so
Garaudy's was by 1968. It has already been seen how, under the guise of
a pluralist dialectic, Garaudy moved towards a universalizing stance in
which all differences were to be reconciled in a single humanist frame.
The speculative electicism of his philosophy echoed his politics of the
open house from which none should be turned away. In both respects
the late 1960s saw Garaudy propelled along his chosen path to accept its
logical outcome.

When the events of 1968 plunged French Marxists into confusion and
division, Garaudy was unhesitating in his support for the student
movement and the Czech liberalization, seeing them both as
expressions of his own perspective. He outlined the reasons for it in two
books: *Peut-on être communiste aujourd'hui?* published in April 1968 and
republished later that year as *Pour un modèle français du socialisme*; and
Le Grand tournant du socialisme, published in 1969 in reaction to the two
'printemps avortés'.[3] He now identified the development of science and
technology as the major source of oppression, and attempted to define a
theoretical humanism which would direct the struggle against it. As
political means, he adopted the notion of a national strike carried out
with the aid of a new block of social forces which would be able to grasp
and wield the historical initiative and overcome the fundamental
contradiction between the possible and the real. As the leaders of this
movement he singled out the intellectuals and the youth of the world.
Urging this new perspective on the PCF, he also argued that it was time
to abandon the notion of an 'official' philosophy, and that pluralism
required a party to be neither idealist nor materialist, neither religious
nor atheist.[4]

The inadequacies, hesitations and confusions in the PCF's response to
the May and August events gave weight to Garaudy's call for a

reappraisal of the party's global strategy. Neither event was anticipated and neither fitted easily into the policy framework of the party. For Garaudy, on the other hand, they came as if in answer to a prayer, the living embodiment of the direction he was promoting. The fact that both movements ended in failure in no way moderated his enthusiasm but rather served to reinforce his convictions with speculation of what their outcome might have been. This incautious interpretation, however, depended on the evacuation of any notion of fundamental antagonisms between capitalism and socialism internationally, and between capital and labour domestically. Historical materialism was replaced by speculative humanism. The dynamic of history no longer lay in class struggle (between worker and capitalist) but in the overcoming of alienation (man against the machine); the decisive forces were no longer the exploited (workers) but the alienated (all men); and their leaders were not the most exploited (proletariat) but those most conscious of their alienation (youth, students, intellectuals).

On a theoretical level, Garaudy's development followed its inner logic which was also the logic of his politics: the dismemberment and liquidation of Marxism. He declared the need for a radical separation of philosophy from politics, scarcely distinguishable from the separation of theory from practice. Having removed this keystone of Marxism, he urged the extension of pluralism to the extent of declaring philosophy a matter of personal preference, and politics a matter of individual initiative. Neither, he thought, should be subject to institutional forms. Though he did not explicitly discount the possibility of a role for the Communist Party, it was clear that Garaudy was not far from proposing the elimination of parties from politics, a position he effectively adopted in his subsequent book L'Alternative (Paris, 1972). And though he did not explicitly dismiss the possibility of rational knowledge, it was apparent that he already considered it an inadequate mode of cognition, ready to be superseded, as he later suggested, by faith and creative imagination.

The dissolution of Marxism and the Marxist party to which he belonged were not openly declared objectives of Garaudy in 1968 and 1969, but they were stitched into the fabric of his writings for any who cared to look. Nor could his religious conversion and burgeoning Catholic faith come as a surprise when they were eventually disclosed, for they were wholly consistent with his development. At what stage they occurred, how far they were causes, and how far effects, these are interesting, but secondary, biographical questions. At all events, they were not explicitly invoked in the incidents which terminated Garaudy's career as a communist. Nor, for that matter, was his general philosophical evolution a major factor. His exclusion from the PCF was primarily based on political divergences concerning May 1968 and Czechoslovakia and his publication of growing numbers of contributions and attacks directed against his party's policies both domestic and international, against the world communist movement as a whole, and against socialist countries in particular. His book *Le Grand tournant du socialisme* precipitated the culmination when he was expelled by the party's 19th Congress in February 1970.

Though Garaudy nailed his flag to the Prague and Paris springs of 1968, they confirmed and accelerated a development which had begun a dozen years earlier. But the movement was neither smooth nor linear. Political events played a vital role in the evolution of his conceptual apparatus, which in turn gave a kind of coherence to his political options. The comprehensive rejection of dogmatism which he initiated in 1956 gradually came to dominate his thought and became its guiding principle, gradually transforming itself into a rejection of any constraints, even conceptual ones, on thought or action. Eventually it led to the rejection of any order or organization, ultimately denying rationality and concerted political action, and any link between the two. In place of an integrated synthesis, Garaudy offered dissolution and disintegration. Similarly the rejection of sectarianism led him to seek dialogue with non-Marxists, but in his pursuit of agreement he gradually came to water down disagreements and divergences, searching for a convergence at the most general level in which all beliefs would be reconciled. By this path too he was led to break down distinctions and differences of belief or behaviour, eventuating in a dream of human oneness sharply at odds with reality and serving at best as an opium substitute.

The tragedy was that Garaudy's problems were real ones: democracy, spontaneity, the strategy for socialism, political alliances, the integration of contemporary scientific and conceptual advances, the emergence of new social forces, new forms of organization, new modes of awareness, new types of social and international relationships. But real problems are not settled by imaginery solutions. The speculative all-reconciling humanism Garaudy proposed was an illusory synthesis, whose practical incapacity was reflected in its theoretical confusions. It is true that some of his suggestions and analyses have been taken up by French and other communist parties. But since he adopted a very eclectic attitude to ideas circulating around him, it is by no means surprising that some of his views are stimulating and valuable, and that others can be developed and adapted to become such. There is no preordained frontier separating that which can be synthesized with

Marxism and that which cannot. Moreover, it is not excluded that other Marxists may, to a greater or lesser extent, share the general perspectives outlined by Garaudy without sharing his philosophical or political fate. In France, in 1970 at least, Garaudy's position had the practical and conceptual consequences which have been outlined. Their outcome in other circumstances, in a different place, or at a different time can only be hypothesized.

Development of Althusser's Theory

Nous pouvons avancer la proposition suivante: la philosophie serait la politique continuée d'une certaine manière, dans un certain domaine, à propos d'une certaine réalité. La philosophie représenterait la politique dans le domaine de la théorie, pour être plus précis: auprès des sciences – et *vice versa*, la philosophie représenterait la scientificité dans la politique, auprès des classes engagées dans la lutte des classes

Louis Althusser, Lénine et la philosophie (Paris, 1972), 42

C'est dans la téléologie que gît le vrai Sujet hégélien. Otez, *si possible*, la téléologie, reste cette catégorie philosophique dont Marx a hérité: la catégorie de *procès sans sujet*. Voilà la dette principale *positive* de Marx à l'égard de Hegel: le concept de *procès sans sujet*.

Louis Althusser, Lénine et la philosophie (Paris, 1972), 69–70

Following the trenchant essays of *Pour Marx*, Louis Althusser applied his conception of the materialist dialectic to an analysis of Marx's masterwork, *Capital*. The result was elaborated together with a team of young associates, Etienne Balibar, Jacques Rancière, Pierre Macherey and Roger Establet, and published in 1965 as *Lire le Capital*. Proposing a philosophical reading of Marx to unearth the theoretical framework supporting *Capital*, Althusser and his colleagues enunciated an uncompromising redefinition of Marxist philosophy which aroused a storm of debate and controversy. Though their interpretation coincided substantially with *Pour Marx*, the bluntly assertive expression it now found posed sharply the question of philosophy's relation to science, and in particular the science of history and society with which *Capital* was concerned.

Underlying the philosophical reading of *Capital* was Althusser's division of the social formation into four main practices: economic, political, ideological and theoretical. Theoretical practice was conceived as a process of transformation of mainly ideological generalities into knowledge by means of a theoretical apparatus; and Marxist philosophy, as understood by Althusser, was defined as the theory of theoretical practice. The elevation of philosophy to the decisive moment in the knowledge process raised the spectre of theology, once designated the queen of the sciences. The 'theory of theoretical practice' could all too readily be translated as 'science of sciences'. Such a view is consistently condemned throughout the Marxist tradition, which rejects the implied subordination of science to philosophy, and the idealist posture of founding knowledge in thought. To condemn idealism is easier than to avoid it, and Althusser was obliged to acknowledge the error of his conception. He appended a note to the second edition of *Lire le Capital* (1968), recognizing what he described as 'une tendance "théoriciste" certaine', and regretting the speculative or positivist echoes it necessarily provoked.[5] The speculative danger is the obvious one of idealism, the positivist danger is that of eliminating philosophy and assimilating its functions to science. Althusser argued that the mistake did not substantially affect the analysis of Marxism as the science of history. But he was left with the problem of assigning a different place to philosophy and consequently a different status to the materialist dialectic.

Within the Althusserian framework, the problem did not easily resolve itself. He had made a radical distinction between ideology and science, had equated science and theory, and was effectively faced with the choice of locating philosophy either inside knowledge as science or outside knowledge as ideology. He had initially opted for the former, but realizing the 'theoreticism' it entailed, had now to reconsider. To opt for ideology would be humiliating and self-defeating, since it automatically excluded any cognitive value and would bring the 'philosophical' reading of Marx crashing down about his head. He was therefore compelled to find a different point of insertion. During 1967 he evolved the view that philosophy was a discipline different in nature from both science and ideology. In a course of lectures to science students, later published as *Philosophie et philosophie spontanée des savants* (Paris, 1974), Althusser outlined his notion of philosophy as parasitic on the sciences and having the function of tracing a line of demarcation between science and ideology. Early the following year he extended this watchdog role to include the function of representing politics.[6] He centred his new conception on the existence of two nodal points, between philosophy and the sciences on the one hand, and between philosophy and politics on the other.

In a paper on Lenin to the Société française de philosophie, he offered the view that philosophy represents politics in the sphere of theory, and science in the class struggle.[7] The queen of the sciences became a go-between. A certain ambiguity subsists in this view, however. Philosophy is apparently still included in the domain of theory, but theory is now divided into the sciences and philosophy. The question therefore arises as to the cognitive status of theory, whether it does or does not constitute knowledge, and if it does, what type of knowledge philosophy produces. The answer appears to be that it produces knowledge of what counts as science and what counts as ideology. Althusser stresses that philosophy itself has no object such as a science has – it cannot therefore be knowledge. But can it produce knowledge without giving itself an object? And without being scientific? The conflicting possibilities have no obvious resolution within the model of society which Althusser has outlined. It is not clear that the concept of non-scientific and non-ideological theory is tenable in those terms, and as a result philosophy is situated outside the purview of historical materialism.

Althusser's further assertion that philosophy has no history consequently takes on a significance beyond that envisaged by Marx or Engels. They suggested in *The German Ideology* that morality, religion, metaphysics, ideology and corresponding forms of consciousness had no history independent of material production and intercourse.[8] Althusser seems to suggest that philosophy, as distinct from ideology, has no history whatsoever, and in some way therefore escapes the processes of historical change. Such a conclusion may be an extrapolation from his position, but it is consistent with his attribution of a place of special privilege to philosophy. From its place in the wings philosophy intervenes in the historical process with a double authority. In politics it carries the emblem of scientific authority, and in scientific research it bears the seal of political necessity. The precise lines of this dual mandate are not elaborated, but it is evident that it permits philosophy to evade questions of its own legitimacy by the simple device of infinite referral. The eternal go-between is always representing someone else: the philosopher is the politician among scientists and the scientist among politicians.

The change in Althusser's conception was from philosophy as the supreme science, to philosophy as hand maiden of the sciences, and then to philosophy as the intermediary between science and politics. It followed the direction of a retreat from cognition and a growing incorporation of political factors. The upheavals of 1968 contributed in due course to a further step along the same path, which led him to encapsulate his position in the formula: 'la philosophie est, en dernière instance, lutte de classe dans la théorie'.[9] In a polemical reply to criticisms put forward by an English Marxist, *Réponse à John Lewis* (Paris, 1973), Althusser explained the significance of his formulation. Philosophy, he said, is not science or a science, though it is in close relation with the sciences, since its abstract, rational and systematic character places it within theory. Unlike science it is closely related to the class tendencies of ideologies, which are practical rather than theoretical, and it is ultimately, though not exclusively, a form of class struggle, with political consequences. His insistence that philosophy is class struggle only in the last instance does not disguise its slow gravitation from science to politics. The dual representation is quietly abandoned in favour of a single mandate. It may be observed that this does not exclude a two-way process of mediation, but the infinite referral is eliminated since ultimately philosophy's legitimacy and authority derives from politics.

Elegant and satisfying though this solution is in many respects, there is an obvious similarity between Althusser's new position and the over-politicized conception of the late 1940s and early 1950s, in which science as well as philosophy were in practice often reduced to a class position. Althusser is careful to warn against a reductionist interpretation of his view, but the danger of 'politicism' is quite as deeply rooted in it as 'theoreticism' had earlier been. There are other problems too besetting his account. It does not settle the uneasy question of what now distinguishes philosophy from ideology. If, as Althusser suggests, ideology is not theory because it is, in the last instance, practical, should not philosophy also be excluded from theory since it is, in the last instance, political and therefore practical also? On the other hand, if its abstract, systematic and rational characteristics suffice to place philosophy in theory, are there any grounds for excluding from theory an ideology which exhibits the same characteristics? Althusser recognizes the problem and suggests that 'theoretical ideologies' would, in the last instance, be detachments of practical ideologies in theory.[10] This is not a solution, however, since it concedes the existence of ideology within theory and thereby undermines the only available criteria for distinguishing philosophy from ideology.

Much of the difficulty relates to the distinction between theory and practice which is inscribed in his basic reformulation of historical materialism. Once Althusser has distinguished theory as a particular practice within society along with ideology, politics and economics it is virtually impossible to avoid its becoming the determinant and all-embracing form of practice, implying that the different practices are each dominated by their theory: a theory of economics, a theory of politics and a theory of ideology, and crowned, logically, by a theory of theory. Having rejected these consequences as theoreticism, Althusser does not abandon the system which generated them, but attempts to reorganize it without changing the basic definitions. The result is a crooked system which is compelled to operate against its inherent logic; the crookedness is manifested in the ambivalence of Althusser's concept of theory, which still carries the residual force of scientificity, but is compelled to include non-scientific thought, in the shape of philosophy.

The only solution possible is to dissolve the model in which theory functions as one of the four dimensions of society, a form of practice among others. Instead theory must be replaced in its former matrix in unity with and opposition to practice. Theory is, in a sense, a form of practice, and indeed the most complex and sophisticated form. But it is not one form among many, it is one of the two basic aspects of human activity which are both inseparable and yet distinct. Theory and practice are integral parts of every type of social activity. If one of the two is designated as a separate activity among others a dissymmetry is created in which the remaining activities are necessarily dwarfed by their gigantic fellow. Gross distortion is the inevitable consequence, exemplified by Althusser's theoreticism, and can only be remedied by returning theory and practice to the level of analysis in which they together belong.

It is doubtful how much of Althusser's model can survive the adjustment proposed, but it undoubtedly resolves his problem of describing philosophy as theory without necessarily including it among the sciences, his problem of how to refuse ideology the scientific prestige of theory, and his problem of how to make philosophy dependent on politics without reducing it to ideology. However, the relation of theory and practice now proposed is also a return to a pre-Althusserian concept of dialectical contradiction. His four-fold division of practice, one part being theory, which then determines the other three parts, was an attempt to restate the unity and struggle of opposites in a non-Hegelian form. The reformulation of the materialist dialectic in *Pour Marx* explicitly excludes the possibility of Hegelian concepts being retained in it. But Hegel is easier to denounce than to escape, and in this instance at least it appears that a Marxist solution to the problem cannot dispense with the rational kernel extracted from Hegel's dialectics.

In other ways, too, Althusser was increasingly driven to recognize a Hegelian component in Marxist philosophy, though he endeavoured to limit its importance. In a paper of 1968 to a seminar organized by Jean

Hyppolite, Althusser broached the question of the positive heritage of
Hegel in Marxism.[11] Marx, he said, had adopted non-Hegelian
conceptions of history, the social structure and the dialectic, but had
taken from him the *idea* of the dialectic. Tracing Marx's passage
through the theoretical humanism of Feuerbach, he points to the
latter's weakness in relation to Hegel by virtue of his lack of a concept of
history, or dialectic, the two being synonymous in Hegelian terms. In
escaping from Feuerbach, Marx adopted Hegel's theory of history as a
dialectical process of production of forms. The weakness of this theory,
however, was that in Hegel's hands it was teleological: that is, it was
oriented towards a predetermined goal, inscribed in the structures of
supersession (*Aufhebung*) and the negation of the negation. Stripped of
the teleology, Althusser argues, Marx takes over Hegel's conception of
history as a process. Moreover, in Hegel's view the process was one of
the self-alienation of the Idea, rather than one of the alienation of Man
within human history. The subject of the process was therefore not
Man but the teleology of the process itself and since Marx removes the
teleology, the concept he inherits from Hegel is of a process without a
subject, and without a goal. It is this concept that Althusser
manipulates to deadly effect in his polemical reply to John Lewis,
denouncing the non-Marxist nature of his woolly humanism.

One strength of Althusser's analysis is that it radically excludes the
neo-Hegelian and existentialist conceptions of the dialectic, based on
the interplay of a human subject and its object. That men act in history
as subjects, he does not deny, but he refuses to consider that history
itself has a subject, which acts as the origin, essence and cause of its
development. In this respect he returns to the notion of the dialectic as a
general law of motion, which he even extends, polemically at least, to
include a dialectic of nature. It is true that the concept of process is of
central importance in Marxist theory. Engels uses it to emphasize the
universality of change and movement, pointing out that it is more
accurate to talk about 'processes' rather than 'things', since the latter
conveys a misleading sense of static and fixed identity. So Althusser is at
least right to suggest that Marxism adopts this much from Hegel. But
the universality of change is a prerequisite for a dialectic, it is not yet the
dialectic itself. This is undoubtedly the force of Althusser's comment
that Marx took only the idea of the dialectic from Hegel, that is, the
recognition of change and of the consequent need to develop a logic
which would express its laws. However, since the major part of Hegel's
gigantic system is devoted to elucidating the laws of change, the
dialectic, it is precipitate to assert that Marxism assimilates no more
than the general idea, or project.

In order to support his position, Althusser must account for the fate of the main laws of the dialectic in their transition from Marx to Hegel. The question of contradiction and his reformulation has already been examined, the question of quantity and quality is not dealt with, and the negation of the negation is quite simply discarded. In the case of this latter, he argues that it is the vehicle for teleology. Negation in his view presupposes a future restoration and is therefore governed by a goal-orientation. The negation of the negation is thus the confirmation of a direction already implicit in the process and constitutes its teleology. However, this view hardly corresponds with the analysis offered by Engels, who devotes an entire chapter of his *Anti-Dühring* to the negation of the negation.[12] Far from translating the force of some historical necessity, it is an extremely general law, which describes the way things develop. Everything has a particular way of being 'negated' or transformed in such a manner as to give rise to development. Every transformation takes place on the basis of previous changes. A new stage of development may therefore incorporate features which were negated in earlier stages and which are now restored but in a new context. Without negation the dialectic lacks a vital means of comprehending development. What is a process in which nothing is transformed? Transformation and negation are inseparable, and the negation of the negation is an irresistible consequence of negation. Without it, Althusser condemns himself to a conception of immobility or at best repetition.

Althusser's analysis of contradiction has already been reviewed and discovered to lack the characteristics of movement and change. Eliminating negation has a similar effect, and is compounded by his total silence concerning the transformation of quantity into quality. It is questionable whether what is left may accurately be described as dialectical. Certainly, the concept of a process, with or without a subject, is the first step towards a dialectic. But without any further specification of the forms of change and relation proper to processes, it is still a regression from Hegel, and not far advanced from Heraclitean flux. Here, as in his concept of theory and practice, Althusser has advanced from his initial static theoreticism. Process is not a new concept in his system, but the prominence now given to it reveals an attempt to overcome the stasis which infected his previous position. Whether it can be carried out without a more extensive incorporation of Hegelian concepts, suitably revised in materialist terms, may be doubted. But even that possibility is not excluded.

The *Réponse à John Lewis* advises prudence with philosophical categories since their nature is determined largely by the function they perform in a given theoretical system, rather than by any inherently idealist or materialist essence. Though Althusser still rejects the negation of the negation as carrying 'une charge idéaliste irrémédiable', he admits a limited validity for alienation, a concept previously anathematized.[13] Surrounded by appropriate qualifications, it is not inconceiveable that the categories of the materialist dialectic may yet be retrieved and incorporated into Althusserian theory. If so then Marxist theory may indeed be enriched by what Althusser described in his doctoral submission of 1975 as a theoretical detour.[14] The construction of a neo-Marxist position in the early 1960s may have served to provide a vantage point from which to subject Marxist concepts to stringent testing. Ultimately the deficiencies and slow collapse of that position may prove less important than the enhancement and clarification of Marxist philosophy resulting from the critical appraisal it provoked.

Whatever the intellectual importance of his work, Althusser's political evolution led him increasingly on to the margins of the PCF, where he and the group which shared his views continued to snipe against the predominant policy with diminishing success. His challenge to the parliamentary strategy of left unity found more response outside than inside the party, though a small and often isolated group, composed mainly of students and intellectuals, continued to press vainly for the positions he advocated. Much of his political critique was presented as a left criticism of the remnants of Stalinism, as yet unrenounced by the party leadership, but the Left/Right classification is unhelpful in explaining the frequent convergences between Althusser's stance and that of the avowedly right-wing communist Jean Ellenstein. The political defeat of Althusserianism during the 1970s is undeniable, though there were occasions when his calls for rigour of analysis bore a kind of fruit. The precipitate abandonment of the dictatorship of the proletariat at the PCF's 22nd Congress was such a case. The visible confusion attendant on the event enabled some telling points to be made in the name of conceptual clarity, not least by the leading Althusserian, Etienne Balibar. But the result was a concerted effort to produce a theoretical framework to situate and justify the step in retrospect. Not the result Althusser or Balibar might have hoped.

The shift from a 'theoreticist' to a 'politicist' position in philosophy mirrors shifts in the role of intellectuals. Essentially, the students and intelligentsia of the early 1960s saw themselves on the periphery of the labour and progressive movement, often detached but increasingly intervening in a supportive or advisory capacity. The enormous growth in their numbers and political strength, along with their declining living standards and expectations, enabled them to claim full membership of the movement in their own right, a change which was dramatically demonstrated in 1968. The precise insertion of intellectuals in the struggle for socialism is an urgent and complex question, to which many answers have been offered. But the solution implicit in Althusser's development is that they are no longer advisors or consultants, as the 'theoreticist' position suggested, but are now a major force in the vanguard, using their knowledge and skills as a weapon of the revolution, as the 'politicist' position implies – from backroom boys to front-line men. There can be no doubt that Althusser's shift reflects real changes in the economic and political structure of French society, comparable to those taking place in other countries. It may be asked though whether Althusser has not fallen into a contrary excess to his initial view. Where he once introduced too radical a division between workers and intellectuals, he now offers too complete an integration. Where once theoretical and practical work were, terminology notwithstanding, effectively separated, they are now virtually indistinguishable.

It would be wrong to urge too reductive a view of Althusser's position, though his less cautious followers have frequently fallen into that error. He does not seriously contend that intellectuals have completely joined, much less supplanted, the working class as the vanguard of the revolution. Various unguarded comments might be quoted to suggest otherwise, and it could even be argued that they represent the thrust or logic of his views. But it is unlikely that his excesses, or even his overall system, will stand as Althusser's lasting contribution to French Marxism. Apart from a handful of new concepts, that contribution lies in his articulation of the aspirations of an important and growing social group, the intellecuals; and in the catalytic effect of his work in stimulating theoretical debate at a high level of sophistication.

Sève and the new consensus

Une contradiction antagoniste n'est-elle pas normalement *auto-explosive* du fait que par position l'un des contraires tend à la suppression de l'autre, qui joue par rapport à son développement le rôle *d'obstacle interne?* Mais aussi, dans la mesure où la résolution qualitative de la contradiction est déjà suffisamment mûre et où, du même coup, le contraire parasitaire, dominant, perd de plus en plus la *force* de s'opposer à l'achèvement du processus, n'est-il pas aisé de comprendre pourquoi les formes pacifiques peuvent alors prendre la relève des formes violentes, sans que soit modifié le moins du monde l'essence antagoniste de la contradiction ni remis en cause le fait fondamental que sa solution exige la suppression jusqu'à son terme du contraire parasitaire?

Lucien Sève, in Lénine et la pratique scientifique *(Paris, 1974), 41*

One of the most significant changes in Marxist philosophy since the Second World War has been the growing role of collective reflection and the diminished role of outstanding individuals. Nowhere is this more evident than among communist philosophers. The star system is not entirely dead, but it is increasingly superseded by group researches, and the major figures are increasingly dependent on the work of lesser-known colleagues. In part it is a result of the enormous increase in activity, drawing in larger numbers of intellectuals. In part, too, it is a result of the specialization and professionalization of philosophy. Marxist philosophers lay great emphasis on their theoretical work as a serious contribution to the development of the natural and social sciences, as well as an important instrument in developing political strategy. In this respect the development of Marxist philosophy has responded to the changing social function of the humanities which are faced ever more sharply with the alternatives of integration into economic production or incorporation among the pursuits of leisure. The two alternatives are not in absolute opposition of course, but the drive to draw the humanities closer to science and technology has been a major result of the option, as discipline after discipline seeks to justify its practical and scientific value – some with greater success than others. Marxist philosophy has always prided itself on its scientific basis and is thus well prepared to develop closer relations with scientific research as a whole, both natural and social, without resorting to the panic importation of concepts and models previously foreign to it. It is not therefore surprising that the philosophers tended to adopt the methods of organization and co-operation prevalent in the sciences generally, where the collectivization of research was proceeding apace.

The decline of the star system in France can be traced by the circumstances of three of the most prominent Marxist philosophers of recent times. Henri Lefebvre came close to the picture of the isolated thinker, especially during the mid-1940s when he was at the height of his influence and productivity. After the end of his collaboration with Norbert Guterman, and especially when, during the 1950s, he had become something of a communist dissident, Lefebvre's work was largely the product of individual elaboration. He represented, and was accountable to, no one but himself. Roger Garaudy, in many ways his successor, was formed in the collective activity of the young PCF philosophers of the late 1940s and by the time he achieved pre-eminence among them, he held a number of representative positions. Though he was something of a star philosopher from the middle 1950s, his work was substantially based on synthesizing the ideas of the bodies which, at different stages, he represented. Even during his dissidence of the late 1960s he remained the leader of a tendency, whose views he articulated while adding his own distinctive contribution. Louis Althusser, though he achieved an individual stature greater than that of either of the other two, was from the early 1960s closely identified with collective reflection, to the extent of expounding his views frequently in terms of a 'we' which was genuinely plural. 'His' work *Lire le Capital* of 1965 was the product of a team of five, including Balibar, Macherey, Rancière and Establet, of which he was the senior and leading member. He worked closely with several other young philosophers, who shared his basic views, and who contributed to drawing out their implications in a range of areas. Some of their work was published in the 'Théorie' collection he directed for François Maspéro. One of the most frequent reproaches urged against him has been that he has built up a clan among communist intellectuals, and one which has adopted a more or less dissident and factional posture within the party. The collective nature of Althusser's enterprise at least is clear, even if he himself has tended to become something of a cult figure as result of it.

One observation at least must be added to this sketch. The star status which Lefebvre, Garaudy and Althusser have successively enjoyed has only in small part stemmed from their fellow communist intellectuals. The major impetus in generating national and international acclaim has in each case come as a result of their dissidence within the PCF, and come from the bourgeois media. Lefebvre, until the late 1940s, Garaudy, until the late 1950s, and Althusser, until the late 1960s, enjoyed the respect and attention of most of their comrades but attracted little notice outside that circle. Thereafter, moving towards positions which conflicted with those of the party, they rapidly became the focus for controversy and were elevated by the hitherto indifferent media into figures of misunderstood genius oppressed by philistine apparatchiks. The procedure is by no means unusual, but it sets a false perspective on their work, which for the most part was substantially elaborated in conditions of relative obscurity before the mantle of fame was thrust upon them. The subsequent fame thus serves to cloak the fact that the productive work of Marxist philosophy is not done by outstanding and isolated individuals. However important their individual contribution, it is made in a context where consciously collective work plays an increasing part.

Lucien Sève, who emerged in the 1970s as the leading PCF spokesman on philosophy, did much to promote the shift from individualism. Unlike Garaudy, he did not emphasize his position with a stream of authoritative books outlining his current thinking, but exercised leadership in a more discreet, but more effective manner. From the appearance of his treatise on personality in 1969, to that of his major *Introduction à la philosophie marxiste* (Paris, 1980), he published no book that was not written in collaboration with others. However, the various collective productions to which he contributed included discussions on many of the major theoretical questions of Marxist philosophy and politics. On a philosophical level, the most concise and the most influential statement of his position is the report he drew up on the dialectic in preparation for the Centre d'Etudes et de Recherches Marxistes' Orsay colloquium of 1971.[15] It was itself a result of group discussions, and can be regarded as articulating a new consensus, summarizing the materialist dialectic as it was understood by the majority of French communists during the 1970s.

Noting that the dialectic had been alternately exalted and vilified in recent times, Sève firmly asserted the notion that the Marxist dialectic began with an inversion of the Hegelian dialectic, though this 'setting on its feet' referred purely to the status, not the content. The critical inventory, or demystification which had to follow was a long process in which Hegelian concepts could still play a useful part. He defined the materialist dialectic as philosophical science, suggesting that its categories were not of the same order as even the most general concepts of historical and natural sciences, since they concerned the relation between thought and being, rather than being itself directly. The dialectic, he said, was not an ontology but a means of access to objective essence through a critical theory of knowledge. Admitting the dangers of dogmatism and schematism, Sève argued that there was nonetheless a kernel of absolute truth operating at an extremely general level, and which could not be reformed at the present stage of thought. The three basic laws, contradiction, qualitative leaps and negation of negation, formed the basis of this kernel, though an exact and complete statement of it in the context of modern science and history still left an enormous task. He then proposed a series of analyses which suggested more exact and complete accounts of dialectical categories in relation to logic, history and forms of transition; contradiction and antagonism; and certain contentious concepts taken from Hegel.

Distinguishing the objective dialectic, the movement of being reflected in consciousness, from the subjective dialectic, the movement of consciousness as being, Sève stressed the difference between the real historical order of development and the logical order of the concepts which grasp it. He examined the structuralist distinction of synchrony and diachrony, where methodological priority was wrongly given to structure over process and to external relations over internal organization. Genetic structuralists, he said, tried but failed to overcome the error by explaining a latter stage of development in terms of an earlier stage, an approach which had a limited value within a single qualitative reality but could not explain transition to another qualitative reality. The materialist dialectic contained, in Sève's view, the distinction between the starting point and the basis of any reality. A new quality generates its own basis which gradually replaces the old quality, from which it emerges, and transforms it into a starting point and possibly a functional support. Hence the emergence of a new quality often appears as a negation of the old, as dominance relations are reversed, and contradictions appear between the new and the old.

Examining the vital question of contradiction and antagonism, Sève criticized Mao Tse-tung and Stalin alike for neglecting the relation of Marx and Hegel. To overcome the various comparisons thus engendered, Sève proposed to restrict the notion of antagonism to the content of contradictions, designating an opposition between the old and the new which could only be resolved by the suppression of one term. Non-antagonism on the other hand would describe opposites which had a tendency to separation but could be resolved by their mutual fusion. The use of antagonism to characterize the violent or explosive form of a contradiction should be discontinued, he suggested, since contradictions which were antagonistic in the first sense might not require explosive resolutions if the old quality lost the strength to provoke violence during its suppression. Conversely certain conditions, such as external obstacles, could provoke explosions between terms which were not in the first sense antagonistic.

Finally, Sève identified a series of Hegelian concepts which were frequently excluded from the Marxist dialectic: negation of the negation of the negation, supersession (Aufhebung) and the identity of opposites. Though he did not give detailed analysis of each one, he noted that what they all shared was a notion of internal continuity within dialectical discontinuity, the continuing relation of the new to the old. Those who rejected them were supporters of a radical break theory who wished to keep nothing of any kernel of truth. He argued that the existence of these concepts in Marxist theory was quite irrefutable and that attention would be more fruitfully turned to the transformation of their content than to efforts to disqualify them altogether.

From a purely conceptual point of view, Sève's analysis is highly persuasive. His clarification of the notion of antagonism is attractive in making the much needed distinction between form and content of contradictions and in providing a clear position from which to criticize the interchangeability which Mao's theory proposed between antagonism and non-antagonism. He does not, however, solve the logical anomaly which consists in defining the nature of a contradiction in terms of its possible resolution. That the resolution is an integral part of its conditions of existence is not in doubt, but the resolution is surely first a product of the kind of contradiction in question rather than the reverse. If so, then it is more appropriate to enquire into the role of a contradiction in the processes in which it is found, and the role of their relation in the formation and development of the opposites. On the basis of the antagonism between bourgeoisie and proletariat it might be suggested that their contradiction is constitutive of capitalist society as such, and that the existence of each class presupposes and requires the other at the same time as setting it in an irremediable conflict of interest as the most basic social level – the economic. That other social contradictions have been similarly constitutive of a social formation, mutually generating each other in basic conflict, is historically verifiable and may form a basis for a general definition of antagonism in history. Whether and to what extent it might be applied to natural processes could only be resolved by examination of the types of contradiction they contain, but it would surely be appropriate to use antagonism to describe the relation in general between mutually reproducing but fundamentally opposed forces which are constitutive of a process. At all events, some such notion of antagonism is necessary if the creeping teleology of Mao's and Sève's concept of antagonism is to be avoided. The future, or at least potential futures, may dialectically affect the present, but the present cannot be other than determinant of the future.

Sève's critique of genetic structuralism is compelling and well conceived. He gives a clear explanation of how, having privileged logic, it is impossible to account for history. Rest may be viewed as a special case of motion, but motion cannot be constructed from rest. Likewise his demonstration of how a new stage in a development cannot be reduced to previous stages is most pertinent and gives a convincing account of the withering away of the old under the domination of the new. There is, however, a danger in his notion of the old as starting point and functional support. He warns against the danger of applying such an analysis to relations between the economic base and ideological superstructures, and reducing the former to a mere support for the latter. There would also be good cause to warn against applying it to the succession of social formations, lest remnants of a past age be misguidedly elevated to necessary supports for the present, or more disturbingly, lest condemned features of the present be given a fresh lease of life on the same principle for the future. The very concept of 'support', with its connotations of bearer or medium which is more or less uninvolved in the process, is one which requires careful handling in a Marxist context. No medium is ever ultimately neutral in a process of mediation, and the cases where it can be so regarded, for all practical purposes, need to be duly circumscribed. However, Sève's position here, as elsewhere, is less reproachable in letter than in spirit. The clear and stimulating analysis is a useful development of dialectics, and its faults are remediable.

Underlying the philosophical principles, and explicitly acknowledged in several places, are the political implications which they do or could entail. In every case, the dialectic is related to the strategy for transition to socialism, and the categories Sève elaborates can with little difficulty be transcribed into terms of the types of social and political change needed in France. It would perhaps be an overstatement to say that his report is a philosophical reflection of the 1968 Champigny manifesto in which the PCF's new strategy was outlined, and on which the *Programme Commun* of 1972 was based. But the peaceful transition to socialism by way of advanced democracy is the implicit guide of Sève's argument. The emphasis on the non-violent or non-explosive resolution of even antagonistic contradictions is an evident correlate of the parliamentary road on which the Left unity programme was based. The slow blossoming of the new quality within the old corresponds to the strategy of revolution by democratization of existing structures. It is also possible that the role of functional support (and starting point) may reflect the concept of advanced democracy in which many features of the existing social and political order are guaranteed continuity, and even in some instances given renewed legitimacy. Certainly the defence of continuity within change represents at least the defence of French national traditions, and the union of the French people understood in its broadest sense as preparing, in an important sense, a conservative revolution, that is, one which conserves all that is valuable in the legacy of the past.

Taken at a purely abstract level, Sève's dialectic offers an interesting discussion of some possible types of change. Truth, however, is always concrete; and before any further judgement could be made, it would be necessary to see his dialectic at work. To say that the old survives in some form in the new is scarcely open to challenge, but it is also true that the new excludes some forms of the old. The point is to discover what old, what forms, and what new. In a general sense, Sève's analysis is characterized by its emphasis rather than its novelty. His attention is focused on continuities rather than discontinuities, and gradual rather than abrupt change. If the dialectic is the logic of change as such, then it must offer accounts of slow transitions as well as explosive transformations. The mistake would be to suppose in advance that one or the other is a necessary rather than a possible resolution of a given process. While it is a classical Marxist stance to explore the possibilities of peaceful transition to socialism, and even to promote the conditions for it, only a speculative dialectic could be brought to present it as the only possible transition.

Sève does not fall into this speculative error, but he does err in understating the discontinuity of transitions, the novelty of the new, and the transformations which qualitative change introduces in a process. Conservative politicians of the 1960s and 1970s made much political (and financial) capital in France with slogans of 'le changement dans la continuité', 'le progrès dans le calme', and the like. Change and continuity are inherent in all historical processes, but not all change is progressive, much less is it all qualitative and therefore revolutionary. It behoves a Marxist, and a communist, to emphasize discontinuity as the primary term in transition from capitalism to socialism, and from the old to the new, while recognizing the dimension of continuity which will not fail to be present. The materialist dialectic holds that the two terms of a contradiction are unequal, one dominating the other, and that a shift in the domination provokes qualitative change. Applied to philosophy, it might be said that unity and struggle, continuity and change, are unequal terms in dialectical contradiction. Depending on which term dominates, the result may be either the conservative and justificatory dialectic of Hegelian idealism or the revolutionary guide to action of Marxist dialectical materialism.

The dangers of Sève's philosophical position are the dangers of the PCF's political strategy. In both cases it is the concrete practical results which alone can permit a final judgement, for the proof of the pudding is in the eating. In 1971, at the time of the Orsay meeting, the Common Programme was still unsigned and Left unity was an urgent objective. In 1974, when the proceedings were published, the hopes placed in the new agreement were riding high. The dynamism which the strategy injected into the French Left could well be marked as a major political advance, and there were grounds to suppose that the programme, if fully implemented, might well usher in far-reaching changes amounting eventually to a socialist revolution. Such a perspective, had it been realized, might well have vindicated the dialectics of gradual change proposed by Lucien Sève. Whether the same emphasis could remain appropriate in the later 1970s is more questionable.

References

1   'Pour une démocratie avancée, pour une France socialiste!', *Cahiers du communisme*, janvier 1969, 120 – 142.
2   'Résolution sur les problèmes idéologiques et culturels', *Cahiers du communisme*, mai – juin 1966, 265 – 280, p.279.
3   R. Garaudy, *Le Grand tournant du socialisme* (Paris, 1969), 7.
4   See quotation at the head of this section.
5   L. Althusser and E. Balibar, *Lire le Capital*, I (Paris, 1968), 6.
6   L. Althusser, 'La philosophie comme arme de la révolution', *La Pensée*, mars – avril 1968, 26 – 34.
7   L. Althusser, *Lénine et la philosophie* (Paris, 1972), see also the quotation at the head of this section.
8   K. Marx and F. Engels, *Collected Works*, V (London, 1976), 36 – 37.
9   L. Althusser, *Réponse à John Lewis* (Paris, 1973), 11.
10 *Ibid.*, 12.
11 L. Althusser, 'Sur le rapport de Marx à Hegel', in his *Lénine et la philosophie*.
12 F. Engels, *Anti-Dühring* (London, 1975), 155 – 170.
13 Althusser, *Réponse*, 58.
14 L. Althusser, 'Est-il simple d'être marxiste en philosophie?', *La Pensée*, septembre – octobre 1975, 3 – 31.
15 L. Sève, 'Pré-rapport sur la dialectique', in CERM, *Lénine et la pratique scientifique* (Paris, 1974), 19 – 47.

9

New Directions

1974 – 1980

Jaeglé, science and dialectics

Expliquer ce que sont l'espace et le temps consiste à reconnaitre les propriétés à la fois directes et générales de la matière qui produisent dans la conscience les concepts d'espace et de temps. . . . De telles propriétés, desquelles seront nécessairement absentes les spécificités propres à chaque domaine particulier du savoir, font partie de ce qu'une philosophie scientifique peut à bon droit appeler catégories philosophiques, au sens ou Lénine écrit qu'il existe une catégorie philosophique de matière.

Pierre Jaeglé, Essai sur l'espace et le temps *(Paris, 1976), 19–20*

The later 1970s have been characterized by two divergent currents of Marxism in contention for the support of young communist intellectuals: the remains of the Althusserian movement and the majority view articulated by Lucien Sève. The direct implications of these two positions for the status of philosophy and the dialectic have already been outlined. As time passed, the opposition between them focused with increasing sharpness on questions of politics and historical materialism. The politics of the *Programme Commun* was strenuously attacked by the Althusserians, who resisted what they saw as pragmatic revisions of Marxist theory to suit political expediency, and equally strongly defended by the Sèvians who urged what they saw as the creative development of Marxist theory to deal with new historical realities. The most vehement controversy was inevitably aroused by the central political questions of the state, power and the nature of revolution. The decision of the 22nd Congress of the PCF in 1976 to abandon the notion of dictatorship of the proletariat provided a focus for the differences to crystallize on. The alternatives are well stated in two opposing studies: *Les Communistes et l'état* (Paris, 1977) written by Sève jointly with Jean Fabre and François Hincker, and published by Editions sociales; and *Sur la dictature du prolétariat* (Paris, 1976) written by Etienne Balibar and published in Althusser's 'Théorie' collection by Maspéro. Both were published in the wake of the 22nd Congress, one to defend, the other to criticize its decisions. It is not within the scope of this study to examine the details of this burning question, but merely to point out that the two conceptions of dialectics were related to fundamental political divergences.

To a large extent, the Althusserians were content to limit their researches to these questions. Althusser's view of philosophy as class struggle in theory, as ultimately determined by politics, clearly sanctioned such a restriction. The tendency of his followers was increasingly to deny any generality to philosophy, and subsume it to historical materialism. Georges Labica's study *Le Statut marxiste de la philosophie* (Paris, 1976) is an example of this tendency, and is analysed in the next section. Categories became increasingly specified and confined to a limited range of meaning within the science of history. The Sèvians, on the other hand, continued to use the categories of philosophy as generalities which could be used in relation to thought, society or nature, and developed a close relationship with the natural sciences. Following in the wake of Engels, whose *Dialectics of Nature* explored the operation of dialectical categories in the natural sciences, a number of natural scientists applied themselves to demonstrate the relevance of the materialist dialectic in the discoveries of contemporary science. The Althusserians denied the legitimacy of such an enterprise, since philosophy could in their view only defend or represent science, not have any active function within it. It was therefore largely in the perspective of Sève's dialectic that scientists explored the philosophical significance of their work.

Sève's exposition at the Orsay colloquium of 1971 was drafted as a result of lengthy discussions within the CERM's 'Natural Sciences' group, and the scientists of the group made substantial contributions to the subsequent debate. This co-operation was in no way original in itself, since French Marxism has always been closely associated with the natural sciences. The relationship has been fostered since the earliest times and has been developed by some of France's leading scientists since the time of Paul Langevin, Frédéric Joliot-Curie and Eugène Cotton. In theoretical terms it was expressed in the notion of a dialectics of nature, but that notion was itself under attack from different quarters as a remnant of the philosophical dogmatism of Stalin's day. The debates of the late 1950s and early 1960s set out the issues very plainly, and since that time the different schools of thought have proceeded to implement the consequences of their position. Within the Althusserian framework a dialectics of nature could have no real meaning, though he recognized its 'polemical' value as a confused assertion that processes had no subject. Within the Sèvian framework, on the contrary, natural science was an important field in which the materialist dialectic received confirmation and development.

Recent attempts have been made to effect some kind of reconciliation between the opposed camps. André Tosel, for example, has argued that while Althusser refuses to universalize scientific and political questions, Sève refuses to acknowledge the historical specificity of philosophical intervention.[1] He himself suggests that the specific historical conjuncture demands a philosophical universalization and categorization, and argues for the elaboration of a new logic. His suggestive analysis has, however, little prospect of exciting the agreement of either school, and his own position comes close to proposing a completely new technical beginning in logic for a new theory of nature and society. The Althusserian position has largely restricted its involvement with the natural sciences to discussion of the history of science, or history of knowledge. In this context, the work of Michel Fichant and Michel Pêcheux, *Sur l'histoire des sciences* (Paris, 1969) and Pierre Raymond's works on the history of mathematics, in particular his *Le Passage au matérialisme* (Paris, 1973) represent attempts to situate the development of science within the framework of historical materialism, rather than attempts to enrich philosophy with the results of scientific discovery. The elaboration of a cognitive relationship between science and philosophy has been left to mainstream dialectical materialists.

The work of natural scientists in developing the materialist dialectic has been extensive and influential. The contributions of physicists, chemists, biologists, mathematicians, medical researchers and others have been prominent in journals like *La Pensée*, which has paid close attention to scientific research, and in the debates of the CERM. The 1971 colloquium contains many such contributions, among which the paper by the physicist E. I. Bitsakis exemplifies the fecundity of the exercise.[2] Examining the findings of contemporary microphysics, he traces the contradictory forms of matter represented by mass and energy, the interaction of transformation and conservation, the unity of continuity and discontinuity, and points out how only a theory of contradiction can embrace, for example, the wave and particle properties of light. His exposition demonstrates the continuing value of the laws of dialectics in rendering the multitude of scientific laws more comprehensible, which in turn enriches the dialectic. Bitsakis, one of the many Greeks exiled by fascism who have participated actively in French intellectual life, later published an extensive study of the relation between Marxist philosophy and physics in his *La Physique contemporaine et le matérialisme dialectique* (Paris, 1973). He has contributed regular articles on related subjects in *La Pensée*, most recently offering a vigorous defence of the objectivity of scientific laws against the renewed penetration of positivist conceptions which regard claims for objectivity as metaphysical.[3]

Native French scientists have not been remiss in developing a closer integration of Marxist concepts with their research. The analyses offered by major non-Marxist scientists are frequently cited to demonstrate the inherent need for dialectical concepts in theoretical research. Nobel prize-winners like physicist Louis de Broglie and biologist François Jacob have been taken to offer substantially dialectical viewpoints. The latter's *La Logique du vivant* (Paris, 1970) has especially been acclaimed in this connection. But one of the most sustained and instructive discussions of Marxist philosophy in the natural sciences has come from an atomic physicist, Pierre Jaeglé, whose *Essai sur l'espace et le temps* (Paris, 1976) constitutes a compelling defence of the dialectics of nature.

Recognizing that time and space involve real theoretical difficulties for scientists, Jaeglé rejects the widespread efforts of idealist philosophers to shroud them in mystery, and proposes to explain on a materialist basis the direct and general properties of matter which produce in thought the concepts of time and space. Tracing theoretical approaches to the concepts since Aristotle, he examines the notions of matter and movement proposed by philosophers and scientists, pointing out the dualities they use in attempting to grasp the contradictory nature of reality. He discusses Engels' analysis of the relation between quantity and quality, demonstrating its debt to Hegel, and the value of the notion of measure, seen as quantity determined qualitatively. He proposes to restate it in the light of subsequent scientific work on the conservation of energy and on reversibility and irreversibility. Drawing on contemporary thermodynamic theory, he argues that this nexus of problems reveals the deep internal connection between the major laws of dialectics. Qualities such as mass, length and time combine to produce a new quality, energy. The dimension which measures energy determines it as kinetic, potential, electrical, calorific, luminous or other. Therefore, since energy is conserved as a quality in the various qualitative changes it undergoes, it may be said that the law of interpenetration of opposites underlies the law of transformation of quantity into quality. Moreover, the physical law of conservation necessarily supposes that processes are in some sense cyclical or reversible, that is to say that transformations occurring in them carry their own negation. What is conserved at the end of a process is a negation of a negation. However, some processes at least are irreversible. The concept of entropy marks the irreversible evolution of systems, and even if specific systems maintain constant entropy, they do so by evacuating their surplus and necessarily add to total entropy. Since entropy can only increase, reversibility is only relative, a notion expressed by the dialectical conception of the negation of the negation. The major laws of the materialist dialectic thus support and pass into one another.

Jaeglé pursues his search for fundamental contradictions in matter and movement to elucidate the notions of time and space, identifying periodicity and non-periodicity as a key opposition in relativity physics. Periodicity, the recurrence of movement in which displacement is cancelled by the end of each cycle, is the material support for the notion of time, as well as the principle of stability of objects or systems. Stable objects are, however, composed of parts, and are also parts of larger wholes. The consequent possibility of distinguishing and separating the parts from the whole is the material support for a notion of space. The contradiction between part and whole is universal, Jaeglé argues, and is reflected in thought as the opposition of two points of view: that of the whole and that of the parts. The point of view of the unity of matter, encompassing stability and periodicity, is expressed as time; that of plurality, including distance and displacement, is expressed as space. Obviously, both aspects of matter coexist in practice and can only ultimately be separated at an abstract level. Furthermore though time is based on unity it has a secondary dimension of plurality, especially with Relativity, where the whole can only be envisaged from the point of view of a part. Similarly, though space is based in plurality, its representation in terms of angles introduces periodicity, and gives it a secondary aspect of unity. The twin concepts of time and space therefore reflect the existence of a basic contradiction in matter, which is again reflected within each of the two concepts. He concludes by asking whether, since Relativity uses the secondary aspect of time to incorporate it as fourth dimension of space, physics could not construct a theory of time incorporating the secondary, periodic, aspect of space.

Jaeglé's provocative and informed discussion breathes new life into the conception of dialectics as the science of general laws of development of all material reality. The progress of physics in studying the fabric of universe has given that science a special status in contemporary knowledge, and his use of its theoretical apparatus to elucidate the laws and categories of the materialist dialectic carries considerable weight. The demonstration of how general philosophical principles of Marxism reflect specific scientific theories is made with particular clarity in relation to the laws of thermodynamics, where concepts of conservation, irreversibility and entropy are shown to entail the major dialectical laws in close interpenetration. Arguably his essay also advances the understanding of time and space on the level of philosophy as distinct from physics. His argument for the points of view or the whole and the parts, or unity and plurality, has a general intelligibility which would repay close investigation in its relevance to other sciences or areas of human experience. Similarly his apprehension of the connections between the dialectical laws in physics serves to indicate an important and uncompleted task of Marxist philosophy. The nature of the unity and opposition of the laws has yet to be comprehensively stated: it is even an open question whether it can be defined in detail at a general philosophical level or whether their relationship can only be analysed in particular cases. Their interweaving in physics cannot be directly translated into terms of biology, much less history. The question remains posed whether they can be related more specifically than by their common characteristics of change and interconnection, which are the presuppositions of dialectics.

The stimulating and persuasive application of dialectical thought to the contemporary development of physics gives, at first sight, a powerful support to the argument for a dialectics of nature. The intention to do so is openly avowed and is implied in Jaeglé's subtitle: *propos sur la dialectique de la nature*. At a theoretical level, however, the argument that scientific laws are dialectically structured does not prove that those laws reflect the structure of reality, if indeed such an expression is permissible. A consistent Althusserian may reply that scientific laws are the product of human practice, and that their dialectical aspect arises from the process of their production. A consistent Sartrean may also reply that science is an attempt at totalization and that it takes its dialectical rationality from the dialectic of consciousness which underlies all totalization. The two replies are not dissimilar, and the issue cannot be determined at a purely theoretical level. Jaeglé's view is that reality pre-exists the concepts which represent and appropriate it, but that such a view is philosophical and may therefore not be resolved by the particular sciences. His essay then attempts to show how immediate reality is transformed into thought reality, that is, how reality gives rise to conceptual reflections of itself. In principle it is an infinite enterprise since its exposition must be constantly modified and deepened by the growth of scientific knowledge about the nature of reality. But at least the principle is posed of a process running from the world to thought, and thence from an understanding of the world to an understanding of thought.

In two senses, Jaeglé's study draws its strength from practical rather than theoretical sources. First, the philosophical principle that thought reflects being is not capable of final proof within thought. The anteriority of being is the basic assertion of materialism and, if true, bears the corollary that the origins of thought lie outside itself. The truth of any proposition therefore rests in its correspondence with the real world rather than in its own internal coherence, even if true thought is also likely to be coherent. The notion of a relationship between thought and the world, in which the latter is determinant, is variously described as correspondence, reflection or representation. Much of Jaeglé's analysis is directed at elucidating the precise nature of the relationship in the light of contemporary science and historical developments. His proof is therefore practical insofar as his position is materialist and consonant with scientific and historical knowledge. His theoretical coherence is an important result, especially for its philosophical implications, but is not in itself proof of its correctness.

In a second sense, the importance of the *Essai sur l'espace et le temps* is practical in that it demonstrates the value of a dialectic of nature for natural scientists, and articulates it in terms of modern physics. Neither the Sartreans nor the Althusserians managed or even tried, to relate their philosophy closely to the natural sciences. At best they sought an external relationship in which philosophy and natural science were counterposed in theory. Conversely, their views held little appeal for natural scientists in their professional activity, whatever about their personal or political options. The mainstream of dialectical materialism has, however, always attracted the interest of scientists anxious to integrate the principles and achievements of their life's work with their progressive political and social commitment. The dialectics of nature, built on Engels' work, offers a fertile means by which a comprehensive Marxist synthesis can be achieved, unifying the knowledge of nature, history and thought with the struggle for socialism. With the rapid growth of scientific knowledge and research, and the increasing numbers of scientific workers in modern society, the importance of Marxism's relationship with science and scientists becomes more acute. Regardless of the theoretical soundness, or the truth of Jaeglé's study, it would still be an important exploration of a key area of Marxist enquiry. And its terms would still be influential in framing future explorations. In this sense too, the value of his work is ultimately practical. But its practical value does not exclude a theoretical value: the two are mutually supporting, and taken together make Jaeglé's book an important and compelling analysis of the materialist dialectic in the light of contemporary natural science.

Labica against philosophy

Mais la philosophie?
Nous n'avons rien fait d'autre, à suivre Marx et Engels, qu'instruire son procès – le plus sévère auquel elle ait jamais été soumise. Revient cependant l'interrogation qui la concerne. Elle exige que soit pris le risque désormais de l'énoncé de quelques résultats, seraient-ils partiels ou contre-posés encore.
Une conséquence paraît découler directement des remarques que nous venons de faire à propos des trois sources: que parler d'une philosophie *marxiste* serait illégitime.

> *Georges Labica*, Le Statut marxiste de la philosophie
> *(Paris, 1976), 364*

Marx's declaration that in *The German Ideology* he and Engels settled accounts with their erstwhile philosophical conscience has continually led commentators to ask whether philosophy could still have any legitimacy within a Marxist framework. The main Marxist tradition, communism, has usually construed philosophy in the broadest sense to include the overall world view of historical and dialectical materialism. On this view philosophy has been, along with politics and economics, one of the three components of Marxism. Within the broad realm of philosophy, the materialist conception of history can hardly be challenged without departing from Marxism. The materialist dialectic, however, has repeatedly been challenged on a variety of grounds, not least as an anachronistic relic of the philosophical conscience which by rights should have disappeared in 1846. The mainstream of communist thought continued, and continues, to hold Engels' view of materialist dialectics as 'the science of the general laws of motion and development of nature, human society and thought',[4] but the legitimacy of such a conception has been a subject of constant debate with writers both inside and outside the Marxist tradition.

Henri Lefebvre's position of 1958 was one type of attempt to liquidate philosophy. The notion put forward in his *Problèmes actuels du marxisme*, that the ultimate nature of the world could only be broached in poetry, was not the *boutade* it may have appeared. It was rather one option for the dissolution of philosophy: that its functions should be taken over by some non-conceptual discourse. Lefebvre himself went on to develop the notion of a 'metaphilosophy', arising from a radical critique and supersession of philosophy.[5] It was to be a new type of global investigation into the inexhaustible totality, based on a *poiesis*, the creative principle of human activity. The intricacies of Lefebvre's conception need not be dwelt on since they lie substantially outside a Marxist framework at this point. What it shows is that if philosophy is to be abolished, by Marxists or anyone else, the functions which it formerly carried out are redistributed elsewhere either consciously or unconsciously. Lefebvre makes conscious provision for them in a 'poietic' metaphilosophical realm. But others may not make any provision. Historically and ideologically, this latter position has been pre-eminently adopted by positivism.

Following in the wake of Auguste Comte, the positivists have generally denied validity to any propositions which do not belong to the 'positive' sciences. Such propositions are dismissed as either theological or metaphysical, and dealt with by being dissolved (as false problems), redistributed (as misdirected enquiries), or reduced (to matters relating to a specific scientific discipline). At most, formal logic is allowed a degree of validity when it is not in its turn reduced to mathematics. Otherwise the only function conceded to philosophy is its own abolition. Among the many Marxist objections to positivism is the criticism that its abolition of philosophy is only apparent. It in fact rests on a range of philosophical presuppositions which are no less real for being unacknowledged. The necessary functions of philosophy continue to be carried out in a hidden, confused and unexamined fashion, all the more difficult to challenge because their existence is denied. Positivists reject as superstition and mystification everything that is not directly verifiable by the 'positive' sciences, some even extend the rejection to what is not falsifiable. But paradoxically they are apt to fall victim to the most crass ideological illusions, as did Comte himself with his 'scientific' religion of Humanity.

Like positivists, Marxists have constantly been aware of the dangers of mystification which philosophy holds, and of the need to set knowledge on a scientific basis in order to ensure its truth and reliability. To meet this need has been one of the principal motivations for Marxist criticisms of philosophy, beginning with Marx and Engels themselves. The production of a scientific critique of philosophy without falling into positivism is easier to aspire to than to achieve. And though it does not entirely avoid the dangers, one of the most thorough recent attempts to redefine philosophy within a scientific framework is that produced by the Marxist scholar and theorist Georges Labica.

Labica, in his book *Le Statut marxiste de la philosophie* (Paris, 1976), offers a detailed analysis of Marx's and Engels' work from 1835 to 1848 to substantiate his view that there can be no such thing as a Marxist philosophy. Taking the classical triarchy of France, England and Germany, representing the three generally acknowledged sources of Marxism, he suggests that the corresponding contributions of socialism, political economy and philosophy have been too hastily assumed into completed Marxism. He traces the development of all of the three aspects in all of the three countries and concludes that the Marxist synthesis constituted a revolutionary leap in which a new and single science was born: the science of history. Philosophy, he says, played an important mediating role in the birth but was sloughed off like a snake's skin when its usefulness was at an end. Examining the period of 1843–46, he argues that Marx embraced Hegelian philosophy as a conscious step in his own formation, expecting to go beyond it as rapidly as he had dealt with Kant and Fichte. But he found the process more difficult than anticipated and could only escape Hegel by penetrating more deeply into his thought. His first attempted *Ausgang* allied philosophy to the proletariat, thus valorizing the former; his second combined philosophy and political economy but degenerated into a purely philosophical alliance between criticism and the masses; finally, viewing philosophy as ideology, he related it to history and thus escaped from philosophy altogether into a science of history in which the major alliance was between the proletariat and political economy.

Labica's view is therefore that philosophy was eliminated from a Marxism constituted as the science of history. He rejects as 'philosophism' any attempt to suggest a conceptual systematization, a world view, a scientific philosophy, a metaphilosophy or even the need for a Marxist philosophy as yet unformulated. Moreover, he argues, the old problem of relating science and philosophy as modes of cognition is simply dissolved, since the latter has now lost all scientific value. Philosophy as such has not been abolished, he agrees, but as a specific domain of ideology it can readily be dealt with as an object of analysis and a field of class struggle. He admits that his conception of the end of philosophy can be seen as the beginning of a new philosophy under a different name, just as the 'death of God' did not end theology but rather gave it new impetus. But he considers that such a new philosophy would at least have to begin by facing the problems of historical science, which is at any rate an advance.

The intricate and detailed analysis of specific texts makes Labica's argument a challenging and provocative one, supported by a wealth of information and evidence. There can be no question of examining its full complexity here. But several general comments are called for. His conception rests heavily on a passage in *The German Ideology* which is both crossed out in the manuscript and susceptible of differing interpretations. Entitled 'Ideology in General, and Especially German Philosophy', the passage reads:

> We know only a single science, the science of history. One can look at history from two sides and divide it into the history of nature and the history of men. The two sides are, however, inseparable; the history of nature and the history of men are dependent on each other so long as men exist. The history of nature, called natural science, does not concern us here; but we will have to examine the history of men, since almost the whole ideology amounts to a distorted conception of this history or to a complete abstraction from it. Ideology is itself only one of the aspects of this history. [6]

Labica takes this to mean that there is only science, the science of history, divided into natural and human history; and that philosophy is a form of ideology which must therefore be studied scientifically without itself having any scientific validity. [7] But in fact, the passage does not exclude the possibility of even ideology having a cognitive value. It states that 'almost the whole ideology' is a distorted conception of history, suggesting that some ideology, or some of the (German) ideology, may not be distorted. Moreover, the fact of being historical does not exclude all scientific value, since even science develops historically and can be studied as an object. Labica adopts the dichotomous view that ideology is entirely illusory, whereas science is not. Marx and Engels on the other hand also admit the conception of ideology as a consciousness of reality which may or may not accurately reflect real relations. Labica adopts the reductionist view that philosophy is purely ideological, that is, to be understood exclusively in terms of its social origins and function. Marx and Engels, however, recognize a cognitive role for it: even in *The German Ideology* they accept the need for a 'summing-up of the most general results' of historical science. Certainly, they declare the end of 'self-sufficient philosophy', but not of a philosophy closely dependent on science and real history. [8]

Even in terms of Marxist thought in 1846, Labica's view of philosophy is one-sided and over-dismissive. He then concludes by admitting that more needs to be said of later Marxist writings on the subject, but he does not confront them. In particular, he ignores Engels' crucial works, especially *Anti-Dühring* (1878) to which Marx contributed and which he followed closely during its production. For this reason, the very admission of possible objections to his conclusion holds more of a threat than Labica recognizes. Philosophy can readily be dismissed from Marxism in name, but it is a different matter to dismiss the activities and functions which were assembled under that name. To some extent Marx and Engels made that discovery in their own development. The 'settling of accounts' with German philosophy was indeed followed by a period during which they paid little attention to philosophy of any description. But the continued need for summing-up, generalizing, and defending their scientific achievements compelled them to return to philosophical questions in various forms. The most developed expositions were, by mutual agreement, undertaken by Engels. In the absence of any confrontation with these works, Labica falls far short of presenting a Marxist view of the status of philosophy. But then, his tendentious interpretation of *The German Ideology* virtually forecloses the matter. Or it would do, if the matter were not inherently resistant to foreclosure.

Perhaps the most productive aspect of Labica's study is the critique of what he calls the triarchy. French socialism, English political economy and German philosophy are commonly identified as the 'three sources and three component parts of Marxism', as a famous essay by Lenin declares.[9] What Labica usefully emphasizes is that the components are radically transformed in Marxism and integrated with each other; that the three sources are not the only three, even if they are the major ones; and that the three were already linked to each other in a variety of complex ways. In so doing, he also reformulates and resituates the relation of Marx and Hegel. Ostensibly, he banishes Hegel and philosophy by posing a radical discontinuity between the triarchy and Marxism, an action he describes as 'couper le cordon ombilical'.[10] In this, his position differs little from Althusser. But the more complex view he takes of the triarchy itself suggests that the supersession of it is also considerably more complex than the simple severance he proposes. Labica's whole essay replaces the Marx – Hegel matrix with a different set of problems: the emergence of Marxism from the history and ideas of its time. 'Hegel' is shown to be a convenient simplification of the philosophical processes at work, and is put in the context of the other processes which mediate it and are mediated by it. This view can be adopted without following Labica's conclusion that no philosophical process subsists in the eventual Marxist synthesis. Indeed, that conclusion betrays and weakens the demonstration by cutting the product off from its process of production. Even his metaphors play him false: cutting the umbilical cord does not end an infant's relationship with its mother, on the contrary, it inaugurates a new relationship; the snake admittedly grows by casting off its old skin, but it does not cast off its entire skin as such. Labica is right to broaden and complexify the question of Marxism and philosophy beyond the relation of Marx to Hegel; this is his major contribution. But in seeking to abolish philosophy from Marxism he casts a veil of obscurity over part of Marxism's history and amputates a whole section of its living present.

D'Hondt on contradiction and difference

Pourquoi le salariat s'opposerait-il au capital si le salaire et le capital n'avaient une origine identique? Alors qu'il serait apparamment si simple, s'il s'agissait de différence et de contrariété, et non de contradiction vivante, d'aller s'installer ailleurs en une paisible Icarie?

La vie, les événements, les crises, les révolutions ne naissent pas *par rencontre*, selon Marx, ni d'ailleurs selon Hegel, ils ne proviennent pas pour l'essentiel de la fusion de facteurs exterieurs les uns aux autres, mais ils résultent – et aussi l'éventuelle fusion de facteurs extérieurs – d'un *aiguisement* des contradictions.

Jacques D'Hondt, L'Idéologie de la rupture *(Paris, 1978), 80–81*

In a suggestive study of 'l'étrange situation (persistante) faite à Hegel', the young Marxist philosopher François Ricci points to a constant feature of Hegel's position in France.[11] Fighting on two fronts, against woolly romanticism and narrow-minded positivism, Hegel appears as 'Guelph to the Ghibellines and Ghibelline to the Guelphs'. The consequent complexity of his influence leads in Ricci's view to the paradoxical observation that for all his long presence in France, Hegel still appears as a somewhat unfamiliar avantgarde thinker whose possibilities remain relatively unexplored.[12] The strangeness of this view is to some extent explained by the changes in French intellectual life since the post-war Hegel boom. The 1970s saw a general abandonment of the phenomenological and existentialist frames of thought in favour of the new 'post-structuralist' and aphilosophical writings of Foucault, Derrida, Deleuze, Lacan and others: a shift in many respects from Kierkegaard to Nietzsche, concomitant with the beginnings of a positivist revival. Hegel was not passed on from the earlier currents to the later, or if he was, it was in a radically altered form with a quite new emphasis.

Though Marxists have maintained a consistent tradition of attention to Hegel, the changes around them have also been reflected in the development of Marxist philosophy and its view of Hegel. The tendencies inherited from Garaudy and Althusser continue to echo the earlier debates in which Ricci's 'two fronts' are plainly recognizable. A minority of Marxists still sail close to the shoals of positivism and, like Georges Labica, try to eliminate Hegel and philosophy with him. But the majority stay on the main routes of Marxist philosophy, many of them looking to Hegel to make better headway through the difficult waters of dialectics. For these latter, Hegel appears as a rich source of teaching, albeit not without certain dangers. Some of the most stimulating philosophical writing of contemporary Marxism has come from this group. To discuss all of the writers who might be evoked in this connection would be too lengthy an undertaking. The work of two of them, Jacques D'Hondt and Solange Mercier-Josa will stand, not only as representative of the new dynamism of a Marxism eager to learn from Hegel, but also as significant contributions to the conception and elaboration of materialist dialectics in recent years.

Jacques D'Hondt is perhaps the most informed and scholarly of the pro-Hegelian Marxists. A philosophy lecturer in Poitiers, he has published several academic studies of Hegel and his philosophy. His *Hegel en son temps* (Paris, 1968) offers an examination of the complex relationship between historical developments and Hegel's philosophical and social position during his tenure of the chair of philosophy in Berlin at the end of his life. *Hegel secret* (Paris, 1968) uncovers the lesser-known sources of Hegel's thought and sheds new light on the dynamics of his intellectual evolution. *Hegel, philosophe de l'histoire vivante* (Paris, 1966) studies the relation of his philosophy of history to the events of his own time, with a view to retrieving something of the reputation which this aspect of his thought has lost. D'Hondt has also been responsible for several conferences and symposia on Hegel and directs in Poitiers a state-sponsored institute for research and documentation on Hegel and Marx. Since the mid-1960s D'Hondt has written extensively on the relations between Marxist and Hegelian philosophy. His essays, collected in two volumes, *De Hegel à Marx* (Paris, 1972) and *L'Idéologie de la rupture* (Paris, 1978), represent an elegant and incisive response to the anti-Hegelians, as well as an exemplary use of Hegelian analyses to enrich the concepts of dialectical materialism.

Responding to the criticisms of Althusser and others, D'Hondt attaches considerable importance to the notion of inversion. While he recognizes the changes which followed Marx's inversion of the Hegelian dialectic, he insists that Marx did not either abandon or strangle the dialectic. He also rejects any attempt to define the Marxist dialectic by its specific difference from Hegel's, arguing that Marx had no theological feeling of being an absolute new beginning. He defends the view that Marx and Engels shared with Hegel a dialectics of nature, distinguished from his by the primacy of development over repetition, where Hegel acknowledged development as a limited, partial aspect of basic repetition. Considering it an entirely legitimate exercise to separate the dialectic from Hegelian idealism, D'Hondt points out that Hegel himself applied various dialectical approaches to a single relation, such as domination and servitude; that in a given work, particular analyses are readily separable from the main argument; and that in his early writings Hegel developed several 'dialectiques régionales' before ever he conceived his notion of the Absolute Idea.[13] He recalls the comment of Lenin, described as 'le moins conciliant des matérialistes', on the final chapter of Hegel's *Logic*, devoted to the Absolute Idea: 'in this most idealistic of Hegel's works there is the least idealism and the most materialism'.[14] D'Hondt is well enough versed in Hegel to see how much Marx had to reject, but he also sees the other side, and the Marxism he presents in *De Hegel à Marx* is deeply suffused with Hegel's dialectic.

Turning to the offensive in *L'Idéologie de la rupture*, he deploys a sharply dialectical criticism against the 'rupturaliste' interpretation of Marx represented by Althusser and his school. Their rejection of unity and continuity appears to him as a fetishization of 'breaks', which disregards the content of what is being replaced and what it is replaced by. Ultimately he considers it as a refurbished dogmatism taking its revenge on the dialectic. He accepts that a purely continuationist view of the development of knowledge is correctly criticized, but suggests that it is a typically ideological illusion to imagine that knowledge springs from nowhere, has no sources. Such illusion, he adds, is tailored to a class with no interest in the future, content to forget its past: the bourgeoisie, particularly its anguished youth. Their non-dialectical 'rupturalism', he suggests, is a form of metaphysics which surreptitiously installs a mystical transcendence in the guise of discontinuities, recalling Paul Ricoeur's description of structuralism as a 'transcendantalisme sans sujet'.[15] Examining in detail a series of conceptual problems, D'Hondt's book offers subtle and provocative analyses in which the Hegelian heritage of Marxism is contrasted to the peremptory solutions proposed by his opponents.

There is much that deserves comment in Jacques D'Hondt's discussion of inversion and its role in the generation of what is new; of the dialectics of dependence and autonomy; of the notion of the beginning and its implications for a conception of totality. But his general position is asserted with particular pertinence in his analysis of the key concept of contradiction. Recalling Marx's and Engels' repeated recommendations to study Hegelian logic, he indicates Hegel's importance in their criticism of the limitations of formal logic which is based on the principle of identity, or non-contradiction. Deprived of a dialectical theory of contradiction, he argues, formal logic tends to regard differences as absolute, ignoring their unity and denying them the possibility to change or even to come into contact with each other. D'Hondt quotes widely from Marx's economic writings to show the practical value of a theory of the unity of contradiction. Whereas, for example, classical economists saw the three sources of income (rent, interest and wages) as separate and independent elements, D'Hondt shows that Marx saw their difference, their identity and the contradictions between them, arising from a common basis, which would eventually lead to their collapse. Simple difference excludes struggle, he points out, but wage-labour and capital are opposed because they have an identical origin. Life, events, crises and revolutions do not, he argues, arise from encounters between different elements: for Marx as for Hegel, they arise from a sharpening of contradictions. He concludes that the project of 'sharpening' contradictions presupposes the unity of difference and identity. Formal logic, based on identity and non-contradiction can therefore have no absolute validity.

D'Hondt's persuasive dialectic is an unblushing defence of the Hegelian component of Marxism against the attacks of Althusser, Godelier and their supporters. His polished prose is no less barbed, however, than their apodictic assertions. His work is especially rewarding in his informed discussion of Hegel's philosophical position, often caricatured by his opponents. Particularly valuable is his suggestion that Hegel's work does not have the monolithic, indivisible quality so often attributed to it. If this is accepted, it confirms the respect which Marx and Engels had for Hegel's work. It also helps to explain how they, and Lenin after them, should have incorporated so much Hegelian philosophy into their own writings without abandoning a consistent materialism in the process. Theoretically, however, the most crucial point he raises is the nature and importance of difference.

Saussurian linguistics has been largely responsible for setting the notion of difference at the centre of analysis in the human sciences. In its wake, structuralist and post-structuralist writers have adopted as a fundamental tenet that phenomena are to be defined in and by their specific difference, a view taken by both Althusser and Godelier. D'Hondt is correct in arguing that such a view belongs strictly within the sphere of formal logic, where precise and unvarying distinctions can be drawn between both concepts and realities. While he recognizes the relative value of formal logic, he insists that it is unable to define its own limits since its founding principle, non-contradiction (or identity), only has validity if and when the more fundamental principle of contradiction (a unity of identity and difference) is disregarded. On this view formal logic is a special case of dialectics. But if it is elevated to primary status, it can only lead to metaphysics and the reduction of contradiction to mere static difference, excluding the unity or identity which gives dialectics its dynamism.

The fundamental threat of D'Hondt's dialectics to structuralism is then not in denying it all validity, but in restricting its validity to the study of phenomena in which movement can, for most practical purposes, be disregarded. Claude Lévi-Strauss, a founding father of structural analysis, already acknowledged the difficulty in *La Pensée sauvage* (Paris, 1962), where he declares that 'la raison dialectique nous apparaît comme la raison analytique en marche'.[16] Conceding the need for a dialectic to grasp the nature of historical movement, Lévi-Strauss attempted to construct it from a base of formal logic, his 'analytical reason'. But where Marxism diverges from structuralism is in its assertion of the primacy of change and movement. It cannot share Lévi-Strauss's view of history as a 'méthode . . . pour inventorier l'intégralité des éléments d'une structure quelconque', since to do so would entail accepting movement as an aspect of structure.[17] At best it may recognize structural analysis as a useful method for analysing the configuration of historical movement within limited parameters. Likewise Marxism cannot accept the reduction of contradiction to simple opposition after Lévi-Strauss's fashion which, as D'Hondt points out, eliminates the source of interaction. Godelier's attack on the identity of opposites and Althusser's decomposition of contradiction can be seen to come under this criticism since the unity of opposites which they propose excludes identity at any level. The elements of their 'organic totality' are radically differentiated. D'Hondt's example of wage-labour and capital is particularly telling since it renders intelligible the necessity of their struggle where a structural analysis only asserts it as contingent. The two are poles in a single process, locked together but having diametrically opposed interests. They are not unrelated entities thrown together by the vagaries of fortune. Hence there is no amicable agreement available whereby they could 'sink their differences' or even 'agree to differ'.

Although he successfully demonstrates the limitations of structural analysis and its failure to recognize the dialectic, Jacques D'Hondt's own account has its limitations. Most of them stem from his tendency to equate the Marxist and Hegelian dialectics in practice, even when he has made the necessary disclaimers. His attack on 'rupturalism' is a case in point. Extracting one fundamental idea, that of the break, he analyses it dialectically, but primarily at an abstract level, drawing out its implications in terms of intelligibility and presuppositions. His conclusions, while valid enough at that level, lose much of their force when confronted with the analysis of any of the specific writers whom, by implication, he attacks. His creature of reason, the rupturalist, lacks the features of a real opponent. His attack is to that extent misdirected.

The level of abstraction also limits the force of his analysis of contradiction. His assertion of the ultimate identity of such opposites as capital and labour is a salutary reminder of the root of their struggle. But it is at a high level of generality which does little to elucidate the mediations through which the contradiction passes or its relationship with other contradictions. As a result his attack bears largely on the general framework of the anti-Hegelian writers, but does not confront the detailed analysis which is their most striking achievement. D'Hondt's position therefore needs to be completed by the application of his general principles to a close study of specific problems of Marxism.

Mercier-Josa and the detour via Hegel

Ou bien faire de l'histoire de la philosophie serait – et c'est la fonction que nous voudrions assigner à notre propre activité philosophique – tenter de trouver la bonne distance pour mettre en perspective, donc pour éloigner quelque peu un texte, celui de Marx qui parce qu'il ne nous paraît en rien dépassé nous prive en un sens du plaisir de dire vrai tout en disant autre chose et autrement. Nous avons essayé de ressaisir par une série de coups de sondes comment précisément Marx à partir de Hegel et de l'hégélianisme avait tissé un discours propre mais dont nous ne pensons pas finalement que le sens soit dans son épaisseur radicalement séparable du texte dont il est sorti. Nous avons trouvé une façon de faire rentrer quelque peu dans l'histoire des textes, un texte que n'a pas fini de se donner à nous comme le langage même de notre expérience du réel et de notre pratique.

Solange Mercier-Josa, Pour lire Marx et Hegel (Paris, 1980), 10

The entry of women into French intellectual life did not await 1980 to be noticed. But the assertion of their importance in philosophy has been perceptibly slower than in other domains. A few exceptional women have always been present in intellectual debate, but much less evident in the field of philosophy than elsewhere. In post-war France a figure like Simone de Beauvoir was very much an isolated exception, and of her writings, the philosophical work was probably the least successful.

The eruption of the women's movement of the 1960s, coinciding with arrival at adulthood of a new, articulate and educated generation of women, born in the immediate post-war years, rapidly challenged the traditional male dominance of cultural life. *La Nouvelle critique* recognized the importance of these changes with a special number in December 1964 devoted to 'Les intellectuelles', and as the years passed reviews and publishers' lists reflected the growing numbers of women taking up intellectual work. Philosophy has usually tended to respond more slowly than other disciplines to the endeavours of younger writers. It is not surprising therefore that women established their reputations first in schools of thought which were at the time considered most innovatory and which attracted young intellectuals impatient with the established patterns of thought. These schools were largely to be found on the margins of Marxism and within the ambit of structuralist theory.

Among the first and perhaps best known of the women philosophers of this type was Julia Kristeva, who first wrote for *La Pensée* in 1966, and whose semiological analyses won her wide acclaim in the late 1960s and early 1970s. The supporters and successors of Althusser too counted among them women of considerable stature as philosophers, such as Christine Buci-Glucksmann and Danielle Kaisergruber who were prominent from 1973 in the review *Dialectiques*. Claudine Normand, like Kristeva concerned with the semiology, wrote for *La Pensée* and then for *Dialectiques* from the early 1970s while her contemporary Nicole-Edith Thévenin wrote regularly on Hegel and philosophy from the same period and from a similar perspective. Solange Mercier-Josa did not adopt an Althusserian viewpoint but worked broadly within the mainstream Marxist tradition and contributed regularly to *La Pensée* from 1970 onwards. Other women writers share her general orientation and are increasingly asserting their presence, as for instance Catherine Backès-Clément in the theory of mind,[18] and Michèle Bertrand in the theory of religion.[19] In view of the growing philosophical strength of Marxist women, and in view of the even greater role they have acquired in other areas of intellectual activity, it may be taken as indicative rather than exceptional that the PCF's newly created Institut de Recherches Marxistes should have a woman, Francette Lazard, as its director. Solange Mercier-Josa's book *Pour lire Hegel et Marx* (Paris, 1980), is therefore representative not only of her generation and of the new level of interest in Hegel, but also of the growing place of women in French Marxism. More important, it is a new and stimulating approach to Marxist philosophy.

Paradoxically, Mercier-Josa begins by admitting the extreme difficulty of saying anything new about Marxism. She articulates the widespread problem of Marxists who have experienced 'la fulgurance de l'évidence' in reading Marx, and can honestly find nothing to add or to change.[20] In large measure the distressing obviousness of Marx's analyses may be ascribed to the fact that we still live in essentially the same historical stage as he did, and that he discerned the way in which it works. But the persistence of this stage holds the danger that Marxism eventually begins to seem stale and over-familiar, losing the appeal of its first discovery. Moreover, philosophers may feel deprived of the joy of speaking a new truth and resent being reduced to textual commentary and history of philosophy, glossing the classics or tracing their emergence. One of her essays explores the consequent dangers of utopianism, arising from the frustrations of these thinkers who perceive that the elements exist for a solution to the historical problems of their society, but who cannot wait for it to be realized. Their impatience drives them to abandon their grasp on the real contradictions, and the concrete forms of negation within them, in favour of an apparently radical negation which is in fact only abstract and therefore inadequate. As a response to the genuine difficulties underlying such attitudes, Mercier-Josa proposes the strategy of a detour through Hegel to explore concepts in their pre-Marxist state. At the risk of straying into Hegelian mystification she hopes to gain a sufficient distance from Marxism to make possible the pleasure of rediscovery, to enable the magnitude of Marx's achievement to appear in a new perspective, and to open the way for fruitful innovation within a fundamentally correct theoretical framework.

Before examining its results, the project itself deserves some comment. The idea that Marxism is stale and over familiar has always been characteristic of commentators who know little of it, have read less, and would prefer it to go away. Actual contact with Marxist writings tends in such cases to come as something of a revelation. Even people who have real familiarity with Marxism commonly experience a sense of freshness and discovery in reading the original works. But it is undeniable, certainly in France, that the number of Marxist works which have appeared in the last quarter century has left many intellectuals, even Marxist intellectuals, with a sated feeling and a desire for novelty. Mercier-Josa's aspiration is to meet this desire without abandoning a position which remains no less valid for being familiar. The recognition of pleasure as a legitimate part of philosophical activity is in itself noteworthy, though not in any absolute sense new. On the one hand, it has clear ideological importance, as a factor in the social implantation of ideas, especially among intellectuals, for whom fashion and novelty are important arbiters of allegiance. On the other hand, pleasure in any textual activity has in recent years been rehabilitated by structuralist and post-structuralist writers to the extent that it has been widely adopted as an inescapable criterion of worth, even if not the primary criterion. Roland Barthes, with his *Le Plaisir du texte* (Paris, 1973) has been a foremost advocate, though he and others have conceived the pleasure in a more immediate, sensual form. The pleasure Mercier-Josa envisages is largely conceptual in nature.

The choice of Hegel as a standpoint from which to approach Marx is more than an exercise in intellectual history. Althusser has explained in his *Eléments d'autocritique* (Paris, 1974) how he undertook a detour via Spinoza to try to understand Marx's detour via Hegel, arguing that a philosophy can only define itself in its difference from other philosophies. Mercier-Josa proposes in effect to take the detour via Hegel in order to understand Marx. Explicit in her aim is the view that Marx is not radically separable from Hegel. She does not therefore require an external standpoint from which to separate the two, as Althusser did; what she does require is an internal standpoint from which to reconstruct the passage from one to the other. Whereas Althusser's Spinoza was the hidden principle of his Marxism, Mercier-Josa's Hegel is the avowed inspiration of hers. But in both cases the object of the exercise is a deeper understanding of Marxism, and the standpoint outside Marx is provisional, whatever the eventual dangers it might engender. The adoption of a pseudo-external viewpoint is taken as the only means of situating a conceptual framework by which all other frameworks are situated. But Mercier-Josa's choice of Hegel to fulfil this office, unlike Althusser's choice of Spinoza, is consistent with the Marxist concept of history. Ultimately it amounts to situating Marxism in its own development. Her external viewpoint is simultaneously internal to the history of Marxism: philosophy and the history of philosophy are combined in a single complex operation.

The essays which compose *Pour lire Hegel et Marx* deal with a series of points at which the Marxist and Hegelian positions can be shown in their connection and difference. One essay traces the passage from Hegel's philosophy of history to Marx's theory of history posing the provocative question of whether Hegel's notion of the 'concrete universal' is transcribed in Marx's account in the notion of the classless society. A second essay poses the question of Marx's early critique of Hegel's theory of the state, asking how much of its survives in his mature conception. Another examines the concept of practice found in Marx, showing its originality with respect to Hegel's concept of free will, which has the comparable role of determining the ontological status of mind. The demetaphorizing inversion which characterizes Marx's treatment of Hegel is shown to be a complex process in a long essay which compares Marx's concept of ideology with Hegel's notion of the spirit of a people (*Volksgeist*).

Mercier-Josa analyses the Hegelian notion of a people as an individualized totality distinguished by its morality and customs (*Sittlichkeit*), and bound together by a spirit which produces the various aspects of its life. The nature of the spirit is defined on the one hand by the relation existing between the people or state and the individual, and on the other hand by its relation to the universal spirit – reason – of which it is a moment. In the first place, she argues, Marx accepts Hegel's view that *Sittlichkeit* is composed of different spheres, including religion, politics, morality, law and philosophy. He proceeds, however, to examine them in their own right. He also accepts that *Sittlichkeit* is dependent on something more basic, but instead of the *Volksgeist*, he relates it to the material production of life. In the second place, Marx rejects the view of the *Volksgeist* as the communal product of all individuals in a collectivity, replacing it with the notion that the characteristic thought of a society is the ideology of the dominant class within it. This dominant ideology, produced by and reproducing relations in the society, seeks to pass for a spirit of the people. The resolution of contradictions and the realm of freedom are therefore not in this spirit, but in the historical achievement of a classless society in which all individuals would be able to unite in a real people. In the meantime, she suggests the notion of spirit of a people could be retained to designate the unstable compromise between dominant and opposing ideologies, or the historical gains won in the process of class struggle towards the achievement of a classless society and therefore the creation of a people.

What Mercier-Josa does in this essay is outline the organization of a series of key Hegelian concepts, show how certain of them are reworked and re-ordered by Marx, and suggest how the remainder of them, neglected by Marx, might be similarly reworked and re-ordered. The novelty of her approach is demonstrated by this last step. Whereas many studies have shown how various Marxist concepts emerge from Hegelian origins, she shows how various Hegelian ideas are transformed into Marxist concepts. The difference, though apparently trivial, is considerable. Marx's development is more completely reconstructed and presented in its original movement rather than in retrospect. Hence the end product, Marxism, is reinvested with a dimension of openness and unresolved possibilities. Mercier-Josa's particular treatment of the possibilities can naturally be criticized, but her approach is open and productive. It provides a means of developing Marxism within the logic of its original emergence, calling the history of philosophy into action as a resource for philosophy.

The tasks of philosophy include those of reflecting political questions and clarifying the terms and concepts which express them. Mercer-Josa's analysis fulfils these tasks and is to that extent political. But the content which her conceptual analysis acquires is not conferred by a philosophical position so much as by its relation to theoretical implications at a social and historical level, and by the political ends to which it is harnessed. These aspects are left open in her analysis, though the circumstances in which she is writing provide a context and relevance for her explorations. The specific question of the nature of a people, and its spirit, are clearly important for the strategy of the communist movement, whether it be the Soviet Union, aspiring to build a 'state of the whole people', as its 1977 constitution declares, or the French Communist Party aspiring to 'l'union du peuple de France', which its documents have called for since its 21st Congress (1974). The difference between a people and a nation or nationality, the relationship between a class or classes and a people, the nature of a people's actual or potential existence, the nature of ideology, culture and other institutions in their relation to a people, these are crucial issues in the theoretical framework of historical materialism. They and other questions need to be clarified before the notions of people or spirit of a people can be adequately judged. Mercier-Josa leaves them open, as she must, since the validity of her suggested concepts cannot be tested on the basis of philosophical analysis, however persuasive, but only on the basis of historical theory and practice. The political considerations, particularly the strategy of the PCF, are clearly a major factor in her choice of subject, and the tendency of her discussion is to suggest a theoretical basis for the notion of the union of the French people. Returning to Hegel for assistance in the task holds two opposed possibilities: either it may be a fruitful basis for elucidating a new, or newly perceived, reality in Marxist terms, or else it may be a fertile source of justification for an old illusion resurrected in Marxist dress. Whether the notion of the people represents a further step towards socialist society or a retreat from the politics of class struggle depends on the functional importance given to it both in theory and in practice.

References

1   A. Tosel, 'Le Matérialisme dialectique "entre" les sciences de la nature et la science de l'histoire', *La Pensée*, septembre – octobre 1978, 70 – 94.
2   E. I. Bitsakis, 'Symétrie et contradiction', in CERM, *Lénine et la pratique scientifique* (Paris, 1974), 134 – 153.

3   E. I. Bitsakis, 'Sur le statut des lois physiques', *La Pensée*, mars – avril 1979, 61 – 85.

4   F. Engels, *Anti-Dühring* (London, 1975), 169.

5   See H. Lefebvre, *Métaphilosophie, prolégomènes* (Paris, 1965).

6   K. Marx and F. Engels, *Collected Works*, V (London, 1976), 28 – 29.

7   G. Labica, *Le Statut marxiste de la philosophie* (Paris, 1976), 368ff.

8   Marx and Engels, *Collected Works*, V, 37.

9   V. I. Lenin, 'The three sources and three component parts of Marxism', in K. Marx and F. Engels, *Selected Works* (London, 1968), 23 – 27.

10   Labica, *Le Statut*, 367.

11   F. Ricci, 'L'étrange situation (persistante) faite à Hegel', *Cahiers du CERM*, 141 (1977), 37 – 41.

12   *Ibid.*, 37.

13   J. D'Hondt, *De Hegel à Marx* (Paris, 1972), 13.

14   V. I. Lenin, *Collected Works*, XXXVIII (Moscow, 1972), 234.

15   J. D'Hondt, *L'Idéologie de la rupture* (Paris, 1978), 143.

16   C. Lévi-Strauss, *La Pensée sauvage* (Paris, 1962), 332.

17   *Ibid.*, 348.

18   C. B. Clément and others, *Pour une critique marxiste de la théorie psychanalytique* (Paris, 1973).

19   Michèle Bertrand, *Le Statut de la religion chez Marx et Engels* (Paris, 1979).

20   S. Mercier-Josa, *Pour lire Marx et Hegel* (Paris, 1980), 7.

Conclusion

Mais la vraie question n'est pas de savoir *dire* en quoi consiste la dialectique, c'est de savoir *penser*, et *agir*, tant soit peu dialectiquement.

Lucien Sève, Une Introduction à la philosophie marxiste
(*Paris, 1980*), 524

For the better part of a decade, from the late 1960s until the late 1970s, Marxism dominated social thought and philosophy in the French universities. Though this pre-eminence was constantly under challenge, it was generally recognized that a major part of the country's intellectual life was conducted in Marxist terminology. Very often the terminology was specifically that of Althusser – not surprisingly since it was he who first successfully stormed the academic establishment in the name of Marx. Other Marxist currents were able to take advantage of the opening, but as the Althusserian wave slowly receded in the later 1970s, so the academic acceptability of Marxism as a whole began to decline. Time alone will tell how permanent this reverse has been, but the experience underlines how fragile are shifts in ideological dominance unless accompanied by corresponding shifts in economic and political conditions. It also illustrates the resistance that mainstream Marxist ideas have continued to meet in the university.

Despite the striking successes of the Althusserians, much of the development of Marxist thought continues to take place outside the universities or at least outside their upper echelons. Marxist academics, especially members or sympathizers of the PCF, still find themselves barred from funds, posts and honours to which their work would otherwise entitle them. For publication they are still often forced to rely on the resources of specialist left-wing publishers. A recent case in point is the monumental study of the early years of Marx and Engels, the life-work of Auguste Cornu, who died in 1981 at the age of ninety-three. The original publishers, Presses Universitaires de France, refused to print a new revised edition of this classic, and Cornu was obliged to turn to the PCF house Editions sociales. The consequent tendency to intellectual ghettoization serves to limit the spread of Marxist ideas and to stamp their advocates with a badge of difference. But there is a perhaps unexpected advantage for Marxists in this. The stigma cast on them by the ruling elite becomes a badge of honour among those who themselves reject or distrust that elite. The recognition withheld by a conservative establishment is compensated by the recognition gained among working people who rarely encounter the world of the intelligentsia, and among fellow intellectuals who are likewise estranged from the dominant culture of their peers.

The strained position of Marxism in French culture derives from the class structure of French society. If it is true that on the whole the dominant ideas in a culture are those which suit the dominant class, then it is understandable that the French bourgeoisie should make every effort to limit the penetration of a philosophy profoundly hostile to it. The precise means by which the ideological struggle is carried out are often subtle and complex. But the existence of such a struggle goes a long way towards explaining why Marxist writing is so frequently ignored or contemptuously dismissed by leading commentators in France and elsewhere. In some respects, Marxism functions as the subconscious of French intellectual life. It is that which respectable authors avoid naming, or do so only with distaste; yet it is the dynamic force to which they are directly or indirectly responding much of the time. The analogy is rich with suggestion, but should not perhaps be overdrawn. At all events it is clear that from Nizan and Politzer through Cornu, Lefebvre and Garaudy to Lucien Sève, the mainstream of communist Marxism has flourished largely outside the institutions provided by the French state for intellectual activity. And when it has penetrated those institutions it has met, and still meets, determined resistance.

The importance of this battle for the commanding heights of French culture cannot be disregarded in the broader conflict of classes and social systems, though its outcome will depend ultimately on the broader issue. In the meantime Marxism has continued to consolidate its position outside official culture as an expression of the experience and aspirations of the working class and of other working people, including intellectuals, who share their desire for change. The times are long past when the intellectual needs of the people could be satisfied by simple introductions and crude vulgarizations. But the same potential audience is also unable or unwilling to enter into the arcane discussions of professional philosophers, sociologists, economists and the like. Yet throughout the 1960s and 1970s there was no single work offering an accessible general statement of Marxist principles, presented in some degree of complexity, from a Marxist viewpoint. There was nothing at a level between the much revised elementary manual based on Politzer's pre-war lectures, or Lefebvre's short volume of 1948 in the 'Que sais-je?' series, and Althusser's difficult philosophical re-readings of Marx or the specialist colloquia of the CERM. It was to bridge that obvious gap that Lucien Sève was commissioned to write the comprehensive synthesis which was eventually published as *Une Introduction à la philosophie marxiste* (Paris, 1980).

This bulky volume of over 700 pages was designed to serve as an intelligent layman's initiation, a student's handbook and a contribution to the development of Marxism. Certainly, the brisk sales it has enjoyed suggest that the first two aims are largely achieved. However, the response of specialist opinion has been almost entirely confined to the communist milieu. It is not surprising that these already sympathetic critics should have given the work a warm reception , but the silence of others confirms the isolation of communist Marxism among the intelligentsia. Yet the policy of an ideological 'cordon sanitaire', if continued, is more likely to promote than to inhibit the spread of Sèvian Marxism, albeit in non-academic circles. The main deleterious effect is to deprive Sève and his supporters of the intellectual tussles in which ideas are refined and tempered. But even this deprivation is less severe in the France of the 1980s than was the case in the 1940s and 1950s, since a wide and well-educated audience now provides an alternative arena for debate. And whatever their ideological position, communist intellectuals operate at a higher level of sophistication than earlier generations usually achieved.

Conceptually, Sève's *Introduction* reiterates most of the positions established during the 1960s and 1970s conerning Marxist philosophy and presents the substance of most of the major debates between the various contending schools of thought. In the process, he pushes further the elaboration of dialectical contradiction, providing a more complete account of antagonism and non-antagonism, which owes something to Pierre Jaeglé's analysis of time and space. Antagonistic contradictions are characterized by irreconcilable opposites which succeed one another in time. Non-antagonistic contradictions are composed of reconcilable opposites which are separated spatially. The two types of contradiction are of course interconnected, the first determining the movement, and the second the structure of a given totality. It is therefore only in a formal sense that there are two types of contradiction, concretely it is more accurate to speak of two aspects to any contradiction. Moreover, since the real world should be the primary determinant of a materialist viewpoint, this abstract analysis is not a blueprint from which reality can be deduced; it is a conceptual apparatus by means of which the infinite complexities of reality can be approached and understood.

Within the terms of his conceptual framework, Sève's analysis of contradiction is satisfyingly complete. He establishes a tight network of interrelated concepts which give coherence to the mainstream view of materialist dialectics without falling into the kind of simplistic and schematic presentation which vitiated comparable works of an earlier generation. The theoretical objections to his analysis are the same as may be urged against his position as a whole. From an Althusserian viewpoint, the primary objection must be that Sève develops a conception which is unacceptable in its entirety, basing Marxism on a post-Hegelian dialectic which Marx rejected in his mature works. On this view the entire enterprise is misconceived. Althusser himself is, however, tragically no longer able to articulate criticisms which might confront the finer detail. An internal critique may well find arguments or interpretations of classical sources with which to take issue, but the most serious question is not Sève's reasoning but the use to which it is put. In justice to Sève, he is clearly aware of the abuses to which dialectics can be subjected, and sternly reproves any tendency to use it either as a sophistical means to justify actions after the event, or as a rhetorical means to present conclusions arrived at in a quite different way. The difficulty is to avoid and prevent these abuses, and there is nothing in Sève's dialectic itself which guarantees that. Nor indeed could there be if, as Marxism holds, thought does not determine its own relation to the world.

The problem, then, is not so much in the ideas as in what is done with them. It is the problem which confronts all theory: that of its translation into practice. If thought is to be an effective guide to action it must first understand its own position in the world, and then find a form of expression which will enable it to influence the thought and action of people. Sève attempts to meet these problems both in the content and in the form of his book, summed up in his concluding call, borrowed from Diderot: 'Hâtons-nous de rendre la philosophie populaire.' In harking back to Diderot he also harks back to the brief years of the Liberation and its aftermath: a time when Marxists hoped to embody the renewed spirit of the French Enlightenment. But the desire for a popular philosophy also recalls these years, and earlier times, when the urgent task was to propagate the basic ideas of Marxism among the working people. Although the need for educational work was never disregarded, the major preoccupation of Marxist intellectuals since the mid-1950s has largely been the much-needed effort of raising the level of debate and developing a more sophisticated theoretical apparatus. With Sève, the emphasis now reverts to the project of education. But the reversion is not necessarily a regression. Marxism has come a long way since the 1950s, and the intense debates of the intervening period have largely settled, leaving a much more complex body of thought in their wake. Research continues, but for the time being it takes place in a well-delineated space. What better time then for taking stock and passing on the accumulated lessons? That is the essence of Sève's project.

While it is in many ways less exhilarating than research, education is arguably a more important work for Marxist intellectuals in the early 1980s. If only for the further development of theory itself, intensified education is clearly advantageous in broadening the social base on which debate can take place, and in ensuring that future theoretical controversies at least begin from an advanced level of enquiry. But the main importance of education is political. The prospect of communists in government with social democrats, which was realized in mid-1981, and the enhanced responsibilities of Marxists at all levels of national life, make it an urgent priority that Marxists other than professional intellectuals should be equipped with the most thorough understanding of the philosophy to which they subscribe and by which they claim to be guided. For it is an obvious truth that ideas become material forces only when they are understood and put into action. And after all, the originality of Marxist philosophy, as Marx himself conceived it, was not so much that it offered a better understanding of the world, but that it proposed to change it.

Annotated Bibliography

For reasons of space, the present bibliography is brief and selective. The interested reader will have no difficulty in finding additional material on Marx, Engels and subsequent international Marxist debate, on the Hegelian and existentialist traditions, or on currents of thought in contemporary France, all of which form the background to the foregoing discussions. The following notes are intended to indicate, especially for the reader with little or no French, the main secondary sources available on French Marxism and its historical context.

French history

There is no shortage of literature in English on French history, and useful general surveys from a variety of standpoints can be found in: A. Cobban, *A History of Modern France*, III (London, 1965); D. W. Brogan, *The French Nation 1814–1940* (London, 1957); G. Wright, *France in Modern Times* (Chicago, 1960); P. Ouston, *France in the Twentieth Century* (London, 1972); T. Zeldin, *France 1848–1945*, 2 vols (London, 1973 and 1977); J. P. T. Bury, *France 1814–1940*, revised edition (London, 1976): S. Hoffman and others, *France: Change and Tradition* (London, 1963); D. G. Charlton, *France: A Companion to French Studies* (London, 1972). Most of these works are stronger on the period up to the Second World War than on more recent developments, and need therefore to be supplemented by more specialized studies. A valuable up-to-date study of contemporary France is provided by J. E. Flower (ed.), *France Today* (London, 1972), which is periodically revised and updated.

A particularly useful survey of the Left in France since the end of the Third Republic is given by F.-G. Dreyfus, *Histoire des Gauches en France 1940–1974* (Paris, 1975). A rapid survey of the Left from earliest to most recent times is given by C. Willard, *Socialisme et communisme français* (Paris, 1978). Many studies of the French Communist Party are available, but for the most part are superseded by Ronald Tiersky's *French Communism 1920–1972* (New York and London, 1974), which also contains a critical bibliography of earlier studies. There is still some useful material in J. Fauvet's *Histoire du parti communiste français* (Paris, 1964) and F. Fejto's *The French Communist Party and the Crisis of International Communism* (London, 1967). Probably the most prolific writer on the subject is Annie Kriegel, whose study *The French Communists* (London and Chicago, 1972) is available in English, though her hatred of the movement to which she once belonged colours much of her work. Danielle Tartakowski's *Les Premiers communistes francais* (Paris, 1981) gives a sympathetic and informative account of the party's early years. Also useful are the essays edited by D. Blackmer and S. Tarrow, *Communism in Italy and France* (Princeton, 1977). The most abundant source of contemporary material remains the regular *Cahiers d'histoire* published by the PCF's Institut des Recherches Marxistes (formerly Institut Maurice Thorez). The collective volume *Le PCF: étapes et problèmes 1920–1972* (Paris, 1981) is an invaluable addition to this literature, produced by party historians.

French Marxism

For reasons mentioned elsewhere, there has been little work on French Marxism in English, though individual Marxists have attracted considerable attention. The most extensive general discussion in English is George Lichtheim's interesting but limited *Marxism in Modern France* (London, 1966), usefully supplemented by his later collection *From Marx to Hegel and Other Essays* (London, 1971). David Caute's *Communism and the French Intellectuals* (London, 1964) has a wealth of information and anecdote on intellectuals who were communists or sympathizers in the period up to 1956 and its immediate aftermath. More theoretical is Mark Poster's invaluable *Existential Marxism in Postwar France* (Princeton, 1975) which deals with a wide range of Marxist and para-Marxist debate since the 1940s. Lichtheim, Caute and Poster each provide extensive bibliographical references.

There is naturally more material available in French, though no overall survey exists, and the studies which do exist are inevitably partial in both senses of the word. There are useful surveys from a PCF point of view in Jacques Milhau's *Chroniques philosophiques* (Paris, 1972), the *Cahiers d'histoire de l'Institut Maurice Thorez*, 15 (1976), and Roger Garaudy's *Perspectives de l'homme* (Paris, 1959). The latter has since reappeared in revised form with new material (4th edition, 1969). Lucien Sève's *Une Introduction à la philosophie marxiste* (Paris, 1980) incorporates a historical survey into his theoretical discussions. These works are usefully supplemented by L. Soubise, *Le Marxisme après Marx*,

1956–1965 (Paris, 1967) which deals with four 'dissident' Marxists in detail.

On the earlier period of French Marxism, Claude Willard's scholarly thesis *Les Guesdistes* (Paris, 1965) gives extensive information. Its conclusions are in part contested by Daniel Lindenberg in his provocative *Le Marxisme introuvable* (Paris, 1975). A detailed study from a different point of view is offered by Maurice Dommanget in *L'Introduction du marxisme en France* (Paris, 1967), and there is still useful material in Alexandre Zévaès' older work, *De l'introduction du marxisme en France* (Paris, 1947) and Neil McInnes, 'Les débuts du marxisme', *Cahiers de l'ISEA*, juin 1960, 5–51. The fortieth anniversary issue of *La Pensée* (mai–juin 1979) includes a number of helpful studies of pre-war Marxist activity.

Individual French Marxists

With the signal exception of Althusser, very little has been written individually about the major French Marxist philosophers outside the debates and polemics in which they were involved. Several works quoted in the previous section contain useful discussions of their work but few monographs have been devoted to them. Of the pre-war writers, Paul Nizan has undoubtedly been best served, but largely on account of his novels and his relationship with Sartre. Unquestionably the best-known and most incisive analysis is the latter's preface to the reprint of Nizan's *Aden-Arabie* (Paris, 1960), collected in Sartre's *Situations*, IV (Paris, 1964). There is a useful introduction by Jean-Jacques Brochier to his edition of Nizan's writings, *Intellectuel communiste* (Paris, 1970) and a lively popular presentation in Ariel Ginsbourg's *Paul Nizan* (Paris, 1966). Interesting material can be derived from two literary studies, Jacqueline Leiner's *Le Destin littéraire de Paul Nizan* (Paris, 1970) and W. D. Redfern's *Paul Nizan: Committed Literature in a Conspiratorial World* (Princeton, 1972). A surge of renewed interest is possibly indicated by three recent French studies of Nizan from a non-literary point of view: Youssef Ishaghpour, *Paul Nizan* (Paris, 1980), Pascal Ory, *Nizan, destin d'un révolté* (Paris, 1980) and Annie Cohen-Salal, *Paul Nizan, communiste impossible* (Paris, 1980), which latter contains important contributions by Nizan's widow.

Considering the quality and range of Henri Lefebvre's work it is extraordinary that no monograph has yet been devoted to him, though such a study would be a daunting undertaking. Mark Poster's *Existential Marxism* (Princeton, 1975) and Louis Soubise's *Le Marxisme après Marx* (Paris, 1967) include extensive consideration of Lefebvre, and there is a

clear but limited discussion of his philosophy by Alfred Schmidt in
Howard and Klare's *The Unknown Dimension* (New York, 1972).
Lefebvre's contemporaries, including Guterman, Morhange and Cornu,
remain shadowy and neglected figures. Even Georges Politzer has
received little attention, beyond short prefaces to reprintings of his
works, though there is an interesting study, 'Georges Politzer ou le
retour philosophique' by Jacques Milhau in *La Pensée* (mai–juin 1979),
48–67.

Post-war Marxists have fared little better outside the context of
contemporary debate and most of the work produced during the 1940s
and 1950s lies in the trough of oblivion which accommodates old news
before it is resurrected as history. The rejection of Cold War polemics
has cast further veils over much of the production of the period,
affecting not only writers like Jean-T. Desanti and Jean Kanapa, but also
over most of Roger Garaudy's work before 1959. Even after this period,
Garaudy's work has attracted much debate but no overall appraisal.
Robert Geerlandt's *Garaudy et Althusser* (Paris, 1978) is highly
informative but restricted to the debates over humanism during the
1960s. Serge Perrotino's *Roger Garaudy et le marxisme du XXe siècle*
(Paris, 1969) is a rather hagiographic presentation of Garaudy's writings
during the 1960s, and is counterbalanced by a systematic demolition of
the same in H. N. Momjan's *Marxism and the Renegade Garaudy*
(Moscow, 1974).

Undoubtedly the most widely and passionately discussed of the
French Marxists is Louis Althusser. An invaluable checklist of his
works and of many works on him is appended by Graham Lock to his
translation of a volume of Althusser's *Essays in Self-Criticism* (London,
1976). Material in English has appeared in several journals of the Left,
including *New Left Review*, *Marxism Today*, *Radical Philosophy* and the
short-lived *Theoretical Practice*. But useful studies are available in book
form in Alex Callinicos, *Althusser's Marxism* (London, 1976) and
Miriam Glucksmann's *Structural Analysis in Contemporary Social Thought*
(London, 1974). Of the abundant French material the most useful books
are Saul Karsz's *Théorie et politique* (Paris, 1974), Jean-Pierre Cotten's *La
Pensée de Louis Althusser* (Paris, 1979), and Robert Geerlandt's *Garaudy
et Althusser* (Paris, 1978), though the latter's scope is rather narrow. Two
polemical attacks on Althusser are also widely distributed: *Contre
Althusser* (Paris, 1974), a collection of Trotskyist critiques, and *La Leçon
d'Althusser* (Paris, 1974), a criticism by his former disciple and co-author
of *Lire le Capital*, Jacques Rancière.

Most of the other French Marxist philosophers of the past twenty
years are generally ignored in English-speaking countries and most can

count themselves lucky to have any of their work translated, let alone studied and commented on. Occasional reviews of such translations do contain substantive discussion, however brief, but for the most part silence is the lot even of major figures like Sève and Godelier, not to mention less prominent writers. It is in part to remedy this silence that the present study was undertaken.

Index